Remembering our Ancestors

A Family History
of the
Pointer, Gage, Schenck, Townsend
&
Related Families

Pointer - Gage
&
Related Families

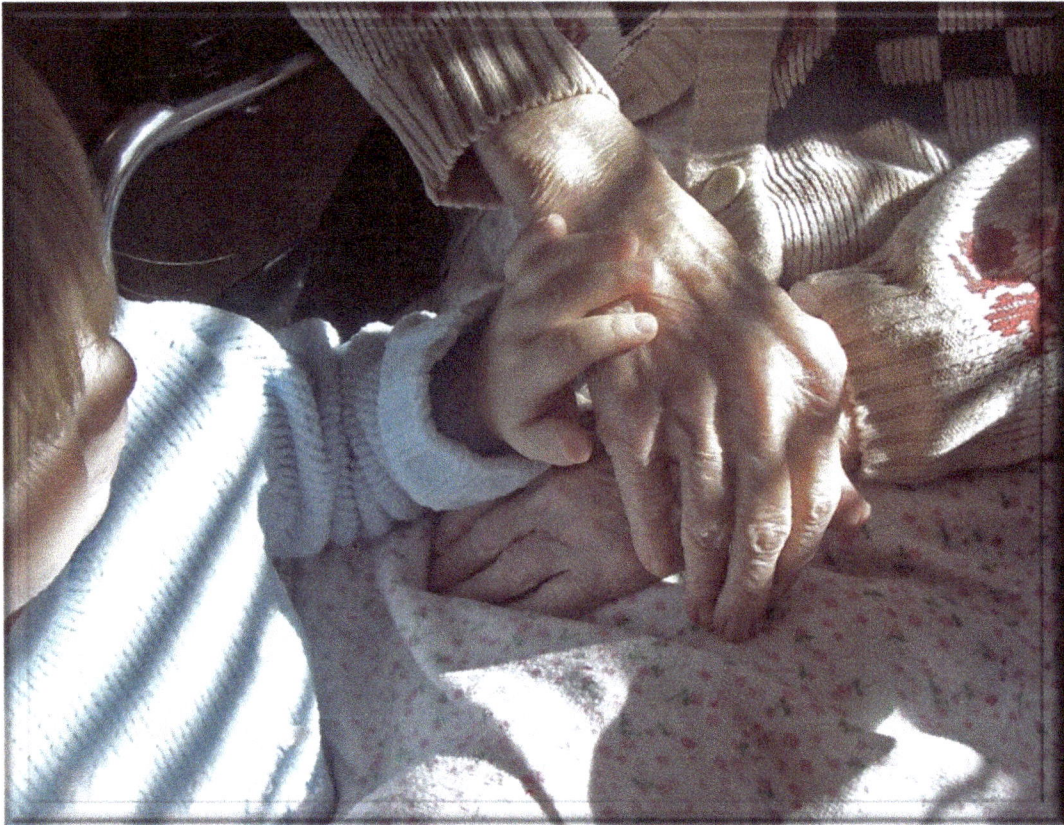

FIVE GENERATIONS

The photograph shows the hands of Daphene Pointer Wall
and great, great granddaughter, Taylor Dawn Chapman.

Remembering our Ancestors

A Family History

of the

Pointer, Gage, Schenck, Townsend

&

Related Families

ISBN 978-1-62137-918-8.

Published by Virtualbookworm.com Publishing, PO Box 9949, College Station, TX 77842.

Library of Congress Catalog Card Number on file with Publisher

Surnames

Anderson, Baugh, Bodine, Burleson, Campbell,

Chew, Cureton, Dorland, Gage, Hageman, Harris,

Hasty, Jans, Ligon/Lygon, Longley, Lupardus,

Moore, Murdock, Oliver, Opdyke, Pearson,

Schenck, Standley, Thomas, Thweatt,

Townsend, Van Couwenhoven, Van Der Vliet,

Van Dorn/Van Doren, Van Voorhees, Walton,

Woodward, Worsham, Wyckoff

Introduction

I have been asked to put down in writing some of the family research I have worked on these past twenty years.

The paths of our ancestors often give us some details as to how they came to be in a particular place at a particular time. Their ancient paths can tell us a lot, not only about the past, but can give us insight into the present. As Abraham Lincoln said, "And in the end, it's not the years in your life that count; it's the life in your years".

My dilemma was where to start. How much do I include and what families should I cover? Since this book is covering the ancestors of our Pointer and Gage families, I have begun there and worked back several generations showing those I have been able to document.

There is no way to find all the details of the lives of our ancestors. It is only possible to guess at what they experienced during their lifetimes. We can research the times in which they lived, as well as the locations, and try and uncover their paths. Much of the history of our families therefore will involve documents recorded during their lifetime and unfortunately this is usually applicable only to the men.

Genealogy is history, nothing more, nothing less. It is the history of a family, a group of families, places they lived, and how they raised their families. There is no way to adequately research the lives of our families without knowing of the times in which they lived. Why? Because the events in their lives caused them to make decisions that influenced where they lived and who they married and those decisions carried down and directly affected each generation after them.

Beginning with the 1850 Federal Census, women and children were named specifically for the first time. Sometimes we are able to find Bible records; sometimes we may find a biography written by a family member. If we are lucky, we may have a family story handed down generation after generation; sometimes we have nothing. We are fortunate when we do find records of our families and I have tried to note that in this book.

Any errors made in compiling this book are unintentional.

© Jean McCullough, 2016

ACKNOWLEDGEMENTS

I would like to take this opportunity to thank the many people who have helped me put together the information in this book. Without their assistance and cooperation, it would not have been possible to complete this work.

I acknowledge that much of the information has come from various sources: my own personal research, family researchers who generously shared their work, websites with information about the times, history and lives of our ancestors and family contributions.

It is my wish to recognize the help given me by family members. First, members of my immediate family who have lived through my time of working on this book: Cynthia and Tim Fish, Cheryl and Mark Walker and Sarah and John Wallis.

Next are my siblings: Juaneice Wall Woodard and Mack Wall who have given me support, pictures and encouragement. To Sam and Jolene Wall, I appreciate your encouragement, editing of my initial work, aid in getting our book published and listening to all my comments. Thanks to each of you.

Next, are my cousins, who generously shared pictures to make the information more complete and interesting. I appreciate the time and effort spent in gathering family photos by James Preston Pointer, Thomas Ray Pointer, Linda Anderson Lisciarelli and Kay Anderson Price.

"Remember me in the family tree
my name, my days, my strife;
Then I'll ride upon the wings of time
and live an endless life."

–Linda Goetsch

Table of Contents

POINTER

Meaning of the Pointer Surname

English: occupational name from Middle English pointer 'point maker', an agent derivative of point, a term denoting a lace or cord used to fasten together doublet and hose (Old French pointe 'point', 'sharp end'). It has been suggested that in some cases Pointer may have been an occupational name for a tiler or slater whose job was to point the tiles, i.e. render them with mortar where they overlapped. Possibly an altered form of German Pointner, a variant of Bainter.

Samuel Thomas & Alta Pearl Gage Pointer

Wedding Portrait

50th Wedding Anniversary

Samuel Thomas Pointer was the son of William Ezra and Nancy Lee Pearson Pointer. He was born in Duffau, Erath Co., Texas on June 4, 1894. He was the seventh child and third son born to his parents.

Sam grew up in Hamilton, Texas and married Alta Pearl Gage on July 23, 1913 in Mills Co., Texas. They were the parents of four children, one son and three daughters. Sam and Alta lived in Hamilton before moving to Marlin, Falls Co., Texas. There Sam was employed as a superintendent of an oil mill.

Alta Pearl Gage was the daughter of James and Elanora Pointer Gage. She was born April 10, 1892 in Giddings, Lee Co., Texas and grew up in that area. At age 18 she left Giddings and moved to Hamilton where she was employed, until her marriage to Sam. Alta was a housewife and an amazing cook. She enjoyed canning and preserving items from the garden Sam always planted.

After Sam retired, they moved to Hamilton County and made their home in that area. After the death of his widowed mother he purchased the family home on Main Street in Hamilton.

Sam died in 1967 and Alta lived until 1980. Both are buried in the I.O.O. F. Cemetery in Hamilton, Texas.

Samuel Thomas & Alta Pearl Gage Pointer

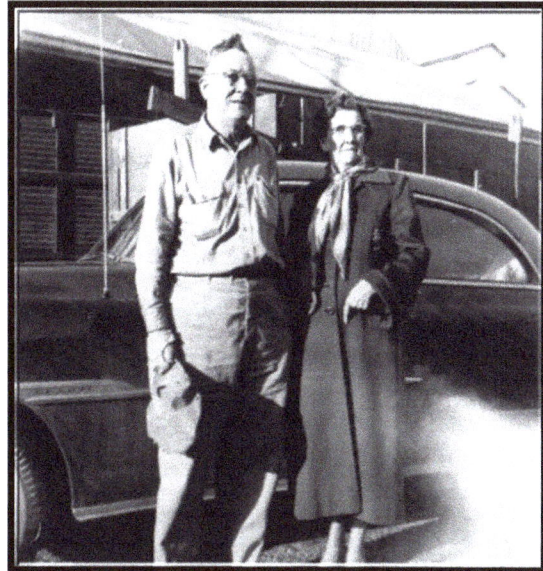

In an accident at the oil mill there was a man caught in a moving belt and in danger of losing his life. Sam rescued him but lost the fingers of his right hand, leaving only his thumb.

The below machinery was the type that Sam had in the mill and quite possibly the type that caused his injury.

Photo provided by Sam Wall

Children of Samuel Thomas & Alta Pearl Gage Pointer

Janie Daphene Pointer Wall,

Born: 17 April 1913, Evergreen, Hamilton Co., Texas

Married: 7 October 1932, to Mack W. Wall, Hamilton Co., Texas

Died: 6 June 2008 in Fort Worth, Tarrant Co., Texas

Buried: Erath Gardens of Memories, Stephenville, Erath Co., Texas

J. T. Pointer

Born: 11 April 1916, Hamilton, Hamilton Co., Texas

Married: 23 July 1938, to Marie Trammel, Hamilton Co., Texas

Died: 11 November 1993, Bosque Co., Texas

Buried: Oakwood Cemetery, Hamilton Co., Texas

Dorothy Merlene Pointer,

Born: 19 September 1924, Marlin, Falls Co., Texas

Married: 1941, to H.W. 'Andy' Anderson, Marlin, Falls Co., Texas

Died: 17 July 2011, San Antonio, Bexar Co., Texas

Buried: Ft. Sam Houston National Cemetery, San Antonio, Bexar Co., Texas

Dorris Alyne Pointer

Born: 5 December 1932, Marlin, Falls Co., Texas

Married: 8 February 1950, to Ray Fry, Marlin, Falls Co., Texas

Died: 15 May 2015, Clifton, Bosque Co., Texas

Burial: Central Texas State Veterans Cemetery, Killeen, Bell Co., Texas

Adult Children & Spouses of Sam & Alta Gage Pointer

Merlene & "Andy" Anderson
Ray & Dorris Fry
Marie & J. T. Pointer
Daphene & Mack Wall

Marie Pointer, wife of J. T. Pointer
Mack Wall, husband of Daphene Wall
Andy Anderson, husband of Merlene Anderson
Ray Fry, husband of Dorris Fry

Sam & Alta Pointer with children
Merlene Pointer Anderson,
Daphene Pointer Wall
J. T. Pointer

Dorris Pointer Fry, Daphene Pointer Wall
Merlene Pointer Anderson & J. T. Pointer

Daphene Pointer
&
Mack W. Wall

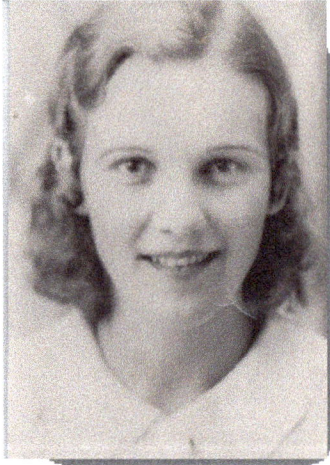

J. T. and Marie Trammel Pointer

Daphene & J. T. Pointer

J.T. Pointer

Alta Pointer, Daphene Pointer,
Unidentified woman, J. T. & Sam Pointer

Daphene & Mack Wall
Marie & J. T. Pointer

Merlene Pointer & Harry Wilton (Andy) Anderson

Dorris Pointer & Ray Fry

**Ray & Dorris Fry with
Daphene Pointer Wall**

GRANDCHILDREN OF SAM & ALTA GAGE POINTER

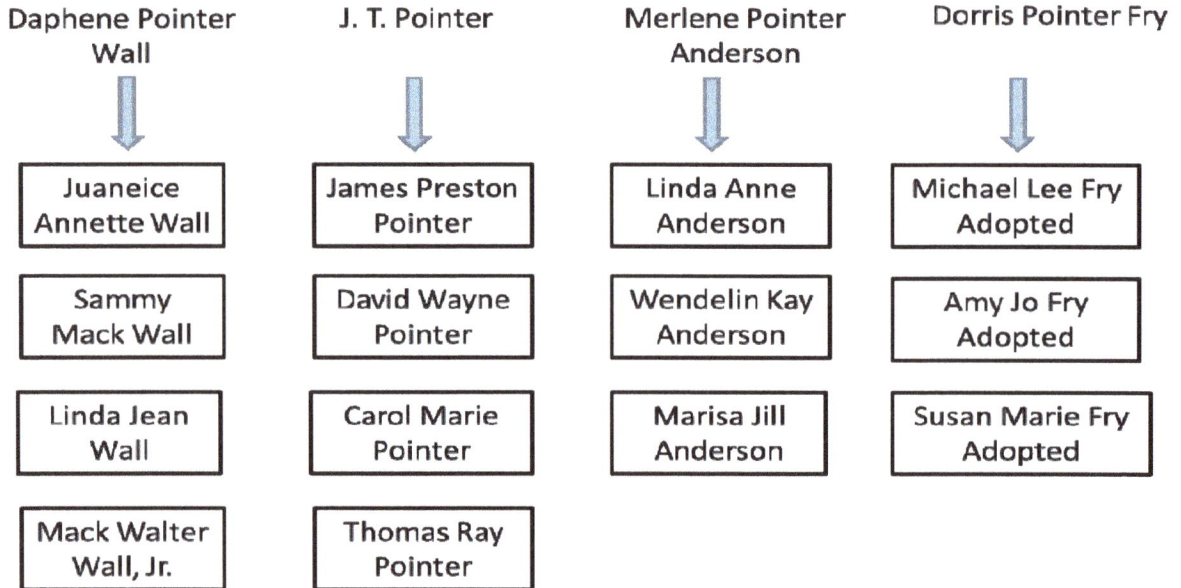

Daphene Pointer Wall	J. T. Pointer	Merlene Pointer Anderson	Dorris Pointer Fry
Juaneice Annette Wall	James Preston Pointer	Linda Anne Anderson	Michael Lee Fry Adopted
Sammy Mack Wall	David Wayne Pointer	Wendelin Kay Anderson	Amy Jo Fry Adopted
Linda Jean Wall	Carol Marie Pointer	Marisa Jill Anderson	Susan Marie Fry Adopted
Mack Walter Wall, Jr.	Thomas Ray Pointer		

Amy Fry Green, Linda Anderson Lisciarelli, Mack Wall, Jill Anderson Lemieu, Michael Fry, Carol Pointer Griffin, Tom Pointer, Juaneice Wall Woodard, Susan Fry, Preston Pointer, Kay Anderson Price, David Pointer, Sam Wall. Missing from the cousins' photo is Jean Wall McCullough.

OBITUARY IN HAMILTON HERALD NEWSPAPER
SAMUEL POINTER BURIED DEC. 3RD

Funeral services for Mr. Samuel Thomas Pointer were held Sunday, December 3rd, in the Park Heights Church of Christ at 2:00 p.m. Mr. Herman Beauchamp officiated. Burial was in the I.O.O.F. Cemetery. Mr. Pointer passed away December 2nd in the Hamilton County General Hospital following an illness of several weeks.

Samuel Thomas Pointer was born in Erath County, Texas, June 4, 1894 to William E. and Nannie Pointer. He was married to Miss Alta Pearl Gage on July 23, 1913. He was a retired oil mill superintendent and a member of the Church of Christ.

Survivors include his wife; one son J.T. Pointer of Hamilton; three daughters, Mrs. Mack Wall of Stephenville, Mrs. Wilton Anderson of San Antonio, and Mrs. Ray Fry of Montpelier, Ohio; one sister, Mrs. Grant Wright of Hamilton; five brothers, Ben of Muleshoe, Charlie of Longview, D.W. of Rule, A.R. of Austin, and Roy of Littleton, Colorado; 14 grandchildren and 10 great grandchildren.

Pallbearers were grandsons of the deceased: Preston Pointer, Glen Griffen*, Sam Wall, Harvey McCullough*, Billie Pointer and Mack Wall, Jr.

*Special Note: Two of the 'grandsons' listed, Glen Griffen and Harvey McCullough were the husbands of granddaughters, Carol Pointer Griffen and Jean Wall McCullough.

Death Certificate
Cause of Death:
Lymphatic Leukemia

Tombstone of
Samuel Thomas & Alta Pearl Gage
POINTER
Located in the I.O.O.F. Cemetery
Hamilton, Texas

Samuel T Pointer Registration

for Draft in World War I

OBITUARY: MRS. POINTER

Funeral services were held Thursday, February 14 at 2:00 p.m. in Riley funeral Chapel for Mrs. Alta Pearl Pointer. Chris Frizzell and Wesley Jones officiated at the service with burial following at the I.O.O.F. Cemetery in Hamilton.

Mrs. Pointer died Feb. 12, in Stephenville, following an extended illness. She was married in Hamilton July 23, 1913 to Samuel T. Pointer. Mr. Pointer died on Dec. 2, 1967. Mrs. Pointer was a devoted housewife and mother and a member of the Park Heights Church of Christ.

She was born April 19 1892 in Giddings, Texas to the late James Gage and Elanora Pointer Gage.

Survivors include four children, Mrs. Mack (Daphene) Wall, Stephenville, Mrs. Harry (Merlene) Anderson, San Antonio, Mrs. Ray (Dorris) Fry, Clifton and J.T. Pointer of Hamilton, by 14 grandchildren and 23 great-grandchildren; and by a brother, Oma Gage of Bryan.

Serving as pallbearers were Preston Pointer, David Pointer, Sam Wall, Mack Wall, Tommy Pointer and Mike Fry.

Death Certificate of Alta Pearl Gage Pointer
Cause of death: Heart Failure

Alta Gage Pointer & Her Daughters

Merlene Pointer Anderson,
Daphene Pointer Wall,
Alta Pearl Gage Pointer,
Dorris Pointer Fry

Ancestors of Samuel Thomas Pointer

Chart no. _____
No. 1 on this chart is the same as no. _____ on chart no. _____

1 Samuel Thomas Pointer
b: 4 Jun 1894
p: Duffau, Erath Co., TX
m: 23 Jul 1913
p: Mills County, Texas
d: 2 Dec 1967
p: Hamilton, Hamilton County, Texas
sp: **Alta Pearl Gage**

2 William Ezra Pointer
b: 17 Oct 1861
p: Indiana
m: 1 Feb 1882
p: Hamilton County, Texas
d: 6 Dec 1935
p: Hamilton, Texas

3 Nancy Lee Pearson
b: 18 Apr 1863
p: Jackson County, Alabama
d: 14 Oct 1955
p: Hamilton, Hamilton County, Texas

4 John Thomas Pointer
b: 29 May 1839
p: Nicholas County, Kentucky
m: 1 Jan 1861
p: Montgomery County, Indiana
d: 4 Sep 1934
p: Belton, Bell County, Texas

5 Kesiah Schenck
b: 14 Dec 1842
p: Montgomery County, Indiana
d: 5 Mar 1928
p: Rule, Haskell County, Texas

6 Charles Mastin Pearson
b: 2 Apr 1832
p:
m: 1853
p: Tennessee
d: 5 Mar 1893
p: Hamilton County, Texas

7 Elizabeth Longley
b: 3 Feb 1833
p: Polk County, Tennessee
d: 19 Sep 1889
p: Millerville, Erath County, Texas

8 Ezra Pointer
b: 27 Dec 1812
p: Kentucky
m: 18 Dec 1833
p: Kentucky
d: 28 Oct 1883
p: Newton County, Missouri

9 Evaline Moore
b: 30 Nov 1813
p: Kentucky
d:
p:

10 Aaron R Schenck
b: 17 Jan 1808
p: Warren County, Ohio
m: 2 Nov 1826
p: Hamilton, Butler County, Ohio
d: 12 Apr 1860
p: Montgomery Co. Indiana

11 Sarah Oliver
b: 8 Jan 1803
p: Warren County, Ohio
d: 8 Nov 1875
p: Montgomery Co. Indiana

12 Doctor Pearson
b: 17 Apr 1787
p:
m: abt 1821
p:
d: abt 1833
p: McMinn County, Tennessee

13 Lovice\Lovey
b: 1808
p: North Carolina
d:
p:

14 Joel Longley
b: 1 Sep 1791
p: Rockbridge, Rockbridge County, VA
m: 1815
p: Centerville, Fairfax County, Virginia
d: 23 Feb 1877
p: Ringgold, Catoosa County, Georgia

15 Nancy Bodine
b: 1797
p: near Manassas, Fairfax Co., VA
d: aft 1846
p:

16 Jonathan Poynter b: 30 Jul 1781 d:
17 Rebecca Hasty b: 1793 d:
18 Thomas Moore b: 1783 d: 18 Apr 1866
19 Nancy Standley b: 1788 d: 17 Sep 1865
20 Roelof (Ruliff) Schenck b: 3 Mar 1766 d: 28 Dec 1831
21 Hannah Hageman b: 7 Oct 1774 d: 21 Oct 1847
22 Ezekiel Oliver b: 1771 d: 12 Apr 1865
23 Mary b: abt 1780 d: 1 Aug 1850
24 Sherwood Pearson b: abt 1743 d: 28 Oct 1816
25 Elizabeth Ligon b: abt 1749 d: 23 Oct 1826
26 b: d:
27 b: d:
28 William Longley b: 1 Sep 1761 d: 7 Nov 1841
29 Mary Ann Bodine b: 1766 d: 9 Jan 1844
30 Francis Bodine b: abt 1768 d: 15 Jul 1836
31 Winifred Young b: abt 1768 d: aft 1807

32 Thomas Poynter
33
34 John Hasty
35 Rebecca Murdock
36
37
38 William Standley
39
40 John Roelofse Schenck
41 Maria (Mary) Van Dorn
42 Adrian Hageman
43 Jannetje\Jane Lupardus
44 Allen Oliver
45 Mary Boyce/Bice/Buys
46
47
48 Charles Pearson
49 Rebecca Walton
50 Thomas Ligon
51 Ann
52
53
54
55
56 Joseph Longley
57 Unknown
58 James Bodine
59 Unknown
60 James Bodine
61 Unknown
62
63

1

Ancestors of Alta Pearl Gage Pointer

Chart no. _____
No. 1 on this chart is the same as no. _____ on chart no. _____

1 Alta Pearl Gage
b: 10 Apr 1892
p: Giddings, Lee Co., TX
m: 22 Jul 1913
p: Mills County, Texas
d: 12 Feb 1980
p: Stephenville, Texas
sp: **Samuel Thomas Pointer**

2 James GAGE
b: 2 Feb 1860
p: Bastrop Co. TX
m: 3 Sep 1882
p: Erath County, Texas
d: 29 May 1941
p: Pleasant Grove, TX

3 Ellanora Pointer
b: 14 May 1867
p: Illinois
d: 1 May 1938
p: Pleasant Grove, Texas

4 William M. GAGE
b: 11 Sep 1827
p: Tipton County, Tennessee
m: 17 May 1855
p: Bastrop County, Texas
d: 20 Mar 1898
p: Bastrop, Bastrop County, TEXAS

5 Elizabeth A. Townsend
b: Feb 1836
p: Mississippi
d: 24 May 1904
p: Bastrop, Bastrop County, TEXAS

6 John Thomas Pointer
b: 29 May 1839
p: Nicholas County, Kentucky
m: 1 Jan 1861
p: Montgomery County, Indiana
d: 4 Sep 1934
p: Belton, Bell County, Texas

7 Kesiah Schenck
b: 14 Dec 1842
p: Montgomery County, Indiana
d: 5 Mar 1928
p: Rule, Haskell County, Texas

8 David GAGE
b: 2 Aug 1801
p: Haywood County, Tennessee
m: 1 May 1819
p:
d: Apr 1847
p: Smithville, Bastrop County, Texas

9 (?) Burleson
b:
p:
d: 1838
p: Pope County, Arkansas

10 Richmond Townsend
b: 1798
p: North Carolina
m: abt 1825
p:
d: aft 1877
p: Bastrop County, Texas

11 Mary Bryant
b: 23 Dec 1808
p: Georgia
d: 9 Feb 1891
p: Bastrop, Bastrop County, TEXAS

12 Ezra Pointer
b: 27 Dec 1812
p: Kentucky
m: 18 Dec 1833
p: Kentucky
d: 28 Oct 1883
p: Newton County, Missouri

13 Evaline Moore
b: 30 Nov 1813
p: Kentucky
d:
p:

14 Aaron R Schenck
b: 17 Jan 1808
p: Warren County, Ohio
m: 2 Nov 1826
p: Hamilton, Butler County, Ohio
d: 12 Apr 1860
p: Montgomery Co. Indiana

15 Sarah Oliver
b: 8 Jan 1803
p: Warren County, Ohio
d: 8 Nov 1875
p: Montgomery Co. Indiana

16 Reuben Gage b: 10 Feb 1770 d: 31 Oct 1844
17 Abigail BURLESON b: 24 Aug 1772 d: 4 Nov 1865
18 b: d:
19 b: d:
20 David Townsend b: abt 1774 d: 1816
21 Tabitha Thomas b: abt 1775 d: abt 1843
22 Alexander Bryant b: 30 Jan 1781 d: 25 Jan 1822
23 Elizabeth Cureton Anderson b: 23 Dec 1790 d: 4 Aug 1821
24 Jonathan Poynter b: 30 Jul 1781 d:
25 Rebecca Hasty b: 1793 d:
26 Thomas Moore b: 1783 d: 18 Apr 1866
27 Nancy Standley b: 1788 d: 17 Sep 1865
28 Roelof (Ruliff) Schenck b: 3 Mar 1766 d: 28 Dec 1831
29 Hannah Hageman b: 7 Oct 1774 d: 21 Oct 1847
30 Ezekiel Oliver b: 1771 d: 12 Apr 1865
31 Mary b: abt 1780 d: 1 Aug 1850

32 David Gage
33 Abigail Burleson
34 Aaron BURLESON
35 Rachel Hendrick
36
37
38
39
40 Solomon Townsend
41 Charity
42 Thomas Thomas
43 Avis Bostick
44 John Bryant
45 Judith Elizabeth Winfrey
46 Benjamin Anderson
47 Rebecca (Polly) Cureton
48 Thomas Poynter
49
50 John Hasty
51 Rebecca Murdock
52
53
54 William Standley
55 Catherine Baum
56 John Roelofse Schenck
57 Maria (Mary) Van Dorn
58 Adrian Hageman
59 Jannetje\Jane Lupardus
60 Allen Oliver
61 Mary Boyce/Bice/Buys
62
63

1

William Ezra & Nancy Lee (Nanny) Pearson Pointer

William Ezra was born on October 17, 1861 in Indiana, probably in Montgomery County, where his mother's parents lived. He was the first born of six children and the only son of John Thomas & Kesiah Schenck Pointer. He was a farmer by occupation and a craftsman. When he left his farm, he built the house shown below in Hamilton, Texas.

Nancy lived in the home after William's death until she passed in 1955. It was purchased by their son, Sam Pointer and wife Alta from the heirs. Alta lived in the home after Sam's death until she became unable to live alone. After her death in 1980, the house was then sold by their children.

Nancy (Nanny) was the daughter of Charles M. and Elizabeth Longley Pearson. Nancy was one of seven children, and she was born in Alabama, during the Civil War.

Nanny and "Billy" married February 1, 1882 in Hamilton County and were the parents of twelve children, seven sons and five daughters.

They were married for fifty-three years ending with the death of "Billy" in 1935.

Children of
William Ezra & Nancy (Nannie) Pearson Pointer

- **Minnie Vivian:** Born 3 Mar 1883; married James Milis Thompson, 29 Dec 1901, Hamilton, Hamilton Co., Texas; died 7 Oct 1965, Long Beach, Los Angeles Co., California.

- **Grizelda "Lula":** Born 17 Oct 1884, Erath County, Texas; married William Martin Weir, 18 Oct 1900, Hamilton Co., Texas; died 4 Jun 1928, Moran, Shackleford Co., Texas.

- **Elizabeth Kesiah:** Born 28 Aug 1886 in Erath Co., Texas. She died on 24 Aug 1889 at the age of 2 in Erath Co., Texas

- **Horace Preston:** Born 27 Feb 1888, Greenville, Texas; married Susan Jennie Johnson, 3 Dec 1905, Hamilton Co., Texas; died 24 Mar 1965, Plainview Hale Co., Texas.

- **Ella Belle:** Born 12 Feb 1890, Hamilton Co., Texas; married Owen Nelson Schooler, 12 Dec 1906, Hamilton Co., Texas; died 12 Nov 1928, Moran, Shackelford Co., Texas.

- **William Benjamin:** Born 12 May 1892; married Hattie Robinson, Sep 1910; died 31 Nov 1972, Muleshoe, Bailey Co., Texas.

- **Samuel Thomas:** Born 4 Jun 1894, Duffau, Erath Co., TX; married Alta Pearl Gage, 23 Jul 1913, Mills Co., Texas; died 2 Dec 1967, Hamilton Co., Texas.

- **Charles McFadden "Charlie":** Born 28 Aug 1896, Stephenville, Erath Co., Texas; married Addie Malone; died 7 Dec 1976, Longview, Gregg Co., Texas.

- **Doctor Willard "Doc":** Born 2 Feb 1899; married Euneice Featherstone, 1 Oct 1916, Hamilton, Hamilton Co., Texas; died 22 Jan 1978, Rule, Haskell Co., Texas.

- **Alonzo Roy:** Born 10 May 1901; married Bessie Mae Ferguson, 18 June 1924; died 3 Feb 1989, Mexico.

- **Roy Mastin:** Born 3 Sep 1903; married Nora Pendleton, 1924, Texas; married Gertrude Idell (Trudy) Lewis, 15 Feb 1944, Yuma, Arizona; died 2 Feb 1996, Littleton, Colorado.

- **Matilda Maude "Tildie":** Born 3 Apr 1906; married Thomas Grant Wright, 17 Aug 1928 in Hamilton Co.; Texas; died 14 Apr 1997 in Hamilton, Texas.

Children and Spouses

Of William Ezra and Nancy (Nanny) Lee Pearson Pointer

Photo Taken Between 1938—1940

Left to right—bottom row: Bessie Ferguson & Lonnie Pointer, Nora Pendleton & Roy Pointer

Second row: Jenny Johnson & Horace Pointer, Vivian Pointer Thompson, Nancy Pearson Pointer, William Ezra Pointer, Ben Pointer

Third row: Eunice Featherstone & Doc Pointer, Addy Malone & Charles Pointer, Tilda Maude Pointer Wright, Alta Gage Pointer, Grant Wright and Sam Pointer

Family Names

Comments on the family names: I have often wondered why William and Nancy (Nannie) Pearson Pointer named some of their children such "different" names. It was only through researching the Pearson line that it became clear where these names came from. Some of the names are Pointer names but many are from the Pearson, Longley & Bodine families.

Pearson family names are shown as underlined:

Minnie Vivian, 1883 – 1965

Grizelda, 1884 – 1928

Elizabeth Kesiah 1886 - 1889

Horace Preston, 1888 – 1965

Ella Belle, 1890 – 1928

William Benjamin, 1892 – 1972

Charles McFadden, 1896 – 1976

Samuel Thomas, 1894 – 1967

Doctor Willard, 1899 – 1978

Alonzo Roy, 1901 - 1989

Roy Mastin, 1903 - 1996

Matilda (Tildie) Maude, 1906 - 1997

**William Ezra
&
Nancy Pearson Pointer**

with the oldest six children.

Obituaries & Death Certificates of William Ezra & Nancy Pearson Pointer

The Passing Of Wm. Ezra Pointer

A man whose sincerity, strict honesty and high sense of honor inspired confidence and esteem in the hearts of all who knew him, has passed out from amongst us and entered into eternal life in the City of God. William Ezra Pointer is dead.

For several years members of Mr. Pointer's family and close friends noted with anxiety the encroachment of feebleness, and in his last weeks of illness watched by his bedside with little hope for his recovery. Death overshadowed the hearts and the old home with sorrow and loneliness, but there was preparation of the lives associated with his for the change brought by the end, which came just after the stroke of twelve on Tuesday morning, December 8.

Mr. Pointer was always interested in life, and made life vital and interesting for those around him. He served others. He was a retired farmer, who had been a resident of Hamilton county for forty-nine years. William Ezra Pointer was born in the state of Indiana, October 17, 1861. He came to Texas about the year 1878, and settled near Hico in the Duffau community. He was happily married to Miss Nannie Pierson on February 1, 1882. Their union was blessed in the birth of twelve children, seven sons and five daughters, and eleven of whom grew to a splendid maturity. Elizabeth died at the age of three years; Mrs. Will Weir and Mrs. Owen Schooler preceded the beloved father in death by only a few years. The widow, seven sons, two daughters, forty-four grandchildren and eleven great grandchildren and his three sisters survive to mourn for him who was well beloved. The sons and daughters are Horace Pointer, Rule, Texas; Sam Pointer, Marlin; Ben Pointer, Lubbock; Charley Pointer, Kilgore; D. W. (Doc) Pointer, Rule; A. R. Pointer, Purmela; Roy Pointer, Stephenville; Mrs. Viva Thompson, Levelland; Mrs. Grant Wright, of the parental home in this city. All were with their mother in the last hours of the life of the father. The sisters of Mr. Pointer are Mrs. Susie Sayles, Belton; Mrs. Nannie Weir, McGregor; Mrs. Jim Cage, of Bokus. These ladies were here last summer on the occasion of the Pointer family reunion.

Mr. Pointer's Christian life was marked with years of devout worship and active service. He made a profession of faith in 1886, and united with the Methodist congregation at Duffau. When he came to this county and settled in the Leesville community, now known as Union, Mr. Pointer was superintendent of the Methodist Sunday School in his community for eighteen years. He knew that he possessed "an house not made with hands, eternal in the skies."

At four o'clock on Monday afternoon the body of W. E. Pointer was borne to the altar of First Methodist church in Hamilton, where impressive memorial services were held, conducted by his pastor, Rev. A. Bryson English. The funeral music was arranged by Mrs. Travis Franks. Burial was in the new I. O. O. F. cemetery, where his father and mother, Mr. and Mrs. J. B. Pointer sleep.

The seven sons performed the loving service of pall bearers.

Anguished sorrow broods in every thought and plan of the lonely widow and her children and grandchildren mourn and friends are grieved that their happy association with Mr. Pointer has been interrupted, but all have the sustaining comfort of the promise of the Father of a joyous and unending reunion in the beautiful City of God when their journey here too shall end.

The Hamilton Herald-News

Apr. 22, 1955

Funeral For Mrs. Pointer Held Friday

Funeral services were held Friday, April 15 at 2 p.m. at the First Methodist Church for Mrs. W. E. Pointer, who passed away Thursday at her home. She lacked only five days of being 92 years old. The Rev. E. C. Carter, pastor of the church, was the officiating minister. Burial was in the I.O.O.F. Cemetery with the Bob Riley Funeral Home in charge. Pallbearers were grandsons of Mrs. Pointer and included J. C., Bill, J. F., Preston, and Wade Pointer and Gayle Weir.

Mrs. Pointer, the former Miss Nancy Lee Preston, was born in the midst of the Civil War on April 18, 1863, the daughter of the late Charles and Elizabeth Pointer. The family came to the Lanham community about 1875, where she grew up, and on Feb. 1, 1882 married W. E. Pointer. Twelve children were born to them. Three of her daughters and her husband have passed on.

She had been a member of the Methodist Church since childhood.

Surviving are 147 descendants. Nine children including Mrs. Vivian Thompson, Bakersfield, Calif.; Ben Pointer, Levelland, Horace Pointer, Anton; Sam Pointer, Evant; Charles Pointer, Hamlin; Doc Pointer, Rule; Lonnie Pointer, Premont, Texas; Roy Pointer, Denver, Colo., and Mrs. Tilda Maud Wright, Fort Worth; 48 grandchildren, 78 great-grandchildren, 12 great-great-grandchildren and two sisters.

Corrections to the obituary:
Nancy Lee Pearson was her correct maiden name and she was the daughter of Charles Mastin and wife Elizabeth Longley Pearson.

John Thomas & Kesiah Schenck Pointer
Parents of William Ezra and Elanora Pointer

Bottom left to right: John Thomas and Kesiah Pointer, William Ezra and Nancy Pointer. Left to right on top row: Unknown man and woman, Addie Malone Pointer, unidentified baby and Charles M Pointer, son of William and Nancy Pointer.

Hamilton County, Courthouse

The first Hamilton County Courthouse was established in 1858. First permanent courthouse was built in 1878, but burned down in 1886. In those days outlaws were so numerous that guards were hired to protect visiting judges. This 1887 structure of native limestone, quarried two miles east of Hamilton, remained unchanged until it was remodeled in 1931.

It has been reported that John T Pointer helped with building the structure with rock as he was a rock mason.

John Thomas & Kesiah Schenck Pointer

John Thomas & Kesiah Schenck Pointer

John Thomas was born on 29 May 1839 in Nicholas County, Kentucky to Ezra and Evaline Moore Pointer. He was the third of nine children. His parents left Nicholas Co., some time prior to 1860 and settled in Montgomery Co., Indiana, where John met and married Kesiah Schenck. By 1870 they had moved into Marion Co., Illinois. Between 1870 but prior to 1880 he and his family had migrated to Missouri but left there and by the 1880 census had settled in Erath Co., Texas. It is not known exactly when this family moved to Hamilton.

John Thomas was a farmer, craftsman and rock mason.

He was married to Kesiah Schenck January 1, 1861 in Montgomery Co., Indiana. Kesiah was the daughter of Aaron R and Sarah Oliver Schenck. She was born December 14, 1840, in or near Ladogo, Indiana. They became the parents of one son, William Ezra and five daughters, Sarah Evaline, Elanora, Sue Elzan, Mary Vivian and Nannie Blanche.

- **William Ezra Pointer** and **Nancy Lee Pearson** were married on 1 Feb 1882 in Hamilton Co, Texas.

- **Sarah Evaline** was born on 6 Dec 1864 in Indiana. She died on 19 Oct 1886 at the age of 21. Sarah Evaline Pointer and **Calvin Gage** were married in Erath Co., Texas by R. J. Miller, minister of the Gospel.

- **Elanora Pointer** was born on 14 May 1867 in Illinois. She died on 1 May 1938 at the age of 70 in Thrall, Williamson Co, Texas. Elanora and **James Gage** were married in Erath County by John Wilson, minister of the gospel.

- **Sue Elzan Pointer** was born on 16 Jun 1874 in Missouri, probably Jackson County. She died on 14 Dec 1969 at the age of 95 in Hamilton Co., Texas. She married **Albert Sydney Sayles** in Cass Co., Missouri on the 24th of December 1890.

- **Mary Vivian Pointer** was born in 1877 in Newton, Missouri. She died in 1890 at the age of 13.

- **Nannie Blanche Pointer** was born on 25 June 1885 in Drexel, Cass Co., Missouri. She died on 17 May 1964 at the age of 78 in Hamilton, Texas. She and **Samuel Levi Weir** were married on 16 Jun 1901 in Hamilton Co, Texas. After the death of Samuel Weir, Nannie married William E. Tipton.

Children of John Thomas & Kesiah Schenck Pointer

Elanora Gage
William E Pointer
Sue Elzan Sayles
Seated is
Nannie Blanch Weir

J. T. POINTER BURIED HERE

J. T. Pointer, ninety-five years of age and a former longtime resident of Hamilton County, died at the home of his daughter, Mrs. Susie Sayles, at Belton, Texas, on Tuesday, September 4 at ten o'clock in the evening.

The body, accompanied by a company of mourning relatives and friends, arrived in Hamilton Wednesday afternoon and funeral services, conducted by Eld. Ozro Newton, of Pottsville, were held in the Church of Christ in this city at five o'clock in the afternoon.

The body was laid to rest in the new I.O.O.F. cemetery with tenderly, comforting commitment ceremonies for those left behind, and honoring the "Old Soldier of the Cross".

A long, long span of earthly years were allotted to this man of God on the earth, and he had used them well. Until the feebleness of advanced years laid hold on him he was active in all the duties that make a well-rounded life of service. He was always cheerful, kind and generous toward his loved ones, and all those with whom he came in contact along the pathway that led to the City of the New Jerusalem.

J. T. Pointer was born in the state of Kentucky on May 26, 1839.   He was married to Kezziah

Schench [sic] on January 1, 1861. Death claimed his loyal and loving companion on March 5, 1928. They were the parents of six children, four of whom survive. They are W.E. Pointer, Hamilton; Mrs. James Gage, Beaukiss, Texas; Mrs. Susie Hayes, Belton, Texas; Mrs. Nannie Tipton, McGregor, Texas. His descendants number twenty-nine grandchildren, eighty-seven great grandchildren, and fifteen great great-grandchildren.

The Herald-Record is not informed of the date of the coming to Texas of Mr. and Mrs. Pointer, but they lived in Hamilton County for many years. "Grandfather" Pointer was a member of the household of his son, W. E. Pointer, in this city up until some twelve months ago, when he went to spend a while with other children.

Loved ones and friends find great consolation in their loneliness in the knowledge that his feeble body is at rest and his spirit is at home with God for he was a consecrated Christian. He had walked unfalteringly in the faith since 1899, when he was converted and united with the Church of Christ. May sweet memories of the past and hope for the future bring surcease of sorrow to the bereaved.

Cause of Death:

Intestinal

Influenza Age: 95

MEMORIES,

Written by Irene Pointer Westbrook, John & Kesiah Pointer's great granddaughter

Daddy's Grandpa and Grandma Pointer had come to live with us as no one else would take them. They wrote Daddy that they were going to the poor farm if he couldn't take them. Roy, Daddy's brother, brought them to our house. Mama had more than she could possibly do, but like her Daddy she never complained.

She gave them a room and Preston cut wood to keep them a fire. They never gave no one any trouble. They sat by the stove all day. Grandma had a stroke and then we had to hand feed her, and help her over the slop jar. We had no bedpan, and an outdoor toilet. It was my job to feed Grandma while Mama and Preston went to milk. I had went and spent a week with a friend. So when I propped Grandma up and was giving her breakfast, I said "Grandma, did you miss me." and she said "Yes" or tried to and then she fell

back in my arms and was dead before I could lay her down. I hollered at Bill to go tell Mama and Daddy.

We had no undertakers. Mama washed her and laid her out. When they did all they could, Daddy went and got Grandpa. He was sick in bed and Daddy said "I want you to go see her.' and Grandpa said "No Horace No. I would rather not. If you say she looks all right I know she does", but he did not go see her.

Daddy and Uncle Dock took her to Hamilton and Grandpa must have gone with them because he went home with his daughter, Mrs. Susie Sayles in the Tennessee Valley. He lived to be ninety-five years old.

He and Great Grandma Pointer had six children, twenty-nine grandchildren, eighty-seven great-grandchildren, and 15 great-great-grandchildren.

Cause of Death:

Cerebral Hemorrhage

Age: 87

Pointers Honor Ancestors

There is a new marker on the graves of a pioneer Hamilton couple who had a big hand in the physical development of this community. An attractive tombstone now stands at the head of the parallel resting places of John Thomas Pointer and his wife, Kesiah Schenck Pointer, in the Odd Fellows Cemetery in Hamilton.

Mr. Pointer was a stone mason who did his work in Hamilton before and just after the turn of the present century. Many of the native stone buildings still in use in Hamilton and environs were erected by him.

Mr. and Mrs. Pointer had six children: William E., Sarah Ebeline, Ellanora, Mary Vivian, Sue and Nanny Blanch.

Descendants of Mr. and Mrs. John Thomas Pointer, clear down to two great-great-great-grandchildren, chipped in donations to pay for the permanent monument at the grave site in I. O. O. f. Cemetery.

A spokesman for the family said, "It was with a lot of love and pride and a family effort that this memorial has become a reality."

Those from the family of William E. Pointer who contributed were: Mr. and Mrs. A. R. Pointer, Mr. and Mrs. Grant Wright, Mr. and Mrs. J. T. Pointer, Mr. and Mrs. Mack Wall, Mr. and Mrs. Ray Fry, Mr. and Mrs. H. W. Anderson, Sam Pointer (memorial), Audie Pointer Russell (memorial), Myrlene Summerfield, Gladys Dawson, Wanda Garton, Mr. and Mrs. Roy Pointer, Mr. and Mrs. Doc Pointer, Mr. and Mrs. J. C. Pointer, Mrs. Leota Pointer, Mrs. Anna Bell Hancock, Ezra Weir, Wesley Jones, Mrs. Preston Pointer, Mr. Bill E. Pointer and Lisa and Randy Lisciarelli (great-great-great grandchildren).

From the Sue Sayles family, Mr. and Mrs. E. Dean Schooler and Mr. Elverne Jones sent contributions.

Mrs. Rush Connor and Mrs. Lucille Cummings of the Nanny Blanch family contributed.

Members of the Ellanora Gage family who helped were Mr. Oma Gage, Mrs. Mimie Gage and Hollis, Mr. and Mrs. Gaston Gage and Mr. and Mrs. Wallace Elkins.

Ezra Pointer & Evaline Moore Pointer

Parents of John Thomas Pointer

The photo is of Evaline Moore Pointer.

Discrepancies have been associated with Evaline's name. Many show it as Ebaline, but a court document in Kentucky shows her name as Evaline.

No death record for her has been found. She is recorded as living with her son Stanley (Standley) in Texas on the 1880 census.

Family Record of Ezra Pointer
Ezra Pointer was born   Dec. 12, 1812
married Ebaline Moore   Dec. 28, 1833
Ebaline Moore Pointer was born Nov. 30, 1812

Stanley Pointer was born Dec. 29, 1834
Mary A. Pointer was born May. 20.   1837
John T. Pointer was born May. 26.   1839
Kitty F. Pointer was born July. 31,   1841
Martha H. Pointer was born Aug. 16. 1843
David   ntr was born Aug. 12. 1846
Joly Jas ointer was born July. 11. 18
Ida   tr was born Nov. 17. 18
Benjam   no Pointer was born March 27. 1853

Stanley Pointer was married to
Caraline Pointer   June 17   1860

John T. Pointer was married to
Kesiah Skank   January 1st. 1861

(coppied from the original by)
(Pearl Pointer Brown Nov. 28, 1924)

Bible Record of Ezra Pointer

Ezra died 28 October 1883 in Missouri.

Death records indicate that Ezra was buried in Crouches Cemetery, which is now called Greenwood Cemetery, located in Diamond, Newton Co. Missouri.

Jonathan and Rebecca Hasty Pointer
Possibly the parents of Ezra Pointer

Research for the ancestors of Ezra Pointer has been conducted by several Pointer researchers. It is thought that Ezra was a son of Jonathan Poynter/Pointer and wife Rebecca (Reby) Hasty. This is based on where they all lived at the same time and the connections between the Poynters and Pointers of that area.

Jonathan Poynter is shown on the 1850 Nicholas Co., Kentucky census record as being blind. He is 68 years old and gave Maryland as his birth state. His wife Reby is shown as being 67 and gives her birth state as Maryland. The census shows them living with William Poynter, thought to be one of their sons. Jonathan died sometime after 1850.

Rebecca (Reby) Hasty was the daughter of **John Hasty** and wife **Rebecca Murdock**. The Hasty family was in Delaware, then Maryland and moved into Virginia.

John Hasty was born in 1753 and died February 2, 1826, at Stepstone, Montgomery Co., Kentucky. He had three known sisters, Elizabeth, Nancy, and Jane Harris, and possibly a brother named Clement.

Both John and Clement fought in the Revolutionary war from Virginia. They entered the militia while in Fauquier Co., Virginia, in August 1776, and served in the Company of Captain Wm. Blackwell and later of Captain Marshall, of 11th Virginia Regiment. He was discharged in August 1779, and was in Battles of Brandywine (PA.), Germantown (PA.), Oct 3 1777, Stony Point (N.Y.), July 1779, and Monmouth (N.J.) and other battles.

Since John Hasty served under John Marshall, he quite possibly was one of the Minute Men of which there were 107 men. Culpeper County was formed out of Fauquier County.

The Minute Men were mostly farmers who fought and trained for a year before it was formed into a company or regiment. John Hasty enlisted in 1776 in Fauquier County and was probably about 23 years old and would have been fighting or rather training since he was 22. Receiving bounty land in Kentucky, he also received a pension at age 65 years. The men of Virginia Line were given grants of land in Kentucky because the Continental Congress had no money to pay.

John married **Rebecca Murdock**, in Culpeper Co., Virginia. Of their 9 children, Catherine, (maybe born 1783), Murdock, William, and John, preceded their parents in death. Rebecca Hasty also died in Stepstone, Kentucky, on September 7, 1844, at the home of their daughter, Nancy. Other surviving children were Clement, Reby, Elizabeth, and James.

For his Revolutionary War service he received a land grant of 100 acres in Kentucky.

Note: THE MURDOCK FAMILY:

Members of the Murdock family do not make their appearance on our colonial records until late in the seventeenth century. The family is unquestionably of Scottish origin, but the name is not uncommon in the northern part of England, and appears frequently in Ireland, especially in Ulster. There was but little emigration to America from these sections in the early years of the seventeenth century, New England and Virginia being settled from the south and east of England.

Thomas Moore and Nancy Standley Moore
Parents of Evaline Moore Pointer

At this time, I have been unable to determine Thomas' parentage. Nancy Standley was born in 1791 in Virginia. She was the daughter of William Standley and the name of his wife has not been documented.

Their marriage bond was found in Boone Co., Kentucky dated 18 January 1806. How long they lived in that county is not certain but by 1820 they are living in Nicholas County and are enumerated on that census record.

The 1850 Nicholas Co., Kentucky, census page 412 lists Thomas Moore, 69 a farmer, born in Virginia and Nancy Moore, 62, born in Virginia. Just to confuse the issue, the 1860 Nicholas County, Kentucky census states Thomas was born in Pennsylvania. Research leans toward Virginia at this time.

In an updated one-page history of the Moore family written by their grandson Luther (1858-1933), son of Hiram and Rebecca Wilson Moore, states: *'Grandfather Thomas Moore was of Irish descent. He died in 1865, lived to be 96. Grandmother Moore died at the age of 86. There were 16 children, 9 males and 7 females of whom 14 lived to adulthood and married.'*

According to this account, Thomas would have been born in 1769 instead of 1781 which is indicated on the 1850 census, so both dates should be examined before reaching any conclusions.

Thomas served in the Revolutionary War from the state of Virginia. There were two land certificate in Kentucky for Thomas and a possible explanation for being awarded two, is that he served as first a private and later as a sergeant in the war. Kentucky land grants were awarded for service in the Revolutionary War only to those who served in the war from Virginia.

Rev War Pay Record & Land Grants

Thomas received two land grants for his service in the Revolutionary War.

One grant for 100 Acres for time served as a private and the second for 200 Acres for time served as a sergeant

Marriage Bond between Thomas Moore and Nancy Standley

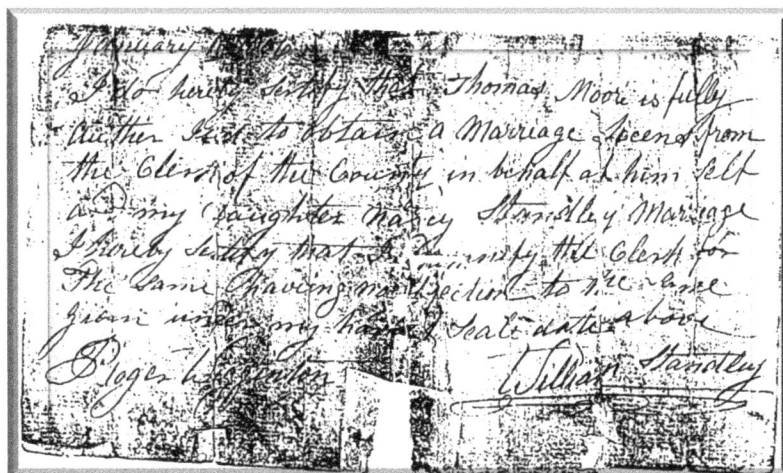

Transcription of marriage bond:

January 15, 1806

I do hereby sertify that Thomas Moore is fully authorized to obtain a marriage license from the clerk of the county in behalf of himself and my daughter Nancy Standley marriage. I hereby sertify that I_____the clerk for the same having no objection to the same.

Given under my hand and seale date above.

Roger Wigginton   ***William Standley***

William Standley & Wife (Name Unknown)
Parents of Nancy Standley

Little is known about William Standley. We do know that he brought his daughter, Nancy to Kentucky from Virginia. It is very likely that William fought in the Revolutionary War and received land for his service. This was the land the State of Virginia used to reward the soldiers for their service.

Some researcher think William Standley was a son of John Standley and Edith Hutchins. The Standley/Stanley families and the Hutchins families intermarried during this time period. The Hutchins family ancestors were Nicholas and then his son Strangeman Hutchins. They were early settlers in Virginia and Strangeman along with his family and some of the Standley families migrated to Yadkins County, North Carolina in the mid 1700s.

The Hutchins and the Standley families were Quakers and there are many records of them in the Monthly Meeting Notes. This relationship has not been proven but is considered a possibility.

Some researchers think William married first Nancy Bowman, but I have not found a record to support this. He later married Catherine Baum but his marriage to Catherine is dated 18 November 1806 in Boone County, Kentucky. This date would prove she was not Nancy's mother.

Thomas and Nancy Moore's family had the following children:

Permelia b. 1806,
John b. 1808,
Standley b. 1809,
Katherine Ann b. 1810,
Thomas b. 1811,

William b. 1812
Evaline b. 1813,
Elizabeth b. 1816,
Montgomery b. 1818,
Charles b. 1816,

Hiram b. 1819, Eli b. 1821
Nancy Ann b. in 1826,
Margaret Jane b. 1829

On July 23, 1828 Permelia married Andrew Mers and their children were:

Hannah, b. 1829
Samuel T Mers, b. 1831
Aud H Mers b. 1833
Stanley F Mers b. 1834
James W Mers b. 1836
Sarah E Mers b. 1839
Luther Mers b. 1846
Luzerne Eaton Mers b. 1849
Susan Mers b. 1851
Andrew Mers b. 1853

The 1830 Census shows Thomas and Nancy still residing in Nicholas County, Kentucky where Thomas and his sons who were old enough were still farming.

On March 29, 1830, Katherine Ann Moore married John Thomas Wilson and their children were:

Ebaline Wilson b. 1830
Nancy Jane Wilson b. 1832
Michael T Wilson b. 1836
Catherine Elizabeth Wilson b. 1838
Andrew Merse Wilson b. 1840

1830 John married Anna Blount and their child was:

Mary Moore b. 1833

In 1832 Standley Moore married Francis Medlin and their child was:

Kitty Moore b. 1827

In 1833 Elizabeth Moore married William Payne and their children were:

Berry Payne b. 1835
James Frank Payne b. 1836
Permelia Payne b. 1841,
Artemesia M Payne b. 1842,
Hiram M Payne b. 1843,
John W Payne b. 1848
Louisa Payne b. 1849
William Payne Jr. b. 1851,
Thomas J Payne b. 1853
Christopher Payne b. 1856

On December 28, 1833 Eveline Moore married Ezra Pointer and their children were:

Stanley Pointer b. 1835
Mary A Pointer b. 1837
John Thomas Pointer b. 1839
Kitty T Pointer b. 1841
David Pointer b. 1846
Job M Pointer b. 1848
Nancy Pointer b. 1850
Benjamin Pointer b. 1853

January 15, 1838 William Moore married Mary Polly Scott and their children were:

Charles Moore b. 1838
Thomas Moore b. 1839
John W Moore b. 1840
Eli F Moore b. 1842

June 23, 1840 Charles Moore married Amazetta Ellen Shulse and their children were:

> Abraham Thomas Moore b. 1841,
> Lydia Francis Moore b. 1843 and
> Nancy J Moore b. 1847
> Lorenzo D Moore b. 1850,
> Mary Ann Moore b. 1852
> Margaret C Moore b. 1854
> Stanley Hayden Moore b. 1857
> Sarah P Moore b. 1860
> Mary Elizabeth Moore b. 1862

November 8, 1843 Hiram Moore married Rachel Wilson and their children were:

> Oliver S Moore b. 1843
> Mary Elizabeth Moore b. 1846
> John L Moore b. 1849
> Hannah Moore b. 1850
> George Ross Moore b. 1852
> Charles William Moore b. 1854
> Thomas Luther Moore b. 1858
> James T Moore b. 1860
> Nancy Catherine Moore b. 1863

On January 29, 1839 Montgomery Moore married Patty Laughlin and their children were:

> Kitty Ann Moore b. 1849
> John S Moore b. 1852
> James William Moore b. 1855

On August 20, 1846 Eli Moore married Elizabeth M Utterback and their children were:

> Mary A Moore b. 1847
> Benjamin D Moore b. 1848

On 18 February 1847 Nancy Moore married Lorenzo Dow Cameron and their children were:

> John Thomas Cameron b. 1848
> Charles Whaley Moore b. 1849
> Eldridge Kelly Cameron b. 1851

The 1850 Census lists Thomas and Nancy Moore still residing in Nicholas Co., Kentucky where William was still farming. His real estate was valued at $900. The 1860 Census shows Thomas and Nancy Moore still living in Nicholas Co., Kentucky, but with no land holdings. Living right next to them is his son Charles and his family whose real estate is valued at $1200 and personal estate at $500. It is possible to assume that Charles now owns his father's land. Some of their other children are living in the following places in 1860:

- Katherine and John Wilson were living in Boone in Bates Co., Missouri.
- Montgomery and Patty Moore had moved to Bourbon Co., Kentucky.
- Charles and Amazetta Moore were still residing in Nicholas Co., Kentucky.
- Hiram and Rachel Moore had moved and were living in Fleming Co., Kentucky
- Eli and Elizabeth Moore were living in Clinton in Boone Co., Indiana.
- Evaline and Ezra Pointer lived in Nicholas Co., Kentucky.

Nancy Standley Moore died on September 17, 1865, at the age of 74 and Thomas died 18 April 1866 at the age of 83, in Nicholas Co., Kentucky.

Eventually, some of the Wilson, Mers, Standley and Pointer families were on the 1880 census in Erath and Hamilton Counties, Texas. Many of them settled permanently in that area.

Aaron R & Sarah Oliver Schenck
Parents of Kesiah Schenck Pointer

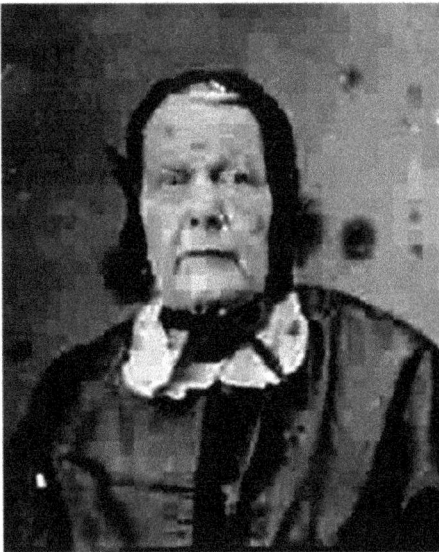

Ohio, County Marriages, 1789-1997
Butler Marriage records 1803-1834

Aaron R Schenck was born on 17 Jan 1808 in Warren Co., Ohio and died on 12 April 1860 at the age of 52 in Montgomery Co. Indiana. He was buried at Whitesville, Montgomery Co., Indiana in the Old Oliver Cemetery.

Sarah Oliver, was the daughter of Ezekiel and Mary Myer Oliver, and was born on 8 Jan 1803 in Warren Co., Ohio. She died on 8 Nov 1875 at the age of 72 in Montgomery County. Sarah was buried at Union (South) Township, Montgomery Co. Indiana in the Old Oliver Cemetery.

Aaron Schenck and Sarah Oliver were married on 2 Nov 1826 in Hamilton, Butler Co., Ohio.

By 1834 Aaron and Sarah had left Ohio and migrated to Montgomery Co., Indiana.

Sarah's parents had already settled in that county with a land purchase in 1824. Ezekiel Oliver had purchased 160 acres in Montgomery County, on 25 July 1820 and an additional 80 acres on 1 November 1830.

Aaron settled near his wife's family and purchased 155 acres in one transaction and 160 acres in a second transaction both dated 14 October 1834.

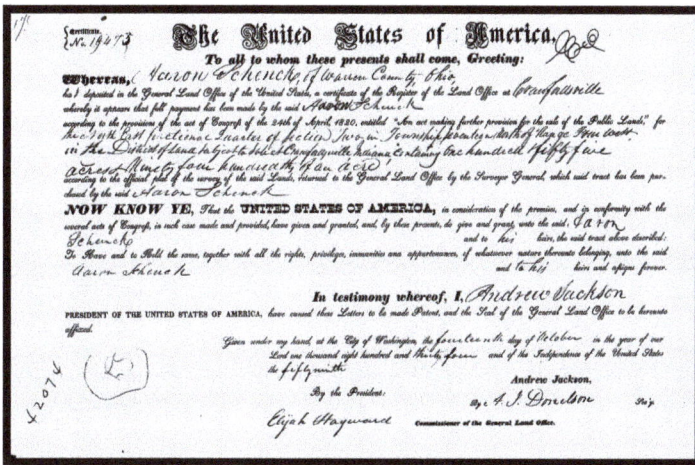

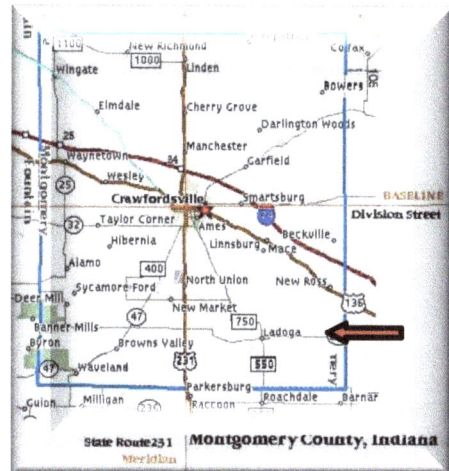

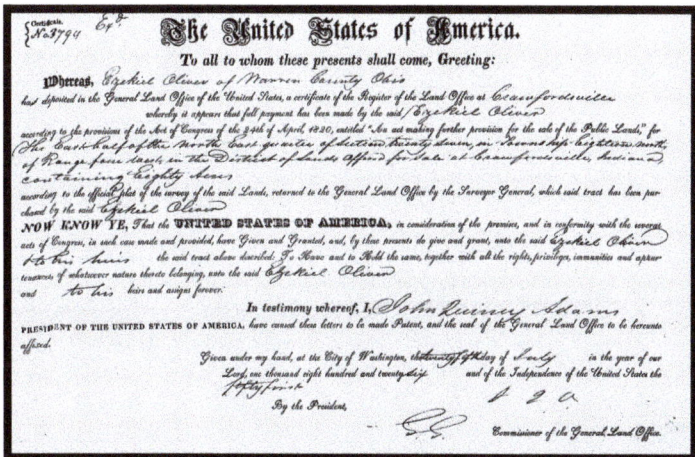

Ezekiel and Aaron each purchased three parcels of land. The documents shown are for the first purchases of each of them.

Note that Andrew Jackson signed Aaron's document and John Quincy Adams signed Ezekiel's.

Children of Aaron and Sarah Oliver Schenck

- **Ezekiel Oliver Schenck**, born 1 Nov 1827, Ohio; married T. Mary Hicks, 19 Apr 1848; died 8 Aug 1865, Vicksburg. (Union soldier who died during the Civil War).

- **Jacob A. Schenck**, born 12 May 1830, Ohio; married Frances Tilley, 3 Jan 1854; died 3 Feb 1899, Montgomery Co., Indiana. (Twin)

- **Isaac A. Schenck**, born 12 May 1830, Ohio; married Mary Jane Thompson, 22 May 1852; died 6 Nov 1909. (Twin)

- **Mary J. Schenck**, born 31 Dec 1831, Ohio; married David Richey, 19 Aug 1850; died 23 Dec 1897.

- **Hannah Schenck**, born 17 Nov 1833, Indiana; married Solomon Kessler, 3 Dec 1857; died 2 May 1863, Montgomery Co., Indiana.

- **Abraham Schenck** was born on 18 July 1835 in Indiana. He died on 12 Dec 1859 at the age of 24 in Montgomery Co., Indiana. He was buried in Oliver Cemetery, Union (South) Township, Montgomery Co., Indiana.

- **Sarah A. Schenck** was born on 12 Dec 1836 in Indiana. She died 23 Nov 1853 at the age of 16.

- **Aaron A. Schenck** was born on 11 June 1840 in Indiana. He was buried in 1860 at Oliver Cemetery in Union (South) Township, Montgomery Co. Indiana. He died 11 Apr 1860 at the age of 19.

- **Kesiah Schenck**, born 14 Dec 1842, Montgomery Co., Indiana; married John Thomas Pointer, 1 Jan 1861, Montgomery Co., Indiana; died 5 March 1928, Rule, Haskell Co., Texas.

- **William Oliver Schenck**, born 7 Nov 1844, Indiana; married Emily J Adams, 6 Sep 1874 in Bates Co., Missouri; died 23 May 1906 in Kansas City, Jackson Co., Missouri.

An interesting note is that **Hannah Schenck, sister to Kesiah,** married **Solomon Kessler** in 1857 and they had four children: Benjamin, Elizabeth, Rena and Milton, who died as an infant. Hannah died in 1862 and in 1863 Solomon married **Martha Hannah Pointer**, **sister of John Thomas Pointer** and a daughter of Ezra and Evaline Moore Pointer. They had seven children: Thomas, George, Charles, John, Mary, Laura and Walter who died at a young age.

Isaac and Jacob Schenck were twins.
They were brothers of Kesiah and Hannah Schenck.
(Picture contributed by Elaine Harper)

Solomon and Hannah Schenck Kessler

Several letters were written to Aaron from family members dating from 1834 to 1856. These letters were in the possession of Elaine Harper of Indianapolis, IN and she graciously shared them with me. The letters are typed, but the wording and spelling are shown as they were written. Copies of the original letters are in Elaine's possession and she shared her copies with me.

A letter written to Aaron Schenck living in Indiana from his brother, John R Schenck, living in Warren Co., Ohio

By the blessing of God in hoom I trust have the opportunity to inform you that the friends are all well as far as we know. We are all well at preasant. We was vary glad to get your letter. It was good 2 hear from you. We have had a great deal of wet weather. It is 9 o'clock a.m. It is freezing a little and spitting snow and looks like as if we might have more.---

I will now give you a short history of our travels. I was gone 7 wks and one day and spent $51 3/4 and time and ware and tare is at least $100.

We went from your house to Ezekill Rynearsons he is adooing exclent well. Now he is agetting a fine farm open and plenty of stock. Thence to Eli Hendricks 3 milds this side of Covington. Staid there all night. they have a fine farm and are well fixed but they have a great deal of trouble with one of their daughters that has fits every night.

Thence we went to Covington. Crost the river one mild above town went N of west to Danville in Illinois good roads sean some elegant land. Thence to the salt works. salt fork of the Vermillion. thence to Urbannah at the big grove at the head of the salt fork. had beautiful prairie roads. sean but little timber and that was along the streams of water. sean elegant land. thence to Bloomington on the head of the Sangamon river. Sean good land. Thence to Chillecotha on the Illinois above peoria. Thence to Indiantown on the big Beaurow, fine country.(*there is today a Bureau Co. [eh])* Across the country and over the beautiful prairies, over the hills to Rock river, a distance of 60 milds To the Crigan (?) city, come to the river found nobody ameediately living on this side. Called over for a ferryman.

Crossed over into Town found Isaac the first man that I come to. Isaac expressed a great gladness. Isaac not married yet but welcomed us up to his lodgeing in ---gan city a Town of 3 or 4 houses situated in a beautiful valley on the west side of the river, it will soon be a fine place. It has a fine rich prararies and groves of timber around it and has got a convenienancy to water the town from an el(g)ant Spring just above Town.

Isaac is making w and 3 dollars a day working at the carpentes trade. It is a righ country and produces wonderfull. I was thare 2 or 3 days and Started for Chicaugo...80 milds sean vary fine prararie land and timber In thre or four days we found ourselves at Chicaugo. It is a handsome town on the SW side of the Lake Michigan. Stands about thre feet out of the water. Lake on the oneside and prarairs on the other, the Lake is a vary handsome sight We traveled around the Lake on the Beach sometimes in the edge of the water to Michigan City Three days tramp (?...trip?)) Visited friends thare.

Michigan City is growing vary fast. thence to Tarrie Cope to find my land was much pleased with it . it is improoving in value vary fast it is exlant land well timbered a big Road running right through it. it is with in 9 milds of a Commercial Town, Niew buffalow, at the mouth of the Galena, I was in that neighborhood three or 4 days then Started for home by Lay Port. Cauled for my Deed it had not come then persued my horse for home had desperate bad roads, had like to .... Most killed my horses got home alive. found all well.

Continued from previous page:

Letter from John R Schenck to brother Aaron R Schenck.

I come now to Religious matters I drempt last night That you and I was in a prayer meeting and that you was Called apon to pray, and that you excepted the invitation Pleas to except a brothers advice and never rest till you make a humble Confession of Christ before the World for he declares that he that will not Confess me before Men him will not I confess before my father and before the holy angels. I would like to see you an talk to you. we want you to right back to us as soon as you can. We want to hear your welfare we can't right much more at preasant but remain your Cincear friends.

John R. Schenck Warren Co. Ohio
Anne Schenck
Palmyra Kirkwood post office
Warren Co., Ohio

To Aaron Schenck
Crawfordsville PO

This letter is from Aaron's sister, Sarah Schenck. Sarah was apparently dyslexic as she used "d"s for "b"s.

My Dear Brother and sister

I take this opertunity to inform you of our wellfaire it has pleased God to restsore me to tolerable health I have had some very dad (*she uses d for b in several places.[eh]*) spells since you went away dut I am deter: Mother is in deter health than she was when yu went away: Jacod has had a tolerable dad spell he was taken the fifth of January he has got pruty smart (I think this means he is better! [eh]) I have ben wanting to write to you ever since we got you leter wich was the Sixth of January dut I was hindered: George said he wanted to write and he would write fore us dut he concluded he had not time. Isaac has ben to Jaake Brineys he said tey ware in tolerable good health Isaac wanted to com oute but has ben disappointed: John is in as good a health as common, but Elizabeth has a very soar time with that canser on her side: Mariahs is in tolerble good health. She calls her son Richard: All the conection is at preasant as well as comon cousin Aaron S has lost wan of his children: their has been a good many Deaths and a Greate many Marriages this winter: it has ben very weat but it is tolerable dry now. we all remember our best respects to you and yours we hoap that you remember us to all inquiring friends if we have any I have more that I wanted to write but I cant now we want you to write to us as quick as you can and let us know about Sarahs eye I want you to look over my maney mistakes and bad writing.
I remain your afectionate sister

Sarah Schenck
March the 27th (maybe) 1834

Roeloff/Ruliff Schenck and Hannah Hageman Schenck
Unity Cemetery, Warren County, Ohio

Roeloff & Hannah Schenck are buried in Unity Cemetery, Deerfield Township, Warren Co., Ohio. Unity Cemetery is located on the north side of Bethany Road, in Deerfield Twp., very close to the Warren-Butler County line.

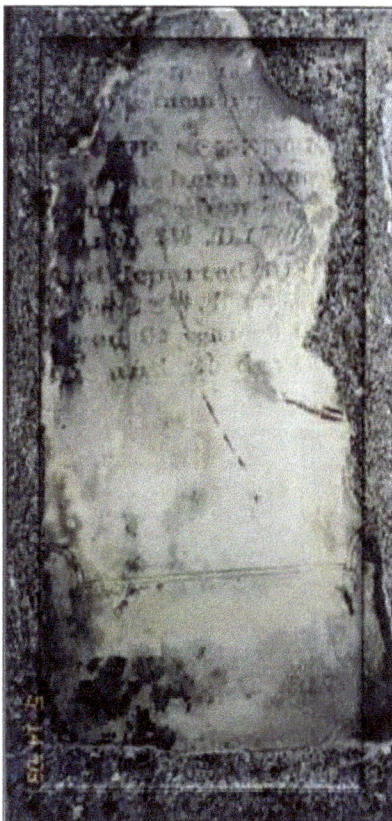

It is named after the community "Unity", which Judge Lowe tried unsuccessfully to start in 1815. The cemetery is on land donated by Judge Lowe for that purpose and stood next to an adjacent Presbyterian church.

The first burials were in 1813 and it is the oldest cemetery in Deerfield Twp.

About 1981, a restoration of the cemetery was undertaken since it was in extremely poor condition. The broken scattered stones were recovered and placed in a cement structure.

Ruliff Schenck
Tombstone

Hannah Hageman Schenck
Tombstone

Ruliff Schenck, & Hannah Hageman Schenck
Parents of Aaron Roeloff Schenck

Roeloff (Ruliff) Schenck was born 3 March 1766 in Monmouth Co., New Jersey and removed to Warren Co., Ohio sometime after 1794 to settle on land he had inherited from his father, John Schenck, whose will states:

"Son, Ruliff, 340 acres, part of my purchase in the Western Territory in Simses (Symmes) Settlement of Miamies (Ohio); the same being valued at 111 lbs. and so charged against his share of my estate."

Ruliff is listed in the 1820 and 1830 U.S. Census records as a resident of the Deerfield Township, Warren Co., Ohio.

According to *'History of Warren County (Ohio)'*, page 632, it states' 'Ruloph Schenck was one of the earliest (settlers) in the western part of the township, settling on Section 6. He was known in the area as "Old Injun" for his Indian-like ways'.

Ruliff died 28 December, 1831 and left estate papers filed in the Warren Co., Ohio court house. According to this court document, Chancery Book 4, pages 306-311; February Term 1833. The estate of Ruliff Schenck having 340 acres in Warren Co, Ohio were partitioned off to the widow Hannah Schenck along with the surviving children and their spouses.

The document was signed by: Hannah Schenck wife of deceased; Jacob R Schenck, son of deceased; Aaron R Schenck, son of deceased; John R Schenck, son of deceased; John D Briney, son in law of deceased; Jane Schenck Briney, daughter of deceased; Peter Verbryke, son-in-law of deceased; Maria Schenck Verbryke, daughter of deceased; Sarah Schenck, daughter of deceased and A.H. Dunlevy court appointed guardian ad litem of Isaac Schenck, minor son of deceased.

Hannah Hageman was the daughter of Adrian and Jannetje/Jane Lupardus Hageman. Hannah was born 7 October 1774 in New Jersey. She died 21 October 1847 in Warren Co., Ohio. It is not known where or when she and Roeloff married but estimates have the date about 1797. Ohio records indicate that Hannah's parents were in Hamilton Co., Ohio by 1783, it is likely that Roeloff and Hannah were married in Ohio. Roeloff was eight years older than Hannah. She remained a widow for sixteen years until her death.

Children of Roelof & Hannah Hageman Schenck

- **John Roelof Schenck**, born 1 July 1799; married Ann Lamb, 1835, Warren Co., Ohio; died 26 May 1846, Warren Co., Ohio. John was 47 when he died.

- **Jane Schenck**, born 6 Feb 1802, Ohio; married John D Briney, 20 Oct 1820, Warren Co., Ohio; died 10 Aug 1888, Adams, Mahaska Co., Iowa. Jane was 86 when she died.

- **Jacob R. Schenck**, born 1805, Warren Co., Ohio. He married Frances Tilley on 3 January 1854 in Boone Co., Indiana. Jacob died 3 February 1899 in Montgomery Co., Indiana. Jacob was 94 when he died.

- **Mariah\Maria Schenck**, born 1807, Ohio; married Peter Verbryke, 14 Aug 1832, Warren Co., Ohio. Maria died 2 February 1886 in German Township, Allen Co., Ohio. She was living with her son Ruliff Verbryke at the time of her death. She was 79 when she died.

- **Aaron R Schenck**, born 17 Jan 1808, Warren Co., Ohio; married Sarah Oliver, 2 Nov 1826, Hamilton, Butler Co., Ohio; died 12 Apr 1860, Montgomery Co. Indiana. Aaron was 52 when he died.

- **Sarah Schenck**, born 17 Dec 1810; married Alexander H. McCowin, 14 Mar 1839, Warren Co., Ohio; died 10 Oct 1880. Sarah Schenck McCowin died January 1 1883 in Dark Co. Ohio. Sarah Schenck and Alexander Hugh McCowin are buried at Greenville Union Cemetery, Darke Co., Ohio. Sarah was 73 when she died. *There were various spellings of Alexander's surname.*

- **Isaac R Schenck**, born about 1812, exact date is not known nor is his date and place of death. Last information about him is contained in his Brother John's letter to Aaron stating that Isaac was in Illinois.

Sarah Schenck McCowin

Sarah was the sister of Aaron R Schenck and the writer of the letter dated 1834.

It is not known if Sarah and Alexander McCowin had any children.

Division of the estate of Roelof (Ruliff) Schenck

In settling the estate of Roelof (Ruliff) the division of his property is as follows to his heirs: We Jacob Hall, James Baxter, & William Coulson commissioners appointed by the court of common pleas for Warren County state of Ohio to make partition of the following described real estate of Ruliff Schenck late of the county and state aforesaid decd. amongst the children & heirs said deceased and also to set off and assign to Hannah Schenck widow of the said Ruliff her dower in the same towit 358 acres situate lying & being in the Miami purchase in the county and State aforesaid, being the West part of section No. 6 in the second entire Township east from the great Miami river and second entire range being part of the lands purchased by John Cleves Symes Esq. from the United States - and also 84 acres & 52 hundreths of an acre situate in the south half of section No. one in the third Township and third entire range in the Miami tract, in the county of Warren and State of Ohio have agreeably to the requisitions of said order made partition of the same in the following manner:

first by setting off to the widow **Hannah Schenck** her dower in the same as follows to wit 120 acres & seventy six hundreths of an acre in section number six including the mansion house in full of her dower in the two several tracts above described as will more at large appear by reference to the foregoing plat.

We set off and assign to **Aaron R. Schenck** one of the children and heirs of the said Ruliff Schenck dec'd, 67 acres & 36 hundreths of an acre in section number 6 designated No. 1 in the foregoing plat in full of his share in said real estate.

We also set off & assign to Jacob R. Schenck 53 acres & 59 hundreths of an acre in the said section No. 6 in full of his share as one of the heirs of the said Ruliff Schenck decd. in the real estate of said deceased being No. 2 as

designated on the foregoing Plat.

We also set off & assign to **John R. Schenck** one of the heirs aforesaid 63 acres and 81 hundreths of an acre in said section No. 6 in full of his share in said real estate being number 4 as designated on the foregoing Plat.

We also set off and assign to **Isaac Schenck** one of the heirs as aforesaid 69 acres & 60 hundreths of an acre being fractional lot No. 6 in section number 6 and fraction number 8 in section number one as designated in the foregoing plats of said real estate in full of his share of said real estate.

We set off to **Jane Briney** wife of John Briney 59 acres and 52 hundredths of an acre in section number one in full of her share as one of the heirs as aforesaid of the real estate of the said Ruliff Schenck decd. designated No. 7 on the foregoing Plat.

We set off to **Maria Verbryck** wife of Peter Verbryck one of the heirs as aforesaid 61 acres and 47 hundreths of an acre in section No. 6 in full of her share in said real estate being designated No. 3 on the foregoing plat.

We set off to **Sarah Schenck** one of the heirs as aforesaid 67 acres and 17 hundredths of an acre in full of her share in said real estate designated number 5 on the foregoing plat.

Given under our hands this 16th of February 1833. William Coulson, James Baxter, Jacob Hall Commissioners.

The first chart shows the ancestral lineage of Roelof Schenck, son of Capt. John and Mary Van Doren Schenck and the second chart shows the lineage of Hannah Hageman, daughter of Adrian and Jannetje Lupardus Hageman.

Ancestors of Roelof Schenck

Chart no. _____
No. 1 on this chart is the same as no. _____ on chart no. _____

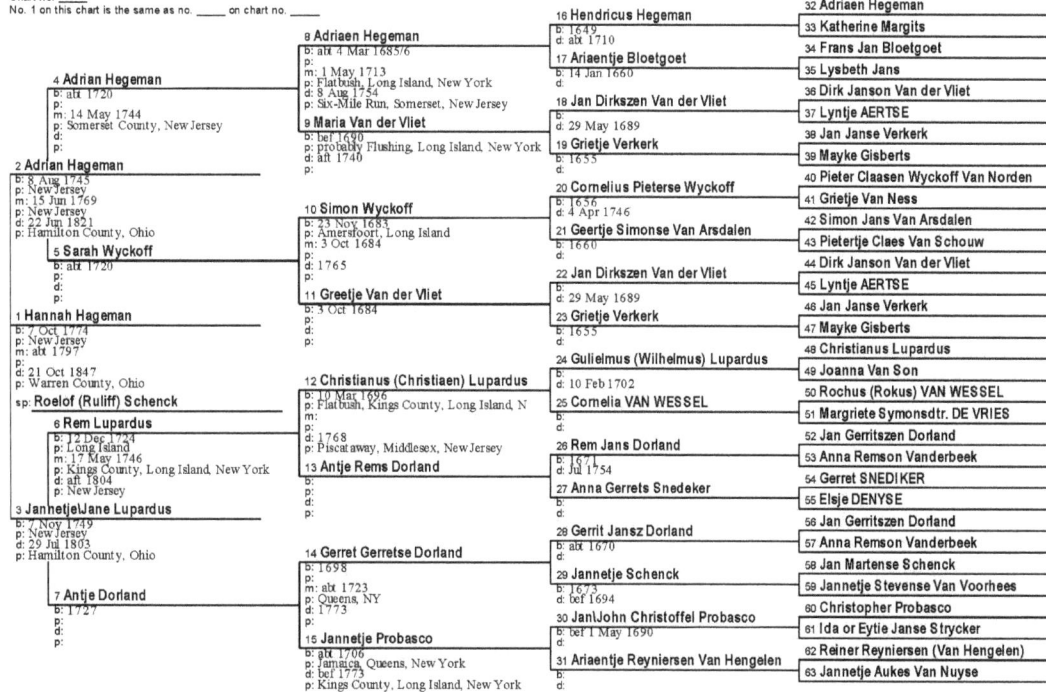

4 Roelof Schenck
b: 27 Apr 1697
p: Penn's Neck, Monmouth County, NJ
m: 1718
p: Penn's Neck, Monmouth County, NJ
d: 22 Aug 1768
p: Pleasant Valley, Monmouth County, NJ

2 John Roelofse Schenck
b: 3 Feb 1740
p: Penn's Neck, Monmouth County, NJ
m: 12 Nov 1763
p:
d: 10 Oct 1794
p: Penn's Neck, Monmouth County, NJ

5 Engeltje Jacobse Van Doren
b: 9 Oct 1696
p: Brooklyn, Kings, Long Island, NY
d: 29 Sep 1741
p: Pleasant Valley, Monmouth County, NJ

1 Roelof (Ruliff) Schenck
b: 3 Mar 1766
p: Penn's Neck, Monmouth County, NJ
m: abt 1797
p:
d: 28 Dec 1831
p: Warren County, Ohio

sp: **Hannah Hageman**

6 Jacob Van Dorn
b: 21 Jan 1703
p: Marlboro, Monmouth County, New Jersey
m: 4 Apr 1730
p:
d: 26 Feb 1770
p:

3 Maria (Mary) Van Dorn
b: 3 Nov 1746
p: Hillsdale, Somerset County, New Jersey
d: 8 Mar 1808
p:

7 Marytie Janse Schenck
b: 8 Aug 1712
p: New Jersey
d: 31 Oct 1756
p:

8 Garret Roelofse Schenck
b: 27 Oct 1671
p: Penn's Neck, Monmouth County, NJ
m: abt 1693
p: Penn's Neck, Monmouth County, NJ
d: 5 Sep 1745
p: Monmouth County, New Jersey

9 Neetlje Van Voorhees
b: 1 Oct 1675
p:
d: 4 Aug 1750
p: Pleasant Valley, Monmouth County, NJ

10 Jacob Van Dorn
b: 21 Oct 1668
p: Gowanus, Long Island, New York
m: abt 1690
p: Gowanus, Brooklyn, New York
d: bef 21 Mar 1718/9
p: Marlboro, Monmouth County, New Jersey

11 Marytje Adrianse Bennet
b: abt 1672
p: Gowanus, Brooklyn, New York
d: 1 Nov 1756
p:

12 Jacob Van Dorn
b: 21 Oct 1668
p: Gowanus, Long Island, New York
m: abt 1690
p: Gowanus, Brooklyn, New York
d: bef 21 Mar 1718/9
p: Marlboro, Monmouth County, New Jersey

13 Marytje Adrianse Bennet
b: abt 1672
p: Gowanus, Brooklyn, New York
d: 1 Nov 1756
p:

14 John\Jan Roelofse Schenck
b: 1 Mar 1670
p: Flatlands, Long Island, New York
m: 1 Oct 1692
p: Flatlands, Long Island, New York
d: 30 Jan 1753
p: Pleasant Valley, Monmouth County, NJ

15 Saartje Van Couwenhoven
b: 20 Dec 1674
p: Flatlands, Long Island, New York
d: 31 Jan 1761
p: Pleasant Valley, Monmouth County, NJ

16 Roelof Martense Schenck
b: 20 Jun 1619
d: 1704/5

17 Neeltje Van Couwenhoven
b: 20 Sep 1641
d: 1674

18 Coerte Van Voorhees
b: 1637
d: 1702

19 Marretje Van Couwenhoven
b: 19 Apr 1644
d: 1708

20 Christian Van Doorn
b: abt 1635
d: bef 1686

21 Tryntje Shubber
b: 1635
d:

22 Adriaen Willemszen Bennet
b: 1637
d: abt 1703

23 Agnietje Van Dyke
b: 1644
d: aft 1711

24 Christian Van Doorn
b: abt 1635
d: bef 1686

25 Tryntje Shubber
b: 1635
d:

26 Adriaen Willemszen Bennet
b: 1637
d: abt 1703

27 Agnietje Van Dyke
b: 1644
d: aft 1711

28 Roelof Martense Schenck
b: 20 Jun 1619
d: 1704/5

29 Neeltje Van Couwenhoven
b: 20 Sep 1641
d: 1674

30 William Van Couwenhoven
b: Jul 1636
d: 1728

31 Jannettje Montfoort
b:
d: 1723

32 **Martin Schenck Van Nydeck**
33 **Maria De Borckhurst**
34 **Garret Van Couwenhoven**
35 **Aeltje Cornelis Cool**
36 **Steven Van Voorhees**
37 **Aaltjen Wessels**
38 **Garret Van Couwenhoven**
39 **Aeltje Cornelis Cool**
40 **Pieter Van Dooren**
41 **Catherine Stelting**
42 **Cornelis Shubber**
43 **Adriantje Wallings**
44 **William Bennet**
45 **Mary Badie**
46 **Jan Thomasse Van Dyke**
47 **Tryntje Achias Haegen**
48 **Pieter Van Dooren**
49 **Catherine Stelting**
50 **Cornelis Shubber**
51 **Adriantje Wallings**
52 **William Bennet**
53 **Mary Badie**
54 **Jan Thomasse Van Dyke**
55 **Tryntje Achias Haegen**
56 **Martin Schenck Van Nydeck**
57 **Maria De Borckhurst**
58 **Garret Van Couwenhoven**
59 **Aeltje Cornelis Cool**
60 **Garret Van Couwenhoven**
61 **Aeltje Cornelis Cool**
62 **Pieter Van Monfoort**
63 **Sara DES Planque**

Ancestors of Hannah Hageman Schenck

Chart no. _____
No. 1 on this chart is the same as no. _____ on chart no. _____

4 Adrian Hegeman
b: abt 1720
p:
m: 14 May 1744
p: Somerset County, New Jersey
d:
p:

2 Adrian Hageman
b: 8 Aug 1745
p: New Jersey
m: 15 Jun 1769
p: New Jersey
d: 22 Jun 1821
p: Hamilton County, Ohio

5 Sarah Wyckoff
b: abt 1720
p:
d:
p:

1 Hannah Hageman
b: 7 Oct 1774
p: New Jersey
m: abt 1797
p:
d: 21 Oct 1847
p: Warren County, Ohio

sp: **Roelof (Ruliff) Schenck**

6 Rem Lupardus
b: 12 Dec 1724
p: Long Island
m: 17 May 1746
p: Kings County, Long Island, New York
d: aft 1804
p: New Jersey

3 Jannetje\Jane Lupardus
b: 7 Nov 1749
p: New Jersey
d: 29 Jul 1803
p: Hamilton County, Ohio

7 Antje Dorland
b: 1727
p:
d:
p:

8 Adriaen Hegeman
b: abt 4 Mar 1685/6
p:
m: 1 May 1713
p: Flatbush, Long Island, New York
d: 8 Aug 1754
p: Six-Mile Run, Somerset, New Jersey

9 Maria Van der Vliet
b: bef 1690
p: probably Flushing, Long Island, New York
d: aft 1740
p:

10 Simon Wyckoff
b: 23 Nov 1683
p: Amersfoort, Long Island
m: 3 Oct 1684
p:
d: 1765
p:

11 Greetje Van der Vliet
b: 3 Oct 1684
p:
d:
p:

12 Christianus (Christiaen) Lupardus
b: 10 Mar 1696
p: Flatbush, Kings County, Long Island, N
m:
p:
d: 1768
p: Piscataway, Middlesex, New Jersey

13 Antje Rems Dorland
b:
p:
d:
p:

14 Gerret Gerretse Dorland
b: 1698
p:
m: abt 1723
p: Queens, NY
d: 1773

15 Jannetje Probasco
b: abt 1706
p: Jamaica, Queens, New York
d: bef 1773
p: Kings County, Long Island, New York

16 Hendricus Hegeman
b: 1649
d: abt 1710

17 Ariaentje Bloetgoet
b: 14 Jan 1660
d:

18 Jan Dirkszen Van der Vliet
b:
d: 29 May 1689

19 Grietje Verkerk
b: 1655
d:

20 Cornelius Pieterse Wyckoff
b: 1656
d: 4 Apr 1746

21 Geertje Simonse Van Arsdalen
b: 1660
d:

22 Jan Dirkszen Van der Vliet
b:
d: 29 May 1689

23 Grietje Verkerk
b: 1655
d:

24 Gulielmus (Wilhelmus) Lupardus
b:
d: 10 Feb 1702

25 Cornelia VAN WESSEL
b:
d:

26 Rem Jans Dorland
b: 1671
d: Jul 1754

27 Anna Gerrets Snedeker
b:
d:

28 Gerrit Jansz Dorland
b: abt 1670
d:

29 Jannetje Schenck
b: 1673
d: bef 1694

30 Jan\John Christoffel Probasco
b: bef 1 May 1690
d:

31 Ariaentje Reyniersen Van Hengelen
b:
d:

32 **Adriaen Hegeman**
33 **Katherine Margits**
34 **Frans Jan Bloetgoet**
35 **Lysbeth Jans**
36 **Dirk Janson Van der Vliet**
37 **Lyntje AERTSE**
38 **Jan Janse Verkerk**
39 **Mayke Gisberts**
40 **Pieter Claasen Wyckoff Van Norden**
41 **Grietje Van Ness**
42 **Simon Jans Van Arsdalen**
43 **Pietertje Claes Van Schouw**
44 **Dirk Janson Van der Vliet**
45 **Lyntje AERTSE**
46 **Jan Janse Verkerk**
47 **Mayke Gisberts**
48 **Christianus Lupardus**
49 **Joanna Van Son**
50 **Rochus (Rokus) VAN WESSEL**
51 **Margriete Symonsdtr. DE VRIES**
52 **Jan Gerritszen Dorland**
53 **Anna Remson Vanderbeek**
54 **Gerret SNEDIKER**
55 **Elsje DENYSE**
56 **Jan Gerritszen Dorland**
57 **Anna Remson Vanderbeek**
58 **Jan Martense Schenck**
59 **Jannetje Stevense Van Voorhees**
60 **Christopher Probasco**
61 **Ida or Eytie Janse Strycker**
62 **Reiner Reyniersen (Van Hengelen)**
63 **Jannetje Aukes Van Nuyse**

Captain John Schenck and wife Maria Van Dorn
Parents of Roeloff/Ruliff Schenck

Captain John Schenck was born 3 February, 1740 in Monmouth Co., New Jersey. He was the son of Roelof Schenck and Engeltje Van Dorn and is an heir in the will of his father.

On 12 November 1763 in Monmouth County, he married Maria Van Dorn. Maria was born 3 November 1746, baptized at the New York City Dutch Church on 11 January 1747. She was married by New York license dated 12 November 1763 to Captain John Schenck, son of Roelof Garret Schenck and Engeltie Van Dorn. He signed a will on 29 Sep 1794 in Middlesex County, New Jersey. 1794, Sept 29.

SCHENCK, John Sr. Of Windsor Twsp. Middlesex County, New Jersey

"Wife, MARIAH, 4 horses, 5 milk cows, 5 young cattle, 15 sheep, riding chair, wagon, farming utensils, all household furniture, 1/3 of profits of home plantation and use of house, while my widow. Son, Ruliff, 340 acres, part of my purchase in the Western Territory in Simses (Symmes) Settlement of Miamies (Ohio); the same being valued at 111 lbs. and so charged against his share of my estate. The remaining part of said tract on the Miamies, valued @ 111 lbs., to any one of my sons who will take it as a part of his share. Daughter, Mary Schenck, 100 lbs. above her equal share. Sons, John, William, Isaac and Garret, to be bound out to such trades as each shall choose. Farm to be rented and remainder sold and used for support of children until of age. After wife marries, or dies, plantation to be sold and proceeds divided in equal shares among all the children. Executors-friends, John Schenck, Jr. of Penn's Neck, Peter Vandeveer, of Monmouth, and son Jacob Schenck. Recommends son, Jacob, to take home plantation. Witness-Jonathan Combs, Andrew Bowne, Garret Schenck, Proved Oct 15, 1794."

John died on 10 Oct 1794 at the age of 54 in Penn's Neck, Monmouth Co., New Jersey. He is buried in Holmdel Cemetery, but was originally buried in the Schenck-Couwenhoven Cemetery. The tombstone is reddish-brown sandstone. Note: John was apparently re-interred in Holmdel Cemetery sometime during late 19th Century. Maria died 8 March 1808.

John Roelofse Schenck and Mariah (Mary) Van Dorn had the following children:

- Jane Schenck
- Maryke Roelofse Schenck, born Roelof (Ruliff) Schenck, born 3 Mar 1766, Penn's Neck, Monmouth Co., New Jersey; married Hannah Hageman, about 1797; died 28 Dec 1831, Warren Co., Ohio.
- Antje Schenck was born in 1768. She died on 11 Apr 1769 at the age of 1.
- Sarah Schenck was born in 1770. She died on 16 Oct 1856 at the age of 86. Sarah moved to Alden, New York; then Bennington, New York, and Lapeer, Michigan.
- Jacob Schenck, born 1773; married Maria Lott, 1792; died 12 Apr 1856.
- Rachel Schenck, born 1775; married William Post, 1792; died 20 Sep 1765.
- John Schenck was born in 1780. He died on 3 Feb 1857 at the age of 77. John remained at Penn's Neck, New Jersey.
- Isaac Schenck, born 1783; married Ruth Anna Knox; died 21 Sep 1856.
- Garret Schenck was born in 1788. Garrett moved to Waterloo, New York and the unknown West.

Capt. John Schenck

John assisted in establishing American independence while acting in the capacity of Captain in the 2nd Regiment of Middlesex County, New Jersey from the outbreak of the Revolutionary War until August 9, 1771, when he and six other Captains and their companies were set off, forming the 3rd Regiment, Middlesex County Militia, by virtue of the following order:

"A petition of sundry officers of the 2nd Battalion of Middlesex Co. praying a division of thereof, read and ordered a second reading. Whereupon Ordered that a third Battalion be formed out of the same, consisting of the companies commanded by the Captains Hartyen, Barr, Staut, Schenck, Sendeler, Withersell and Pyatt. Ordered that John Duychink Reg. be Colonel; William Soudder, Esq. be First Major, and the 2nd be appointed on the return of General Heards Regiment." [1]

"John Schenck served throughout the seven years of the war as captain. He raised his own company, equipped, fed and paid them through the Revolution, or a great part of it. Many of them were his own slaves, whom he set free and enlisted. He was well known and trusted by Washington.

His home at Penn's Neck, one and one-half miles from Princeton, was occupied several weeks before the battle of Trenton and Princeton, the latter battle fought within site of his home."

The Schenck house was occupied by British Major Thomas Moncrief, an engineer with the British 7th Regiment of Foot Soldiers for some time.

After the Battle of Princeton, he evacuated immediately and went to the assistance of the British at Trenton, carrying away with them everything of value. [2]

Capt. John Schenck was in the battle of Monmouth and in continuous service until the war was closed.

Sources:

[1] Taken from the minutes of the Provisional Congress and Council of Safety 1775-1776 of the State of New Jersey.

[2] *Officers and Men of N.J. in the Revolutionary War"*, page 408. By General W. S. Stryke, Agt. Gen. of N.J.

The National Society of the Daughters of the American Revolution has recognized his service and his Ancestor number is A100697.

Garret Schenck & Neeltje Voorhees

Parents of Roelof Schenck

Garret was born October 27, 1671. He married, about 1693, Neeltje, daughter of Koert Voorhees. He resided on the farm occupied by Theodore Rapelyea, and built the spacious old mansion still standing there in good order. He acquired a large property and in different parts of the country, among which, in company with John Couwenhoven, was a six thousand acre tract of land at Penn's Neck purchased of John Penn. Then the First Reformed Church of Freehold was organized, in 1709, he was one of the two first deacons, and from 1721 to 1727 he was a member of the Provincial Assembly of New Jersey. He had five sons -- Roelof, Koert, Garret, Jan and Albert -- and five daughters.

Garret died 5, 1745 and Neeltje, August 4, 1750. In his will dated January 13, 1739, he calls himself *'a gentleman of Middletown'*, mentions his wife Neeltje and provides for her care by their son Garret. Sons Roelof, Garret, Koert, John and Albert and daughters Mary, Alkie, Neeltje, Rachel and Margaret are mentioned. Also mentioned were grandchildren, not named, sons and daughters of Anne, who was deceased, and a granddaughter, Nelly. Executors were his wife, his son Roelof and son-in-law Hendrick Hendricksen. The will was proved October 7, 1745.

Garret Roelofse Schenck and Neetlje Coerten Van Voorhees had the following children:

- **Antje Schenck**, born 15 Nov 1694, New York; married Matthias Lane, 1712.

- **Roelof Schenck**, born 27 Apr 1697, Penn's Neck, Monmouth Co., New Jersey; married Engeltje Jacobse Van Doren, 1718, Penn's Neck, Monmouth Co., New Jersey; died 22 Aug 1768, Pleasant Valley, Monmouth Co., New Jersey.

- **Mary Schenck**, born 1 Nov 1699; married Hendrick Smock, Sep 1747; died Sep 1747.

- **Koert Schenck**, born 1702; married Mary P. Couwenhoven, 1724; died 2 Jun 1771.

- **Altje Schenck**, born 1 May 1705; married Teunis Van Derveer, 1723.

- **Neeltje Schenck**, born 1708, Penn's Neck, Monmouth Co., New Jersey; married Henrick Hendrickson, 1725.

- **Rachel Schenck** was born on 2 Apr 1710 in Penn's Neck, Monmouth County, NJ.

- **Garett Schenck** was born on 30 Aug 1712 in Pleasant Valley, Monmouth Co., New Jersey. He died on 20 Aug 1757 at the age of 44 in Pleasant Valley, Monmouth Co., New Jersey.

- **Margaret Schenck**, born 17 Apr 1715, Penn's Neck, Monmouth Co., New Jersey; married Cornelius Couwenhoven, in 1735.

- **Jan (John) Schenck** was born on 7 Dec 1717 in Penn's Neck, Monmouth Co., New Jersey; married Mary Johnson. He died 13 Feb 1775 and was buried in Monmouth Co. New Jersey.

- **Albert Schenck**, born 19 Apr 1721, Penn's Neck, Monmouth Co., New Jersey; married Catryntje (Katy) Van Couwenhoven, 1745; married Angenetje Van Brunt, 1758, Marlboro, Monmouth Co., New Jersey; died 21 May 1786, Middlesex Co., New Jersey.

Garret emigrated in 1696 or 1698 from New Amsterdam to Monmouth County, New Jersey and together with his brother John, and Cornelius Couwenhoven, who married their sister Margaret, settled in Pleasant Valley on a five hundred acre tract of land purchased of John Bowne, merchant of Middletown. This is a copy of the actual land document dated 1697. It is very difficult to read but the signature of John Browne and the date are legible.

WILL OF GARRET ROELOFSE SCHENCK

Extracted from *DOCUMENTS RELATING TO THE COLONIAL HISTORY OF THE STATE OF NEW JERSEY, VOLUME XXX, CALENDAR OF NEW JERSEY WILLS, VOLUME II, 1730-1750*; Paterson NJ, 1918 (Libers 1, 2, etc. are of West Jersey Wills. Those as Libers A, B, etc., are of East Jersey Wills) SCHENCK, page 417:

1739, Jan. 12. Schenck, Garret, of Middletown, Monmouth co., gent. Will of.

Wife, Neelkie. Son, Roeloffe, the great Dutch Bible, meadow at Conascunk Meadows and the third of landing on Chingaroras Creek.

Sons Roeloffe and Garrat, neck of land adjoining Capt. Reids. Son, Koert. Son, Garrat, lot adjoining Hendrick Hendrickson, land bought of John Bowne, March 10, 1705, and testator's home plantation. Sons, John and Albert, land at Brunswick, bought of Koert Van Voorhuyse, Nov. 5, 1723.

Five daughters, Mary, Alkie, Neelkie, Rachel and Margaret, land at Conascunk purchased of Hendrick Hendrickson, and 986 acres at Penn's Neck bounded by Tatamus Swamp, Bear Swamp and Asinpink Creek. Grandchildren, sons and daughters of daughter Anne (evidently eight in number), granddaughter, Nelly. Personal estate after wife's decease to testator's eleven children. Executor's wife, son Roeloffe and son-in-law Hendrick Hendrickson. Witnesses Johannes Bennet, Roelyf Covenhoven and Robert Dodsworth. Proved Oct. 7, 1745. Roelef Schenck and Hendrick Hendrickson sworn as executors. Lib. D, p. 394.

Note: Garret's will is several pages long and the above is a condensed version of the original will.

Roelof Martense Schenck & Neeltje Van Kouwenhoven

Parents of Garret Schenck

Roelof was born on 20 Jun 1619 in Amersfoort, Utrecht, Netherlands. He immigrated before 17 July 1649. Roelof arrived in New Amsterdam having traveled on the ship *Valckenier* (The Falconer). It sailed from Amsterdam 1649, arrived New Amsterdam before 17 July 1649.

He was the son of Martin Schenck Van Nydeck and Maria Margretha Bockhurst. Roelof married Neeltje Gerretse Van Kouwenhoven, daughter of Gerret Wolfersen Van Kouwenhoven and Aeltje Cornelis Cool about 1660 at Flatlands, Kings Co., New York. After the death of Neeltje, Roelof married Anetje Pieterse Wyckoff and had the following children: Margaret; Neeltje; Mayke and Sara. After Anetje died he married a third time on November 19, 1688 to Katrina (Catherine) Cruiger, widow of Stofle Hoogland, and they had no children.

Roeloff obtained a patent for 23 morgens (*1 morgan of land equals $\frac{1}{2}$ to 2 $\frac{1}{2}$ acres*) at Flatlands.

Roelof held the position of magistrate from 1662 until 1664. He was a representative in the Hempstead convention in 1665.

Roelof purchased 200 acres on 19 March 1674 at Amersfoort, Kings County, New York. Roelof purchased/bought of his brother Jan one-half of mill and the island on which it stood on 20 Apr 1688.

He gave oath of allegiance in 1678 at Flatlands, Kings Co., New York. He held the position of justice of the peace, 1684, 1689, and 1692, and held the position of sheriff of the county in 1685. He became Captain of Horse in 1690.

He died 1704 at Flatlands, Kings Co., New York.

Roelof settled in Niue Amersfoort, afterwards called Flatlands, on Nassau Island, afterward called Long Island in 1661, and was prominent where he lived and one of the 6 or 7 wealthiest men on the Island. In 1687 his name appears on the list among those who took the oath of allegiance to the English Government which he subscribed between the 26th and 30th of September.

He obtained a patent for forty-six acres of land and subsequently purchased lands until he must have owned some three hundred acres and the one-half of the mill occupied by his brother Jan (John). At one assessment for taxation his rateables were the next highest in the town, and at another subsequently taken they were the highest. He was among the first enrolled as a member of the church of Flatlands, and no doubt among its principal supporters. When a bill was procured for the church, Roelof's subscription was the highest on the list.

Roelof was appointed by Governor Leisler Captain of Cavalry in Kings County, and at several different times held the office of justice of the peace and once that of schepen, or judge, and in general in public affairs was among the leading men in the colony.

Neeltje Van Kouwenhoven, daughter of Garret Wolfert Van Kouwenhoven and Aeltje Cornelius Cool, was born on 20 Sep 1641 in New Amsterdam, New York. The witnesses at her baptism were Wolfert Gerritszen, Huysen Aertszen, and Hester Simons.

Garret Wolphertse Van Kouvenhoven, was a son of Wolfert Garretson Van Couwenhoven and Neeltje Jens, who came from Amersfoort aforesaid to America in 1630 with the Dutch emigrants who settled Rensselaerwick, near what is now Albany, in the state of New York. In 1630, he helped to settle Brooklyn, New York and area towns.

Aeltie Cornelius Cool was born 1618 and died June 14, 1683 in Flatlands, Long Island, New York. She married Garret Wolphertse Van Couvenhoven, 10 March 1634/35 in Oyster Bay, New York.

Neeltje married Roeloff Martense Schenck in 1660. Soon after their marriage they settled permanently at Flatlands, Long Island. She died in 1674 at the age of 33 in Flatlands, Kings Co., Long Island, New York.

Children of Roelof Martense Schenck and Neeltje Gerretse Van Kouwenhoven:

- Marten Roelofse Schenck, b. 2 Jan 1661 – d. 2 May 1727)

- Annetje Roelofse Schenck b. abt. 1663 – d. 25 Mar 1688)

- Jannetje Roelofse Schenck b. abt. 1664

- Marike Roelofse Schenck, b. 14 Feb 1666/67 died unknown

- John Roelofse Schenck, b. 1 Mar 1670 - d. 30 Jan 1753)

- Garret Roelofse Schenck, b. 27 Oct 1671 - d. 5 Sept 1745

Children of Roelof Martense Schenck and Annetje Wyckoff:

- Margaretta Schenck, b. 16 Jan 1677/78 - d. 16 Dec 1751

- Neeltje Roelofse Schenck (3 Jan 1682 - d. 27 July 1751)

- Mayke Schenck (14 Jan b. 1684 - d. 25 Nov 1736

- Sara Schenck (18 Dec 1685 - d. 1 Nov 1727

- Willampe Schenck, b. abt 1687 - unknown

There were no children from the marriage of Roelof and Catryntyna Crigers.

Martin was left the homestead at Flatlands, and his descendants have principally remained on Long Island.

Note: The spelling of Kouwenhoven is also shown as Couwenhoven in various record. Sometimes the word "van" precedes the surname.

Jan Martense Schenck and Jannetje Stevens Van Voorhees

Jan Martense Schenck, son of Martin Schenck and Jannetje Van Voorhees. Jannetje Stevense Van Voorhees was born at Netherlands. She was the daughter of Steven Coerte Van Voorhees and Willempie Roelofse. She immigrated on ship 'De Bonte Koe' in 1660. She married Jan Martense Schenck, son of Martin Schenck, circa 1672 at Flatlands.

Their daughter Jannetje married Gerret, the eldest son of Jan Gerritzsen Dorland and Anna Remsen. He was born in Brooklyn about 1670. Jannetje married Gerret Jansen Dorland 20 May 1692 in Flatbush in the Reformed Dutch Protestant Dutch Church of Flatbush.

Jannetje is mentioned in her father Jan Martense's will. He passed away on August 27, 1687, in Kings County, New York, at the age of 56.

John Martinse Schenck's Will: In the name of Jesus Christ, in the year which we write 1688 01. 9, the 28 day of January. I, John Martinse at present being sick abed. His wife Jannettie Stevens is to remain in full possession of all the estate, till the youngest child is of age or married. Then shall Martin Johnson take in his possession the old house with the small island and mill, on condition that he render to his mother yearly 600 guilders. The youngest son, Stephen Johnson, shall have the lot of land in the neck with the meadow at Hog Neck. The other children shall have as follows: Stephen Johnson, 100 pieces of 8. Jannettie Johnson, 100 pieces of 8 and 2 cows, and daughter Neltie to have the same. As regards an expected child, if it be a son he shall have the money standing out in New York, 1600 guilders. If it be a daughter, it is to have the same as the other daughters. Dated in Amersfoort in Kings County, January 28, 1688. John Martinse Schenck. Witnesses, John Tan Duyckhings, Win. Gerittse von Cowenhoven. Proved July 5, 1694, and Letters of Administration granted to widow Jannettie Stevens.

It should be noted that "Jan" became "John" after arriving in New Amsterdam. His children used the patronymic "Johnson" meaning the son or daughter of John.

Shown below are the ancestors of Jannetje/Jane Lupardus Hageman, wife of Adrian Hageman, and namesake of her great grandmother, Jannetje Schenck Dorland.

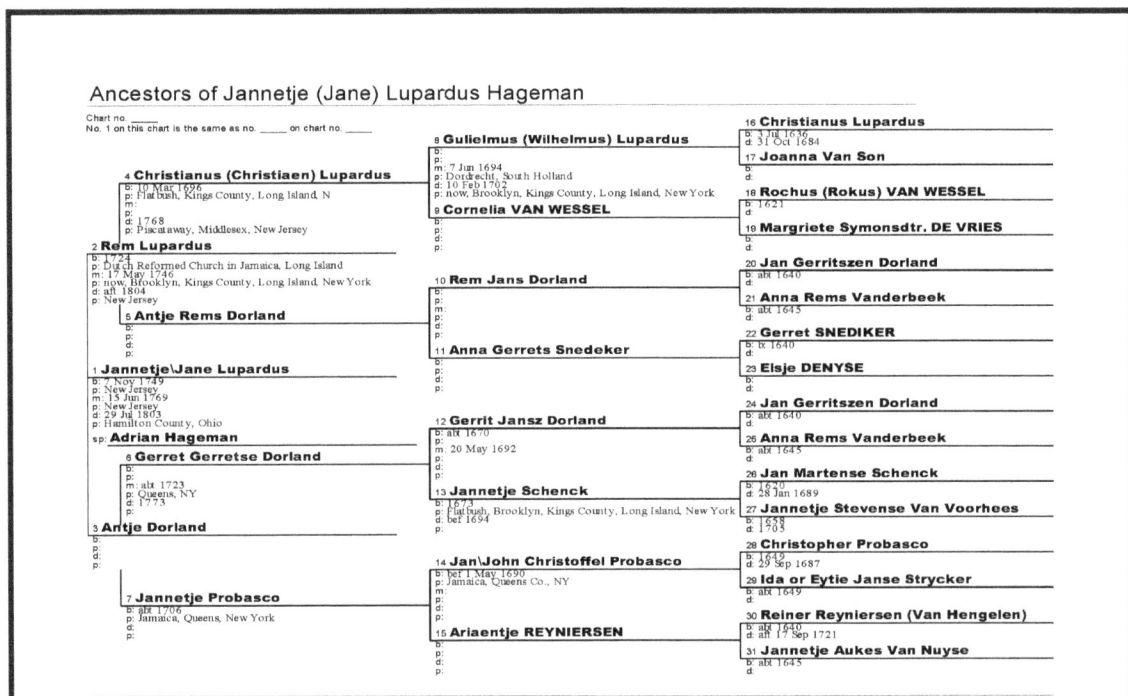

Ancestors of Jannetje (Jane) Lupardus Hageman

Adrian & Jannetje/Jane Lupardus Hageman

Parents of Hannah Hageman Schenck

Hannah was the daughter of Adrian and Jannetje Lupardus Hageman. She was born 7 October 1774 in New Jersey. She died on 21 Oct 1847 at the age of 73 in Warren Co., Ohio.

Adrian Hageman was born on 8 Aug 1745 in New Jersey. Adrian was a son of Adrian and Sarah Wycoff Hageman. Jannetje or Jane Lupardus was the daughter of Rem Lupardus and wife Annetje Dorland and was born on 7 Nov 1749 in New Jersey. Jannetje\Jane and Adrian Hageman were married on 15 Jun 1769 in New Jersey. Jane was mentioned in Rem's will as being deceased and her children were given an inheritance from their grandfather Rem.

'Adrian L. Hageman, a Dutchman from New Jersey cut a wagon way from Columbia, east of Cincinnati in 1794.

The first conveyance in section 30 (of John Cleves Symmes tract of land), west of the Dayton turnpike, and west of Main Street in Sharon, Ohio, was made in 1798 by Johnathan Dayton to Adrian Hageman for the south half of the section, 320 acres. The brick homestead stood just west of the railroad crossing on Reading Road. On April 4, 1807, Adrian purchased another 275 acres from Symmes, making him the owner of 619 acres of land in and around Sharon. Adrian's son Simon (Simeon) was deeded 124 acres of the land in August of 1807. On the same day he (Adrian) conveyed to son Christian Hageman, 100 acres. The Hageman homestead was built from 1818-1822 and was the oldest house in the village for a long time. It was the finest house in town and stood for over 100 years. It was built just west of Reading Road where it crossed the New York Central Railroad in Hagerman town. There is still a street in Sharonville called Hageman Street. The house stood on the site until about 1940.'

Adrian Hageman and Jannetje\Jane Lupardus had the following children:

Adrian Hageman was born on 3 Dec 1771 in New Jersey. He died about 1810 at the age of 39 in Hamilton Co., Ohio. He held the title of Jr. Adrian, Jr. served terms in the state legislature, then at Chillicothe. He married Elizabeth Shank in 1791.

• **Hannah Hageman**, born 7 Oct 1774, New Jersey; died 21 Oct 1847, Warren Co., Ohio and married Roelof/Rulif Schenck.

• **Simon Hageman** was born on 3 Aug 1780 and was baptized on 17 Aug 1780 in the Neshanic Dutch Reform Church in Somerset Co., New Jersey. He died on 2 Jul 1860 at the age of 79. He married Catherine Hercules in 1830.

• **Mary Hageman** was born about 1782. She married John Anderson.

• **Christian Hageman** was born in 1783 and was baptized in 1783. He died in 1835 at the age of 52 in Hamilton County, Ohio. He married Esther Hercules, a sister of Catherine.

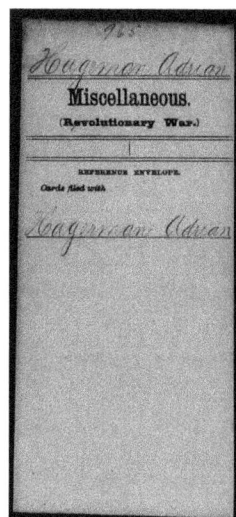

Adrian served in the Revolutionary War in the Somerset Co, New Jersey Militia.

The National Society of the Daughters of the American Revolution has recognized his service and his Ancestor number is A049090.

LAST WILL AND TESTAMENT OF ADRIAN HAGEMAN

No. 135, Filed Aug. 30, 1821, Recorded Vol. 9, Page 467, Sycamore Township, Hamilton County, Ohio

In the name of God, Amen. I Adrian Hageman of the township of Sycamore in the county of Hamilton and state of Ohio do being of sound mind and memory knowing the uncertainty of human life do make ordain and publish this for my last will and testament.

FIRST, I desire and direct that as soon as possibly convenient after my decease that all my just debts and funeral charges be paid and discharged.

SECOND, I give and bequeath unto my children Simon Hageman, Christian Hageman, Hannah Schenck, wife of Ruloph Schenck, each one dollar and to my daughter Mary Anderson, wife of John Anderson, ten dollars, to be paid to them out of my moveable estate by my executors after my decease.

SECOND, I give bequeath and devise unto my dear wife Micah Hageman all the residue of my moveable estate and also all my real estate wherever situate lying or being, to be by her held used and enjoyed until the oldest of her children born in wedlock in the coverture between her and myself shall become of lawful age, when the property shall be divided, and the real estate partitioned into three equal parts, which I do give devise and bequeath unto my three youngest children VIS. Charlotte, Lavina and Lucinda a third each of them one of the parts so as aforesaid divided and partitioned and each part to remain in the hands and possession of my said wife until the children respectively become of age when at which time each is to receive their apportionments - the mother still retaining her dower in the real estate.

Should however it happen that my said wife should again intermarry then and in that case it is my will that immediately on such an event taking place that her dower shall be set off to her and the property both real and personal be placed in the hands of lawful guardians duly appointed for my said three youngest children who shall dispose or manage it to the best advantage that is the moveable property.

The real estate shall remain unsold and partitioned as aforesaid among them and given to each her share on her arriving at lawful age, the proceeds of the real estate and improvements of the moveable estate or it's proceeds to be applied towards the bringing up and educating of my three youngest children as aforesaid.

Should either of my said youngest children die before the youngest arrives at full age, then under that case her share to go to her sisters and second to the remainder, but should they all die before the youngest is of age, then the property to be equally divided among my surviving children, my wife tho, still retaining her dower.

I do appoint my trusty friends John Cummins and Thomas Whalen executors of this my testament and last will.

In witness whereof I have hereunto set my hand and seal this twenty third day of September in the year of our Lord one thousand eight hundred and eighteen.

Signed: Adrian Hagaman (Seal)

Signed, sealed, published and declared by the said Adrian Hageman to be his last will and testament on the day and date aforesaid in presence of us: Samuel Ayers, Mary W. Henderson, Thomas Henderson

Note: Adrian married after the death of his first wife, Jannetje/Jane Lupardus Hageman. His second wife's given name was Micah but to date I have not found her surname. They had three daughters, Charlotte, Lavina and Lucinda.

Lupardus Ancestry

Jannetje (Jane) Lupardus was a daughter of Rem Lupardus and Antje Dorland. This is the same Dorland family that we have in our Jan Martense and Jannetje Van Voorhees Schenck family. The marriage of Rem and Antje took place three generations later.

Antje Dorland's parents were Gerret Gerretse Dorland and Jannetje Probasco.

It was finding Rem's will that led to my identifying Hannah Hageman Schenck's family. As the will is very lengthy, I will only include a portion of it here.

1804 October 15, Lupardus, Rem Of Amwell Twnship, Hunterdon Co.

Will of Rem Lupardus. Copied from the original Will, No. 2152 J., on file in the State.

I, Rem Lupardus of the Township of Amwell, County of Hunterdon and State of New Jersey; being aged, and weak in body, but of sound mind and memory; blessed be almighty God for the same; do make and publish this my last will and testament, in manner and form following Viz.,

First, I do will and ordain, that all my real and personal estate be sold, to the best advantage, as soon as conveniently may be, after my decease, by my executors, hereafter named, or the survivor of them (except my wearing) hereby authorizing my executors, or the survivor of them, to give a deed and conveyance, or deeds and conveyances, for my said estate, to purchaser, or purchasers, as the case may require and out of the money arising from the sale of my estate, I do will that all my debts and funeral charges be punctually and honestly paid.

Second, unto my daughter Anne the wife of Abraham Striker, I give and bequeath the sum

of Twelve pounds, lawful money, yearly and every year during her, my said daughter's, natural life, to be paid as is hereafter mentioned.

Third, unto my grandson Jacob Wycoff Lupardus, son of my son Christian Lupardus, I give and bequeath the sum of five hundred pounds lawful money.

Fourth, unto my grandsons Garret D. Striker, and Peter Striker, the sons of my daughter Anne, I give and bequeath the sum of Four hundred pounds, lawful money, to each of them, my said grandsons. And in consideration of the bequest to my said grandsons Jacob Wykoff Lupardus, Garret D. Striker, and Peter Striker, I do will and ordain, that they my said grandsons do pay the annuity, given and bequeathed unto my daughter Anne as aforesaid, in proportion to the legacies given and bequeathed unto them my said grandsons.

Fifth, unto my granddaughters, Charity, and Hannah, the daughters of my daughter Anne, the wife of Abraham Striker, I give and bequeath the sum of One hundred pounds lawful money, to each of them my said granddaughters.

Sixth, unto my grandsons, and granddaughters, the sons and daughters of my daughter Jane, late the wife of Adrian Hagaman, to wit. Adrian Hagaman, Iunr. Simon Hagaman, Christian Hagaman, Hannah Hagaman and Mary Hagaman. I give and bequeath the sum of One hundred pounds lawful money, to each of them my said grandsons and granddaughters; my will further is, that if any of the sons or daughters of my daughter Jane, should be dead at the time of my decease, that the legacy of the deceased, be equally divided among the surviving children of my daughter Jane.

Four Generations of the Lupardus Ancestry

First Generation

Rem Lupardus was born in 1724 in Dutch Reformed Church in Jamaica, Long Island and was baptized on 25 Dec 1724 in Dutch Reformed Church in Jamaica, Long Island. He lived in Raritan, Hunterdon Co., New Jersey in 1782. He died after 1804 at the age of 80 in New Jersey. He signed a will in 1805 in Hunterdon Co., New Jersey.

Annetje Gerrits Dorland and was the daughter of Gerret Gerretse Dorland and wife Jannetje Probasco. She married her cousin, Rem. She was baptized 30 April 1727 and married Rem Lupardus 17 May 1746 in Flatbush. She died in Hunterdon Co., New Jersey before 1804.

Second Generation (Grandparents)

Christianus (Christiaen) Lupardus was born on 10 Mar 1696 in Flatbush, Kings Co., Long Island, New York. He died in 1768 at the age of 72 in Piscataway, Middlesex, New Jersey.

Antje Dorland was born about 1697 and died 1730-1733. She was the daughter of Rem Dorland and Anna Snedeker.

Third Generation (Great Grandparents)

Gulielmus (Wilhelmus) Lupardus was baptized on 21 Aug 1669 in Nieuwenhoorn, Holland. He died on 10 Feb 1702 in Flatbush, now, Brooklyn, Kings Co., Long Island, New York. Cornelia Van Wessel and Gulielmus (Wilhelmus) Lupardus were married on 7 Jun 1694 in Dordrecht, South Holland.

In October, 1695, the family left Dordrecht, South Holland and arrived in New Netherland, where the Reverend Lupardus served as minister of the Dutch Church at Flatbush, Long Island.

Cornelia VAN WESSEL was baptized on 25 Mar 1663 in Dordrecht, South Holland. She died 26 June 1737.

Rems Dorland was the second son of Jan Gerritszen Dorland and Anna Remsen, born about 1672, probably in Brooklyn. He married Anna Snedeker, the daughter of Gerrit Snedeker and Elsie Teunissen (Denyse).

Anna Snedeker was born about 1671. There are no death records for Rems and Anna Snedeker Dorland.

Fourth Generation (2nd Great Grandparents)

Christianus Lupardus
Joanna Van Son

Rochus (Rokus) Van Wessel
Margriete Symonsdtr De Vries

Jan Gerritszen Dorland
Anna Rems Vanderbeek

Gerret Snediker
Elsje Denyse

Note: The given name of Rem comes from the surname Remsen. Rem Janszen "Remsen" Vanderbeeck "Vanderbeek" was born in Oldenburg, Lower Saxony, Germany. He married Jannetje Jorisse Rapelje "Rapalie" on December 2, 1642, in Netherlands. They had one child during their marriage. He died in 1681. The children went by the surname REMSEN (son of REM) and dropped the Vanderbeek name)

Gage & Burleson

Coat of Arms

James & Elanora Pointer Gage,
Parents of Alta Pearl Gage Pointer

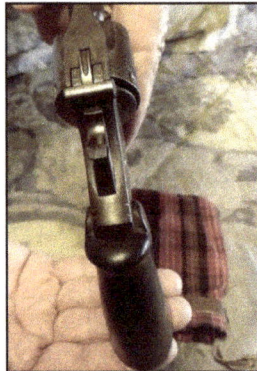

James Gage was the son of William M and Elizabeth Townsend Gage. He was born on 2 Feb 1860 in Bastrop Co. Texas. James Gage was a farmer in Lee County, Texas.

The gun photos were provided by James Preston Pointer and taken by his daughter Vickie Pointer. The gun is now in the possession of the sons of J. T. Pointer: James Preston, David & Tom Pointer.

Elanora Pointer, daughter of John Thomas and Kesiah Schenck Pointer married James Gage and the marriage was solemnized 3 September 1882, in Erath Co. Texas.

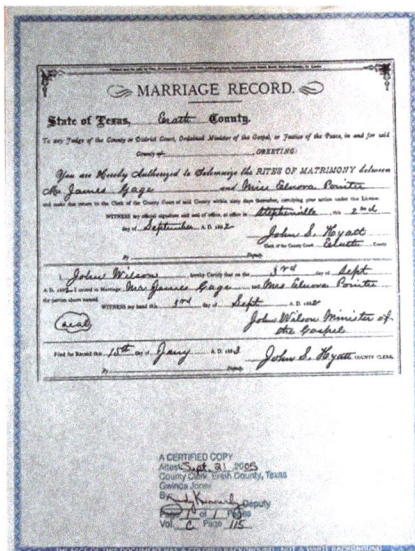

MARRIAGE RECORD OF
JAMES GAGE & ELANORA POINTER

To any Judge of the County or District Court, Ordained Minister of the Gospel, or Justice of the Peace, in and for said county GREETINGS:
You are hereby authorized to solemnize the RITES OF MATRIMONY between. James Gage and Miss Elnora Pointer and make due return to the Clerk of the County Court of said County within sixty days thereafter, certifying your action under the License.

Witness my official signature and seal of office, at office in Stephenville, this 2nd day of September A.D. 1882.
John S Hyatt, Clerk of the County Court Erath County.

OBITUARY OF JAMES GAGE

"Mr. James Gage, son of the late William and Betty Gage, was born in the Pleasant Grove Community, east of Elgin, February 2, 1860, where he was reared and engaged in farming in that vicinity until his retirement a few years ago. He was married September 6, 1881, in Hamilton, Texas to Miss Elanora Pointer. About 1895 he purchased a farm and built a nice home where he has since lived. Mrs. Gage passed on May 1, 1938. September 24, 1940, his son, W.H. Gage, and family went to make their home with him and gave him loving care and companionship. He had been confined to his bed about two months altho a complication of pneumonia of only a few days duration was the attributed cause of his death, which occurred at 1:40 p.m. Thursday, May 29, 1941, at his home.

Last rites were held from the church at Pleasant Grove at 3:30 p.m. Friday, May 30th, with the Rev. Ralph Wolfe, pastor of Central Christian church, Elgin, officiating. Pall bearers were Ray Gage, Wendell Gaston, G.D. Gage, grandsons, C.B. Dildy, grandson by marriage and J.R. Cook.

Interment was in the family burial plot in Pleasant

Grove Cemetery beside his wife and beautiful floral tributes banked his final resting place, sent by relatives and friends who held him in high esteem.

Survivors are six children, namely, L.L. Gage, Austin; Tom, Thrall; Mrs. Sam Pointer, Marlin; Mrs. P.G. Elkins, Houston; W. H. and O.V. Gage, Elgin; one sister, Mrs. Bessie Eggleston, Gainesville; two brothers, Mitt and Will Gage, Elgin.

Mr. Gage was a prominent citizen in his community; he served as trustee in the school district several times and was known for his progressive and aggressive spirit. He was a member of the Pleasant Grove Christian Church and a fine Christian character. He was dependable and trustworthy and inspired the confidence and respect of all who made his acquaintance. He was a generous and kind neighbor; he loved company and the welcome sign was always out at his home. He will be missed by a large circle of friends."

Note: James & Elanora were married in Erath County, rather than Hamilton County.

James death resulted from cancer of the right hand and a complication of pneumonia.

He is buried in Pleasant Grove Cemetery, Elgin, Texas.

Elanora Pointer Gage

Elanora was the daughter of John Thomas and Kesiah Schenck Pointer. She was born 14 May 1867 and died 1 May 1938. Elanora's clothing caught on fire from a wood stove. Her grandson, Virgil, Sr., received burns to the hands while trying to extinguish it. She suffered severe burns and subsequently died from pneumonia.

Memories of Elanora: One of her sons, Oma, referred to her as 'an angel on earth and very beautiful in her youth'.

James Gage and Elanora Pointer had the following children:

- **Elizabeth Kesiah\ Kizzie Gage** was born in 1885 and married Joe B Barber in 1914. She died in 1918 at the age of 33.
- **James Thomas (Tom) Gage**, was born 30 May 1888; died 31 December 1978, and married Jessie Diddle in 1908.
- **Lonnie Lee Gage**, born 23 October 1889; married Mattie Condon, 12 May 1905; died 14 Aug 1957, Austin, Travis Co., Texas.

- **Alta Pearl Gage**, born 10 Apr 1892, Giddings, Lee Co., Texas; married Samuel Thomas Pointer, 23 July 1913, Mills Co., Texas; died 12 Feb 1980, Stephenville, Erath Co. Texas.
- **Wilburn Hurshel Gage** was born on 17 February 1894 and married Minnie Holman in 1916. He died on 25 July 1976 at the age of 82 in Elgin, Bastrop Co., Texas
- **Cohen GAGE** was born on 17 August 1897. He died on 12 January 1899 at the age of 1 and is buried at Pleasant Grove Cemetery in Elgin, Bastrop Co, Texas.
- **Roxie Ora Lee Gage**, born 12 November 1900; married Paul Elkins, 7 March 1920, Lee Co., Texas; died September 1977, Harris, Texas.
- **Oma Virgil Gage**, born 30 January 1902; died 16 November 1990.   He was married to Ruth Lenoir.
- **Gracy Gladys Gage** was born on 17 October 1908. She died on 22 November 1913 at the age of 5. (Twin)
- **Grady Gage** was born on 17 October 1908. He died on 23 Oct 1908 at the age of 0. (Twin)

Cause of Death: Senility and heart failure brought on by severe burns and blisters on the back.

She is buried in Pleasant Grove Cemetery, Elgin Texas.

Gage—Pointer Family Photos

**Tom Gage with Sisters
&
Brothers-in-Law**

Paul Elkins, Roxie Lee Gage Elkins
Tom Gage
Alta Pearl Gage Pointer
Samuel Thomas Pointer

The photo is thought to have been taken
at the Pleasant Grove Cemetery, Elgin,
Texas, and the date unknown.

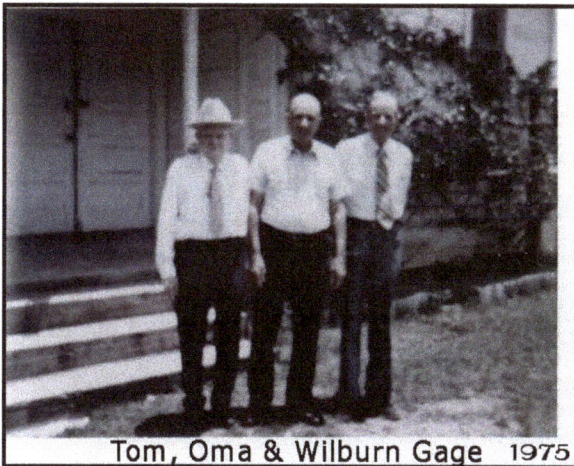

Tom, Oma & Wilburn Gage 1975

5 Generations (1933) L-R Barbara Nell Gage
(Eddie Gage's sister), Tom Gage, John
Thomas Pointer (Elanora's dad), Elanora
Pointer Gage, Tomie Windell Gage hold ing
Eddie Windell Gage.

Photo contributed by Teresa Gage Neal

Back Row: Kesiah Schenck Pointer & John
Thomas Pointer

Front Row: William Ezra Pointer, Nancy
Pearson Pointer , daughter Tilda Pointer,
Elanora Pointer Gage and James Gage.

William & Elizabeth Townsend Gage

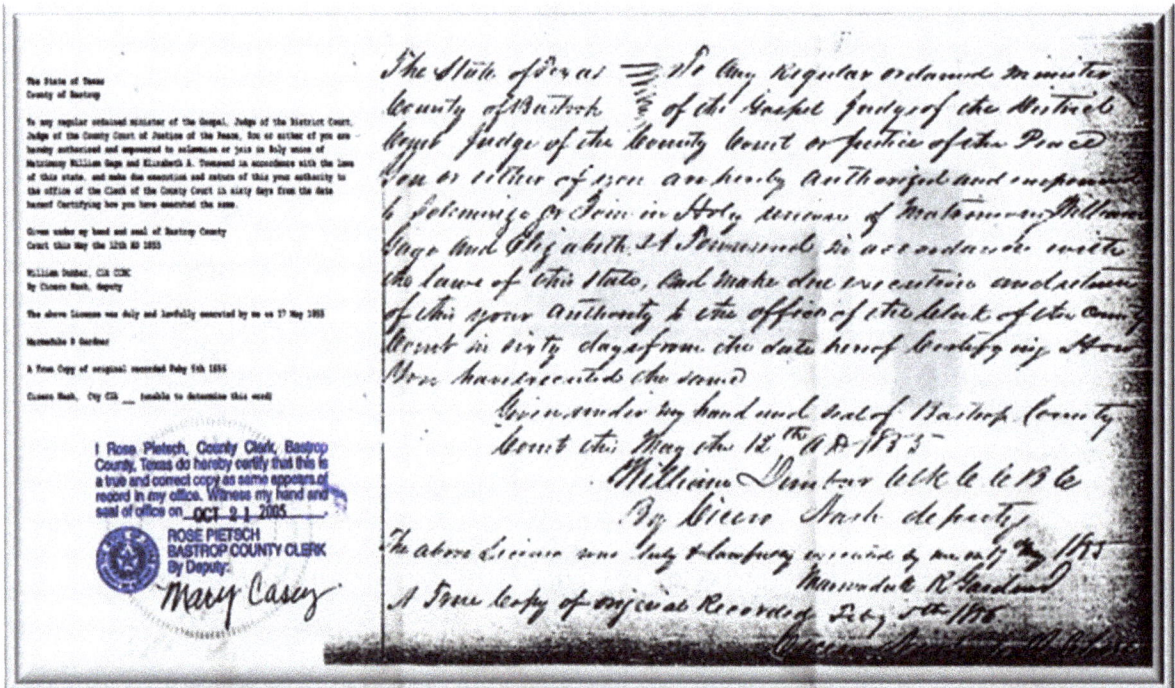

Marriage license for William Gage and Elizabeth Townsend issued in Bastrop County, Texas

Pleasant Grove Cemetery, Elgin, Lee County, Texas

William & Elizabeth (Bettie) Townsend Gage Family
Parents of James Gage

William was the son of David Gage and his first wife who was a Burleson. Research to date has not discovered her name nor the names of her parents.

William M. Gage and Elizabeth A. Townsend had the following children:

- **Calvin Baxter Gage**, born 20 Mar 1856; married first married Sarah Evaline Pointer, 19 December 1883, Erath Co, Texas. After Sarah's death he married Maggie Nash, 12 November 1891, Bastrop Co, Texas; died 29 April 1938, Bastrop Co. Texas.

- **Mary Abigail Gage**, born Mar 1858, Elgin, Bastrop Co., Texas; married John Arnold Davis, 20 December 1880; died 10 March 1928, Elgin, Bastrop Co., Texas.

- **James Gage**, born 2 February 1860, Bastrop Co. Texas; married Elanora Pointer, 3 Sep 1882, Erath Co., Texas; died 29 May 1941, Pleasant Grove, Texas.

- **Nannie Gage** was born in 1862 in Bastrop Co. Texas. She was married to James Davis Delmar.

- **Bessie Gage**, born 16 February 1866, Elgin, Bastrop Co., Texas; married George Marion Eggleston; died 17 Feb 1950, Elgin, Bastrop Co. TX.

- **Milton Gage** was born in 1868, married Delitha Davis and died 27 March 1943 in Bastrop Co. Texas.

- **William Gage**, born 1870; died 1957, Texas. He married Edna Fischer in 1894 and died 8 March 1960.

- **Nora Gage** was born in 1872 and married Thomas Knight Estes on 15 February 18, 1889 and died 29 February 1923. She is buried in Pleasant Grove Cemetery, Elgin, Texas.

- **Walter S Gage** was born in 1876. He died on 13 Aug 1878 at the age of 2 and buried at Pleasant Grove Cemetery in Elgin, Bastrop Co., Texas.

William Gage served in Texas Infantry, Company C, Griffin's Battalion, March 1861, enlisted at Post Oak Island, was mustered out for the sum of $30.00 and was paid for the use of his horses, amount $12.00.

Military records of William Gage, in possession of Merlene Anderson, from Texas Archives, Austin, Texas. Military file from the National Archives, Washington D.C. which has only pay records are in the possession of Jean McCullough. **Note: The 17th Texas Volunteer Infantry Regiment** was one of 22 infantry regiments from Texas. It was organized around January of 1862. The 17th was part of the 3rd Brigade of the famous Walkers Texas division also known as Walkers Greyhounds.

William Gage and two of his brothers-in-law, A. B (Alex Bryant) and A.J. (Andrew Jackson) Townsend fought in this same unit of the Confederacy.

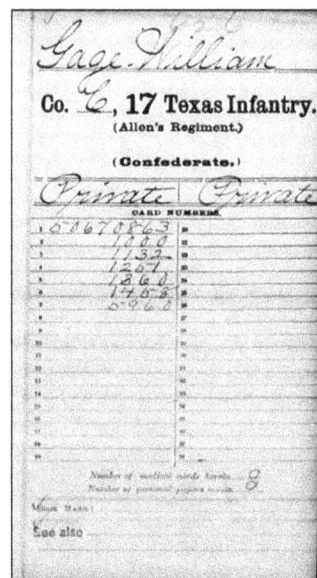

Elizabeth (Bettie) Townsend Gage requested a Civil War pension as the widow of William Gage but was denied because of a small piece of property she owned.

CONFEDERATE PENSION APPLICATION: FORM NO. 2, R 3532

 Name of Applicant: Mrs. B. Gage, Bastrop County

Post Office: Elgin, Texas

Comptroller's File No. 858 216

 I have carefully examined the within application for pension, together with the proof in support thereof, and I recommend that the application be **Disapproved** this 21 day of **Sept** A.D. 1899.

J. R._____,Comptroller

 Fee $2.00 pd.

 THE STATE OF TEXAS,

County of Bastrop

To the Honorable County Judge of Bastrop County, Texas
Your petitioner, **Mrs. Bettie Gage** respectfully represents that she is a resident citizen of Bastrop County, in the State of Texas; that she is the widow of **William Gage**, deceased, who was a Confederate soldier, and that she makes this application for the purpose of obtaining a pension as the widow of said William Gage, deceased, under the act passed by the Twenty-six Legislature of the State of Texas, and approved May 12, 1899, the same being an act entitled, "An act to carry into effect the amendment to the Constitution of the State of Texas, providing that aid may be granted to disabled and dependent Confederate soldiers, sailors, and their widows under certain conditions, and to make an appropriation therefore,' and I do solemnly swear that the answers I have given to the following questions are true.

Note – Applicant must make answers to all the following questions, and such answers must be written out plainly in ink.

Q. What is your name? Answer: Bettie Gage

Q. What is your age?   Answer: Sixty-three (63) years old

Q. In what County do you reside?   Answer: Bastrop

Q. How long have you resided in said County and what is your post office address?

Answer: Since 1839 (making 60 years). P.O. Elgin, Texas

Q. Have you applied for a pension under the Confederate Pension Law heretofore, and been rejected? If so state when and where. Answer: No

Q. What is your occupation if able to engage in one? Answer: Unable to do anything except a little work about the house.

Q. What is your physical condition? Answer: not good.

Q. What was the name of your deceased husband? Answer: William Gage.

Q. Were you married to him anterior to March 1, 1866? If so, on what date were your married to him and where? Yes. Was married May 17 in 1855 in Bastrop County, Texas.

Q. What was the date of his death? Answer: He died March 20 in 1898.

Q. Are you unmarried, and have you so remained unmarried since the death of your said husband for whose services you claim a pension? Answer: Yes

Q. State in what company and regiment your deceased husband for whose services you claim a pension enlisted in the Confederate Army, and the time of his service therein? Answer: Co. C17 in Texas Inf. He served from beginning thru end of the war.

Q. If your deceased husband served in the Confederate Navy, state when and where, and the time of such service. Answer: He did not serve in the Navy.

Q. State whether or not you have received any pension or veteran donation land certificate under any previous law, and if you answer in the affirmative state what pension or veteran donation land certificate you have so received. Answer: None

Q. What real and personal property do you now own, and what is the present value of each property? Give list of such property and value. Answer: 100 acres of land valued about $600.00, about 45 acres in_____, which I rent and get about $50.00 or $60.00 in rent on it each year, and can value $20.00.

Q. What property, and what was the value thereof have you sold or conveyed within two years prior to the date of this application? Answer: None.

End of answers. As shown previously, Bettie was denied a pension.

Obituary of William Gage

GAGE

Entered into rest at his late residence in Bastrop County, March 20, 1889, William Gage, aged 71 years, 6 months and 9 days.

"So He giveth His beloved sleep."

The subject of the above notice, Mr. William Gage, was born in Gifton County Tennessee, September 11, 1827. At an early age he went from there to Marion county, Alabama, and from thence in 1849 he came to Williamson County, where he married Miss Bettie Townsend, daughter of Mr. Richmond Townsend, a Texas veteran, and settled in Bastrop County May 17, 1855. Mr. Gage became a member of the Masonic lodge No. 181 then located at Post Oak Island, in 1857. He withdrew his membership from that lodge six years ago and affiliated at Perryville lodge No. 328. He was a Mason in good standing at the time of his death, and was enterred at Pleasant Grove church with the impressive rights of that order. The Lodge of which he was a member attended in a body, besides Masons from other lodges, who came to assist in the last sad rights and to do honor to the memory of one who had lived according to the high standard of the order. The pall bearers, all of whom were Masons, were as follows: Messrs. Will Straus, Willie Jarmon, Westley Lawhon, John Lawhon, and R. Roemer.

In August 1892 Mr. Gage united himself with the Church of Christ and has since lived a consistent life as a follower of "Him who died that we might live," _____ testifying by his works and word to the faith that was in him, and beloved by all who knew him for the purity of his life, for his devotion to home, wife and children. A wife and seven children survive to mourn his loss, but they do not morn as those without hope for they feel assured that he has "crossed over to the other side" and reached heaven, the heart's true home, there to await his loved ones and to welcome them to that land beyond the skies where there is no more sorrowing no more parting, but peace, eternal peace.

One of the largest processions ever seen in the country followed the body to its last resting place, and the vast crowd of nearly four hundred people who gathered around the grave attested to the high esteem in which the deceased was held. Relative and friend, neighbors and brother Masons, all came to show their respect to him whom they had known and esteemed in life. Time alone can heal the broken heart of his bereaved wife and sorrowing children. Let us hope that they will take comfort when they remember him as he was, busy cheerful, unselfish, always considerate of others, always ready to find a way to comfort those in trouble and to help the poor, the sorrowful and the mistaken ones. Remembering these things may they not hope, and may they not strive to greet him on the other side of

"The fair immortal sea
Where white winged fleets are to have fd'with light from a celestial shore;
Whose passengers have learned the songs and shouts of victory;
And stretch out dear familiar hands.
To lead us to supreme, eternal lands
Where sorrow dies - and parting is no more."

X X X

David Gage, and (Given Name Unknown) Burleson
Parents of William Gage

David was born in 2 August 1801 in Haywood County, Tennessee. William Gage, David's son said his mother was a Burleson but to date her given name has not been found.

The Gages and the Burlesons lived near each other in North Carolina and along with the Shipmans began their travel west through Tennessee, Missouri, Arkansas and finally settled in Texas.

David was in Tennessee on the 1830 census and in Pope Co. Arkansas on the 1840 census. His first wife apparently died in Arkansas. Surviving children from this marriage were William, Henry, Hiram and Thomas.

After the death of his first wife, David married Denisa Harrison in Arkansas and then moved his family to Bastrop Co. Texas where their daughter Mary Abigail was born in 1845. David died suddenly and was thought to have been killed by Indians about 1847. His grave has not been discovered.

```
                                    1st revised page 48
252 David A Gage, born 180- In Haywood Co.Tenn census 1830
    Pope County,Ark census 1840.It is believed that he was
    murdered by Indians in Bastrop County,Texas 4/1847 for his
    death was quite sudden and unexpected and no one could
    confirm when or how he died according to the records.
    Married: 1st--Haywood County,Tenn.about 1821.
    Children
370 A daughter; born Tenn about 1822
371 A daughter, born Tenn.about 1825
372 A son, born Tenn. about 1827
373 Henry Salem Gage, born Tenn 1829.In Bastrop Co.Texas
    census 1850 age 21. Died Fayette Co.Tex 1868
374 A child, born Tenn 1830
375 Hiram Gage, born Ark 1832.In Bastrop Co.Tex census 1850
376 Thomas E Gage, born Ark 1835

    Married: 2nd about 1844 Pope County,Ark. to Denisa--(Note)
    She was born in Ala.1826.
    Child
377 Mary Abigail Gage, born Bastrop County,Texas 1845.
    Married: 6/21/1860 James M.Dancer.
    Note--after the death of David A Gage,Denisa married
    2nd Levi McClure of Fayette Co.Tex and 3rd 1/8/1865
    William N.Matthews in Fayette Co.Texas
```

David was a minister of the Primitive Baptist Church and was ordained in the Mt Tabor church in Tennessee. He transferred his ministry to the New Hope church in Arkansas and then to Plum Grove Baptist Church in Fayette County, Texas

PLUM GROVE BAPTIST CHURCH

Plum Grove Baptist Church constituted March 31, 1839 and called Hopewell according to Elder J. S. Newman in his A History of the Primitive Baptists of Texas, Oklahoma and Indian Territories. Formed with 13 constituent members. On Oct. 25, 1841 the church divided over the mission question. The minority retained the church book and continued for a number of years as Hoepwell. The majority continued as the Plum Grove Baptist Church adhering to missionary principles. On this same date and immediately following the exclusion of the minority the Plum Grove Church received "bro Levi McClure & his wife by letter."

Jan. 4, 1845 "...bro David Gage presented his letter of dismission as a Licensed preacher from New Hope Church Arkansas also his license from Mt. Tabor Church Tennessee, which was received by the church and his license returned to him."

Sept. 6, 1845 "Bro D Gage requested a letter of dismission which was granted"

Land record for David Gage situated in Fayette County, Tennessee.

Transcribed copy is on the following page.

THE STATE OF TENNESSEE --- N° 11121

To all to whom these presents shall come...Greeting:

KNOW YE, That *By virtue of Certificates N° 2670. 2671. 2672. 2673. 2674. 2675. 2676 & 2677 all dated the 6th Day of March 1826 Issued by the Commissioner of Tennessee to the assignee of the Register of the Western District, for 25 acres each, and entered on the 8th day of May 1826, as an Occupant claim under the act of 1825 by N° 2033.—*

There is granted by the said State of Tennessee, unto *David Gage assignee of said Register.—*

A certain tract or parcel of Land, containing *two hundred acres by Survey bearing date the 23d day of February 1827 lying in the Tenth District in Fayette County On the waters of Bear Creek, a south Branch of Big Hatchee river, in range five and Section five, and bounded as follows to wit. Beginning at a stake, with a black Oak and three hickory pointers Seventy six poles East of the South most corner of an entry in the name of Sarah Hutchins for 640 acres N° 1042 runs south two hundred and forty two poles to a white Oak & Dogwood. Thence West one hundred thirty two & three tenth poles to a stake, with four hickories and a black Oak pointers. Thence north two hundred and forty two poles to a black Jack. Thence East passing the South West corner of said Hutchins entry at fifty six and three tenth poles, in all one hundred thirty two and three tenth poles to the Beginning.—*

With the hereditaments and appertenances. TO HAVE AND TO HOLD the said tract or parcel of land with its appertenances to the said *David Gage* and *his* heirs forever. In witness whereof, *Sam Houston* Governor of the State of Tennessee, hath hereunto set his hand, and caused the great seal of the state to be affixed, at *Nashville* on the *5th* day of *November* in the year of our Lord one thousand eight hundred and twenty-*eight*, and of the Independence of the United States the *53.—*

BY THE GOVERNOR:

Sam Houston

Daniel Graham Secretary.

Transcribed from original document on prior page.

Recorded November 10th 1829

THE STATE OF TENNESSEE ---N°. 1112

To all to whom these presents shall come … Greeting:

KNOW YE, *That By virtue of Certificates N°2670, 2671, 2672, 2673, 2674, 2675, 2676 & 2677 all dated the 6th day of March 1826. Issued by the Commissioner of Tennessee to the assignee of the Register of the Western District for 25 acres each, and entered on the 8th day of May 1826 as an Occupant claim under the Act of 1825 by N°2033.*

There is granted by the said State of Tennessee, unto *David Gage, assignee of said Register. –*

A certain tract OR PARCEL OF Land, containing *two hundred acres by survey bearing date the 23rd day of February 1827 lying in the Tenth District in Fayette County on the waters of Clear Creek, a south branch of Big Hatchee river, in range five and section five, and bounded as follows to wit, Beginning at a stake, with a black oak and three hickory pointers, seventy six poles east of the south west corner of an entry in the name of Sarah Hutchins for 640 acres N°1042 runs south two hundred and forty two poles to a white oak dogwood. Thence one hundred thirty two and three tenths poles to a stake, with four hickories and a black oak pointer. Thence north two hundred and forty two poles to a black Jack, thence east facing the south west corner of said S Hutchins entry at fifty six and three tenth poles, in all one hundred thirty two and three tenth poles to the Beginning.*

With the hereditaments and appurtenances. TO HAVE AND TO HOLD the said tract or parcel of land with its appurtenances to the said David Gage **and** his **heirs forever. In witness thereof,** Sam Houston, **Governor of the State of Tennessee, hath hereunto set his hand and caused the great seal of the state to be affixed, at** Nashville **on the** 4th day **of** November **in the year of our Lord one thousand and twenty-eight and of the Independence of the United States the 50.**

  By the Governor:

Daniel Graham, **Secretary**

Sam Houston

Number of Items	Description	Appraised Value
25	Head of cattle	
1 set	_____lings	
1	Log cabin	
-	Household furniture	
1	Bridle	

Bastrop County Inventory

$134.70

11	Cattle (all bought last spring)	
3	Cows without calves	
5	Cows and spring calves	
1	Yoke of work oxen, yoke, bows, ring & style	
1	Mare and colt	
1	Bridle	
1	Gun	
2	Bells	
1	Foot adze	
1	Log chain	
1	Oven & lid	
3	Pots	
1	Skillet	
1	Pr pot hooks	
1	Sack & contents	
1	Wheel without a bench	
	Beds & bed clothing	

Fayette County Inventory

-	Irons of hubs of wagon wheels	
1	3 year old steer, born last spring	

Gonzales County Inventory

1	Cow & calf	
2	Plain bitts (in possession of Zachariah Nettles of Gonzales Co)	
4	Axes	
2	chissels	
1	Auger	
30	Hogs (in possession of Mr Mullen of Gonzales Co)	
1	Paint mare	
1	Gun	
-	Saddle & bridle (in possession of Henry S Gage)	
	There is in possession of A H Wood, admr a bond executec by one W W Ashby of this State for the sum of $400, datec May 1st. 1844 to David Gage	

Transcribed Inventory Of David Gage's Estate

Land Document

This document is for land being purchased by John Burleson in Gonzales County, Texas. Witnessing this is David Gage on October 20, 1845 and was recorded in Fayette County, Texas.

Interesting to note is David's first wife, who was a Burleson, could have been a daughter of any number of Burlesons. She would have been a descendant of Aaron Burleson I and Aaron Burleson II. David's mother was Abigail Burleson, daughter of Aaron Burleson II and wife Rachel Hendricks.

David had assets in Gonzales County, as well as in Bastrop and Fayette Counties, Texas

Reuben & Abigail Burleson Gage
Parents of David Gage

Joseph the son of Reuben & Abigail Gage was born January 25th 1799--

David, the son of Reubes & Abigail Gage was born August 2nd 1801

Burleson the son of Reuben & Abigail Gage was born February 27, 1805.

Jonas the son of Reuben & Abigail Gage was born October 27, 1807.

Sally the daughter of Reuben & Abigail Gage was born October 8th 1810.

BIRTHS [Second Column]

Vany the daughter of Reuben & Abigail Gage was born February 24th 1813

Calvin the son of Reuben & Abigail Gage was born May 1st, 1817--

Abigail the daughter of Andrew & Rachel Thompson was born May 24, 1816--

[Page 3]

BIRTHS [First Column]

Moses Gage son of Jonas and Jane Gage was born March the 19th A.D. 1849°

Margret Ann Owen daughter of cilus lester and Lucinda Owen was born January the 31 A.D. 1853 and was married July the 17th A.D. 1872°

Jane Nancy Gage Daughter of Moses and Margret Ann Gage was born October the 5th A.D. 1873.

Robbert Lee Gage was born (cq) son of Moses and Margret Ann Gage was born April the 23rd A.D. 1894 (cq) 1875°

Jonas berten Gage son of Moses and Margret Ann Gage was born November the 23rd A.D. 1876.°

Maryann gage, Daughter of Moses & Margrett Ann Gage was born March the 12th A.D. 1878.°

[All the above in first column in blue ink, different hand; the 1875 after the marked over 1874 is in brown ink.]

BIRTHS [Second Column]

Reuben Gage was born February 10th 1770

Abigail Burleson was born August 24 1774

Calvin Jeffrey Gage son of Margret Ann & Moses Gage was Born August the 4th A.D. 188_

Jonas Menifee Gage Son of Moses and Margretann Gage was born July the 4, 1882

Marilda Abigal Gage Born December the 24th 1883.°

Rufus Earnest Gage Born Sept. the 6, 1886°

William Moses -- Gage, born June the 4th 1888.°

Transcribed page from Reuben Gage's Bible

Reuben Gage

Reuben was a son of David Gage and wife. He died in Saline County, Arkansas "on or about the last of October A.D. 1844" according to the Letters of Administration on his estate granted to Jonas Gage on the 28th of December 1844. (Saline County Will Book A, p. 52).

Abigail Burleson Gage

Abigail was a daughter of Aaron Burleson, "II" and wife Rachael Hendricks.

Abigail is living with son Moses on the 1860 Federal Bastrop County Census Record.

Abigail was designated as a Citizen of the Republic of Texas.

Cemetery where Abigail Burleson is buried in LaGrange, TX.

ABIGAIL BURLESON GAGE
AUGUST 24. 1771. N.C.
NOVEMBER 4. 1865. TEXAS

Reuben Gage's Bible

(Transcribed from previous page)

MARRIAGES

Reuben Gage and Abigail Burleson were Married Sept1790

BIRTHS

Michel, daughter of Reuben & Abigail Gage was born January 21st 1792

Moses the son of Reuben &Abigail Gage was born July 13th 1796

Joseph the son of Reuben & Abigail Gage was born January 25th 1799

David, the son of Reuben & Abigail Gage was born August 2nd 1801

Burleson the son of Reuben &Abigail Gage was born February 27, 1805

Jonas the son of Reuben & Abigail Gage was born October 27, 1807

Sally the daughter of Reuben & Abigail Gage was born October 8th 1810

Vany the daughter of Reuben & Abigail Gage was born February 24th 1813

Calvin the son of Reuben & Abigail Gage was born May 1st, 1817

Reuben Gage married Abigail Burleson in September 1790 in North Carolina. Abigail was the daughter of Aaron Burleson II and Rachael Hendricks, born August 24, 1774, in Rutherford Co., North Carolina. Abigail died in Texas on November 4, 1865.

In the late 1790's, a group of related families left Rutherford Co., North Carolina, and settled in Warren Co., Kentucky. The families were: Gage, McFadden, Shipman, and Burleson and others. All were related to the Burleson family by marriage.

Reuben Gage and his brother, Moses Gage, applied for a state grant of 200 acres each on Sinking Creek, Warren Co., Kentucky in August 1799. Twenty years later, Reuben Gage lived in Howard Co., Missouri, where his relatives, the Shipman's, tried to talk him into going to Texas.

Wrote Daniel Shipman, *"About this time, a father and an old friend, by the name of Reuben Gage, took a notion to move to the state of Arkansas. They sold out, and on the 5th of June 1821, they started from Howard County,* *Missouri after about 25 miles, we crossed the Missouri River at Boonville, Copper County.*

Father broke a wagon wheel, he and old cousin Reuben Gage managed to have it mended, so that we got to a large creek called 'Mori'; by this time the weather had become very warm and horse-flies so very numerous, that it was almost impossible to travel.

While there, his father heard tales of land on the Red and Sabine rivers and of the generous offers made by the Spanish Government to American settlers. His father was interested but it did not appear to take so well with our friend Gage."

In 1834, while Texas was still a part of Mexico, Reuben Gage did moved his family to Texas and renewed his close relationship with his Burleson in-laws. Before Texas, the Burleson's had been in Alabama where they farmed and fought the Indians."

Texas Land Grants

Under the Constitution of 1836 all heads of families living in Texas on March 4, 1836, except Africans and Indians, were granted "first class" headrights of one league and one labor (**4,605.5 acres**), and single men aged seventeen years or older, one-third of a league (**1,476.1 acres**).

Translated from Spanish

Reuben Gage having given due oath according to the law and as responsible party under the contract of colonization of Benjamin R. Milam, has revealed his name the gentleman above stated, sixty-five yrs of age, married and occupation as farmer. Native of the State of N.Y. and with three persons of the family. In agreement of which has signed with me in the Villa of Mina on the 16th day of Sept. 1835, signed: Talbot Chambers & Reuben Gage."

A labor of land was issued to Reuben Gage, and was returned to Bastrop Co. for recording in September 1846.

Austin's Little Colony & Milam's Colony.

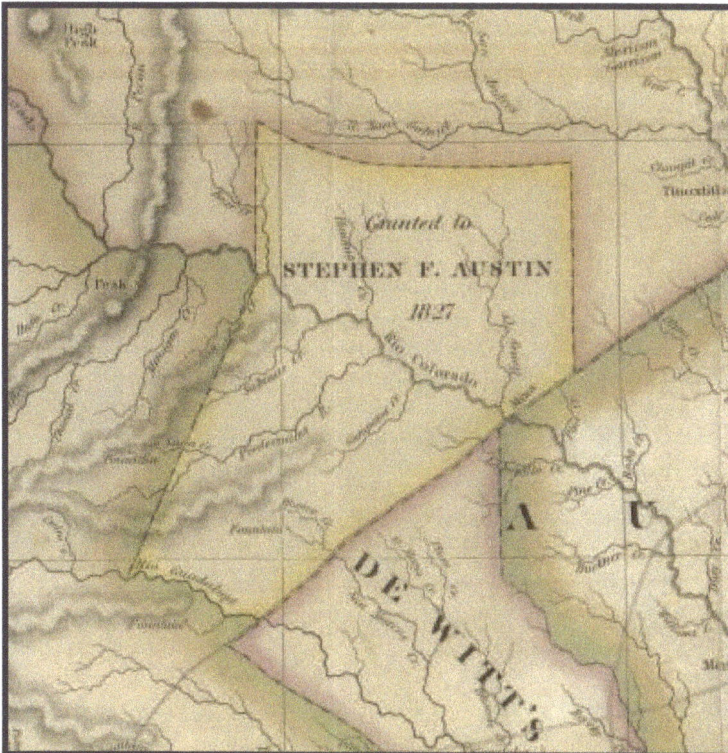

The site was first occupied in 1804, when a fort was established at the strategic Colorado River crossing of the Old San Antonio Road and named Puesta del Colorado.

The Baron de Bastrop obtained permission from the Spanish to found a German colony and selected the site in 1823, but subsequently failed to establish a settlement.

On November 20, 1827, Austin entered into another contract with the Mexican government of the state, for one hundred families to be settled on the east side of the Colorado above the San Antonio Road. The contract was to expire 6 years from that date.

Bastrop County was colonized under terms of Austin's original colony, Austin's Little colony, and Milam's Colony.

MILAM COLONY

Benjamin R. Milam, 10/20/1788-12/7/1835, killed in the Battle of San Jacinto.

January 12, 1826, Benjamin R. Milam was granted the right to settle three hundred families between the Guadalupe and Colorado Rivers, west of the Old San Antonio Road.

His contract ended 13th day of January 1832 with very few families settled and those that did settle had a problem proving ownership.

The government commissioned Talbot Chambers to get titles for the families that were already settled.

In 1835, fifty-two titles in the Milam Colony were issued, seventeen of which were within Bastrop County. Below is a list of original titles for Milam Colony issued by Land Commissioner Talbot Chambers, 1835-1836, as listed in the General Land Office. Name, Date of Title, Quantity, Location

Reuben Gage 9/25/1835 1 League On the waters of Cedar Creek, joins A. Litton.

Bastrop Co, TX - Land Certificates for GAGE family; Calvin 6,174; Reuben --, 175; Moses --, 176; William B. --,183 (Leag. sec, abs)

Reuben Gage and family were early settlers of Bastrop County in Stephen F. Austin's Colony. "One of the earliest settlements in inland Texas, Bastrop was located at the intersection of the Colorado River and the Old San Antonio Road. The settlement, originally called Mina, was first settled in the late 1820s.

Soon after the Texas Revolution, the town was incorporated. Its name was changed to Bastrop, in honor of Baron de Bastrop, an official of the Mexican government credited with aiding Moses and Stephen Austin in securing land grants and enabling the colonization of Texas before the Revolution."

Reuben Gage received $12.00 for loan of wagon and team to the Texas Army forces under General Edward Burleson for 30 days and $4.00 per day voucher 11/25/1836. Reuben also acquired land in Saline Co, and Batesville, Arkansas areas purchasing land there in the 1830-1860s.

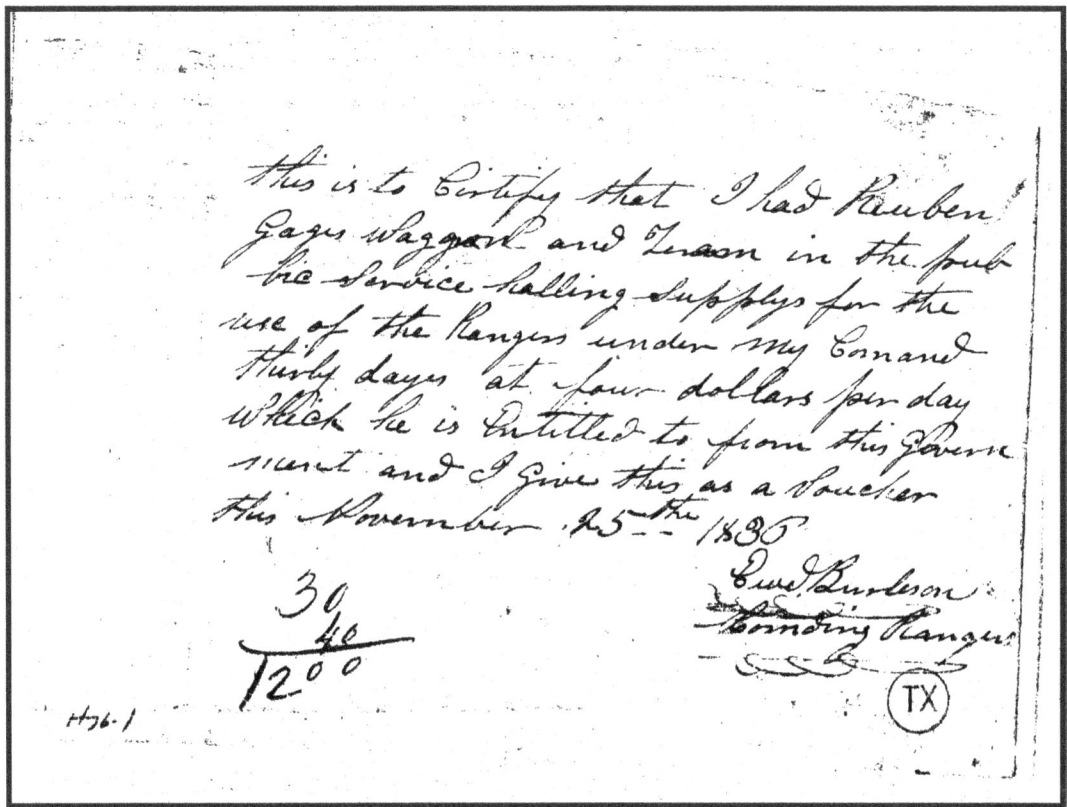

Transcription: This is to certify that I had Reuben Gage's wagon and Team in the public service halling [sic] supplys for the use of the Rangers under my Comand [sic] thirty dollars at four dollars per day which he is entitled to from the government and I give this as a Voucher this November 25th, 1835.

Ewd Burleson
Comding Ranger

Burleson & Gage

Special Note: Information on the Burlesons and Gages taken from pages 183 -189 of, "The Ancestry of David Bracewell, including the Allied Southern Families of Braswell, Brazil, Bay, Price, Passmore, Gage, Prillaman and Allen", book written by Carey Bracewell.

"Aaron Burleson (I), born about 1690 and christened in Caerleau, Manmouth, Wales, immigrated to Baltimore, Maryland in 1726. There he married a woman named Sarah and moved to Lunenburg County, Virginia, in 1748. Aaron died in 1763 in Rutherford County, North Carolina.

Aaron Burleson I had fourteen children, among them Aaron Burleson II, born in Baltimore and married Rachel Hendricks in 1748. At Watauga, now eastern Tennessee, he went out to hunt deer and was killed by Indians on November 16. 1781. Whether this was the start of Burlesons' fight with the Indians, more likely, just part of their fighting heritage from Wales, it began the Burlesons' frontier conflict with Native Americans.

Aaron II was an ancestor of such remarkable Burleson offspring as the founder of Baylor University and the Postmaster-General in President Wilson's Cabinet.

THE GAGES

I only knew Abby as a child. She loved me wholeheartedly so I loved her too. I used to steal flowers and take them to her. Later, as an adult and genealogist, I began to see the aggressiveness of Abby's early Burleson and Gage ancestors as the key to their success. The Burlesons, Gages, Shipmans, and other allied families from North Carolina to Texas were the most closely-knit group of families I ever studied. Moreover, the Burlesons connection with minor gentry back in Wales suggested to me how a fighting spirit and fame seem to go together.

Aaron Burleson's murder by Indians in the Watauga Settlement in 1781 may not have been a cause of their aggressiveness but only a symptom. Wherever the Burlesons lived, they always fought with Native Americans. From North Carolina through Kentucky, Tennessee, Alabama and Texas, Burlesons and their allies battled the Indians. Wherever the family branch of Southern Burlesons lived, they were ready for a fight. To me, their original fearlessness was nature, nor nurture. In 1835, for example, the first shot in Texas' War for Independence, a cannon fired at Gonzales, Texas, at Santa Anna's troops, was lighted by a Burleson.

The Gages were also Welch. Nicholas Gage, Sarah's ancestor, was born before 1683 in Wales. He married Mary and had David Gage, born in Wales in 1701. His son, David Gage, Jr., was born in 1734 in New Jersey and died there in 1805. One of David's children was Reuben Gage, born February 10, 1770, in New York.

While there, his father heard tales of land on the Red and Sabine rivers and of the generous offers made by the Spanish Government to American settlers. His father was interested but it did not appear to take so well with our friend Gage.

Our friend Gage agreed to meet us at Mr. Harrell's (the informant on the free lands in Texas) where we all were to meet and hold a general consultation. The result was that Mr. Gage and his family was to go to Gasconade, Missouri; Mr. Harrell, family, father, and our family went to Arkansas. So in two or three days, we all made a general start on the 23rd of October, 1821."

REUBEN GAGE FAMILY REUNITED
WITH THE BURLESONS IN TEXAS

In 1834, while Texas was still a part of Mexico, Reuben Gage moved his family to Texas and renewed his close relationship with his Burleson in-laws. Before Texas, the Burleson's had been in Alabama where they farmed and fought the Indians.

The Mexican government granted Sarah Gage Brazil's great-grandfather, Reuben Gage, a league of land, 4,428.80 acres in the Milam Grant on May 25, 1835. This made him an original Anglo-American Texan. In his grant application, he gave his age as sixty-five and his place of birth as New York.

On November 25, 1836, Reuben received a voucher for $120 from the Republic of Texas, payment for the loan of his wagon and team to General Edward Burleson, his brother-in-law, who commanded the center division at the Bartle of San Jacinto. Texas won her independence from Mexico in that battle and became the Republic of Texas.

COMANCHE TROUBLE

The year after Texas joined the Union in 1845, two Burleson girls were captured and scalped by Comanches. The girls survived but the Burleson and Gage men went on the warpath against the Comanches. David A. Gage may have paid the price for their lack of forgiveness. David A. Gage (1801-1846), Abby's grandfather, died in Bastrop County under mysterious circumstances. His death was never fully explained in his probate papers. He died in 1846 without a will. His probate papers only say that he died "in the month of April last." His body wasn't found for some time after he died. The Republic of Texas and the state's early years afforded little protection for its citizens. Everyone was on their own. Evidently, Burleson's and Gages' may have been singled out by the Comanches, the tribe everyone white or red hated and feared.

David's father, Reuben, and his brother, Burleson Gage, George Washington Gage, and Jonas Gage all went back east to Arkansas, away from Texas. The Gages settled in Saline County, Arkansas, on the Military Highway to Texas. Reuben bought 123 acres on September 8, 1840, from Abijah Davis, an old Saline County pioneer. He also bought fifty acres from John Lindsey, a Brazil relative. Reuben Gage died in Saline County on Halloween, October 31. 1844. The Brazils and Gages churched together but had no idea they would become relatives in Texas.

David Gage's estate Inventory, dated August 24, 1847 included: "In County of Bastrop: 11 cattle, all bought last spring; 3 cows without calves, 5 cows and spring calves; 1 yoke of work oxen, yoke, bows, ring & style; I mare and colt; 1 bridle, & gun, 2 bells: 1 foot adze, I log chain, I oven & lid, 3 pots; 1 skillet, 1 pr. pot hooks, 1 sack & contents; I wheel without a bench, Beds & Bed clothing.

In Fayette County, David had irons of hubs of wagon wheels, and a 1 three year old steer born last spring.

In Gonzales County, David had one cow & calf. 2 plain bitts, in possession of Zachariah Nettles of Gonzales County; 4 axes, 2 chissels, 1 auger and about 30 head of hogs In possession of Mr. Mullen of Gonzales County; 1 Paint mare, 1 gun, in saddle. & bridle in possession of Henry S Gage.

"There is in possession of A. H. Wood, admr, a bond executed by one W.W. Ashby of this State for the sum of $400, dated May 1st. 1844, to David Gage.

David A. Gage, born August 2, 1801, married about 1821 to a woman even whose first name was lost. David's third child by her was Henry Salem Gage (1829-1857), Sarah Gage Brazil's father.

HENRY GAGE

David Gage's probate papers, dated August 29, 1848, described Henry Gage as "a minor and heir of said deceased (David) who has in his possession a Sorrell and a paint Mare belonging to said estate. A dispute had arisen over ownership of the paint mare. On September 1st, Henry Gage appeared in court, and upon motion of attorney the court appoint Moses Gage, his guardian in the interest of said minor. "It is further ordered that John Burleson, Senr and Joshua V. Stewart, citizens of the County of Gonzales be summoned to appear at said term of court and give evidence in the case at the insistence of said Henry." On October 20, 1848, the probate court "Ordered that Henry Gage, one of the Heirs of said David Gage dec'd return and hold the Sorrell Mare and become chargeable to said Henry at the price of seventy dollars."

David Gage's second wife, Denisa, whom he married before coming to Texas, came up in David's probate proceedings dated July 26, 1847. They only had one child before David died in 1847, Mary Abigail Gage, born about 1845.

The Probate Court in Fayette County on August 27, 1849, ordered Levi McClure to be appointed Guardian of the minor, Mary Abigail Gage, whom he represents as about three years old and he submitted the petition at the request of "the surviving parent."

In January 1851, McClure was summoned by the county to give an account of his guardianship which he ignored. He was arrested and John S. Black "went his bond" for his next appearance.

In his final account, Levi declared that his ward has no property and that he "has had the care and keeping of said ward since being appointed guardian". Mary Abigail Gage relieved Levi of his responsibility by marrying, on June 21, 1860, at the age of fifteen, James M. Dancer."

End of the excerpt from "*The Ancestry of David Bracewell*" book.

Aaron Burleson, II

Father of Abigail Burleson Gage

The author of the following is unknown: "Aaron Burleson served in the War of the Revolution along with six brothers. This is confirmed by the Aaron Burleson chapter of the Daughters of the American Revolution, Longview, Texas. [From *1966 'Sketches of James and Joseph Burleson' written by Irene Bogard-Winton granddaughter of Cornelius Bogard and Caroline Burleson; on file in the Texas Collection at Baylor University, Waco, Texas 76706*]. She is descended from Joseph Burleson.

Aaron Burleson II, lived a very colorful life, and is worth noting in this text. He served as a Minute Man in the American Revolutionary War, and probably served with Isaac Burleson, who was Aaron's nephew. Aaron II was an intimate friend of Daniel Boone and after the Revolutionary War decided to join Daniel in Kentucky. Aaron II's descendants include Captain James Burleson, General Edward Burleson, Dr. Rufus C. Burleson, and Albert Sidney Burleson. Aaron II died in the Blue Ridge Mountains in 1782, being killed by Indians on either Cane Creek in what is now Mitchell Co., North Carolina, or on the Clinch River in Tennessee. In John Preston Arthur's *'Western North Carolina, A History, 1730- 1913'* we find the following:

Samuel Davidson was killed by Indians in 1781 or 1782 at the head of the Swannanoa River, near what is now Gudger's ford, and Aaron Burleson was killed on Cane Creek in what is now Mitchell County about the same time, although the exact date has been lost. He was an ancestor of Postmaster-general Burleson of President Wilson's cabinet in 1914. Aaron Burleson probably belonged to the settlers around Morganton,

and had ventured beyond the Blue Ridge to hunt deer' (Page 250)."

WILL OF AARON BURLESON II, State of North Carolina, Sullivan Co. (later in Tenn.)

*I, Aaron Burleson being in perfect mind and memory considering the uncertainty of life and being desirous of settling of my affairs in a regular manner before I depart this life I do hereby give and bequeath all my possessions as followeth (viz) first I commit my Soul to God that gave it my body I commit to the dust from whence it came and my worldly estate real and personal I give and bequeath to <u>my beloved wife</u> all my real and personal estate during her life except three mares which I give to my <u>son John</u> one to my <u>son Jonathon</u> one to my <u>son Joseph</u> and each of the said sons a good rifle gun which my widow is to give out of the estate to the three sons when they come of suitable age and further I give and bequeath unto my <u>daughter Elizabeth</u> one shilling sterling and to my <u>son Thomas</u> one shilling sterling and to my <u>daughter Sarah</u> one shilling sterling and to my <u>son Aaron</u> one shilling sterling and to my <u>daughter Rachel</u> one shilling sterling and to my <u>daughter Nancy</u> one shilling sterling and to my <u>daughter **Abegail** and Mary and Rhoda</u> each one cow the whole to be paid by my widow out of my estate and to the remainder of all my estate real and personal I give to my <u>son James</u> at the death of my beloved wife or at her next marriage. In witness whereof I hereunto set my hand and seal this sixteenth of November 1781. I do hereby before sealing of the above last will and testament constitute and appoint my beloved wife executrix and my son Aaron Burleson executor to the above will.*

Aaron Burleson (seal)

Witness, Thomas Shields, Patrick Shields, Henry Clark. The foregoing will was proven in Court by the oath of Thomas Williams one of the subscribing witnesses thereto at May Sessions 1782 and ordered recorded.

Townsend

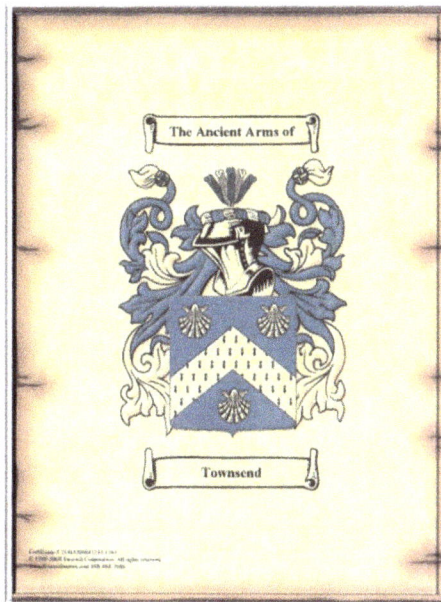

The Ancient Arms of

Townsend

Anderson

Baugh

England

Cureton

The Ancient Arms of

Soane

Related Families
Anderson, Baugh, Bryant, Cureton, OpDyke,
Soanes, Thweatt, Winfrey

Richmond & Mary Bryant Townsend

Parents of Elizabeth 'Bettie' A. Townsend Gage

Richmond was the father of Elizabeth A. (Bettie) Townsend Gage. He was the son of David and wife Tabitha Thomas Townsend. His birth date was in 1798 and he was one of ten children born to David and Tabitha. He grew up in Anson Co., North Carolina. We do not have an exact date of death but know it was after 1877. We can trace his travels through Georgia where his grandmother, Charity lived in Jackson County. It is possible that Richmond met the Bryant family while living in Jackson County. but it cannot be proved at this time. We do know that Mary's parents, Alex & Elizabeth Anderson Bryant, were in both Jackson Co, Georgia and Greene Co. Alabama at the same time as Richmond.

Mary was the daughter of Alexander Bryant and wife Elizabeth Anderson. Born in 1808 in Georgia, she along with her family and maternal grandfather Benjamin Anderson and his family, left Georgia about 1815-1820's and settled in Greene Co., Alabama.

Although no marriage record has been found for Mary and Richmond Townsend it is thought to have been in Greene County, Alabama.

Transcription of Document

This day appeared in court **Richmond Townsend who by marriage with Polly Bryant is entitled to a distributive share of the Estate of Alexander Bryant dec'd** and also Benjamin Anderson Esq. Guardian of the infant children of Alexander Bryant dec'd six in number and the said **Townsend made application to the court that his share of the negroes of the said Estate should be allotted to him**. It is therefore ordered by the court that Thomas J Anderson, David M Deal, Paul Fulton, Richard Harrison and James W Foster be and they are hereby appointed commissioners and are requested and directed as soon as they can agree upon a time to meet and divide into seven lots as nearly equal in value as possible the Negro property of the

Estate of said Bryant in the hands of Benjamin Anderson, Esq. and if they cannot be made equal in division to fix upon each the value to be had in money, these lots to be numbered of which the said Townsend will be permitted to draw one and the lot so drawn to be delivered over to said Townsend the parties to be accountable for any differences in value there may be in said lots. The said commissioners to act under oath and to make due return to this court of the negro as allotted to said Townsend and of their proceedings all of which is accented [sic] to by **Benjamin Anderson Esq. Guardian** as aforesaid. Witness: Wm Murphy, Judge of our said court this 10th January 1825. Attest: Edw Herndon, clk State of Alabama, Greene County January 14th 1825 We the undersigned commissioners in pursuant to an order to us directed from the judge of the county court have this day proceeded to lot out the Negroes of the Estate of Alexander Bryant deceased and these are the lots we have made: Jack No 1 $500, Peter No 2 $625, Arthur No 3 $600, Mary No 4. $270, Nancy & Infant Child, No 5. $500, Clary No 6 $175, Little Peter No 7 $150.

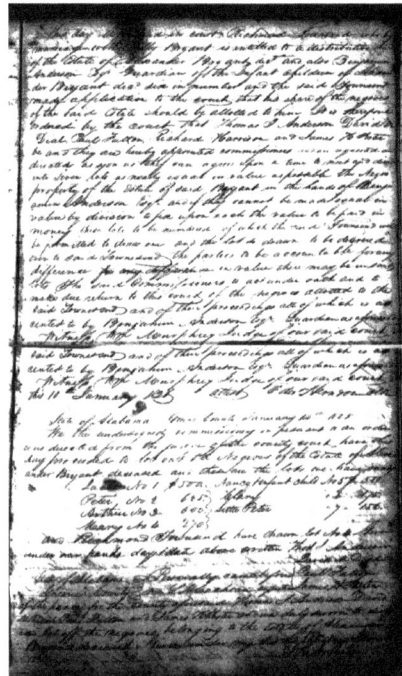

76

Children of Richmond and Mary Bryant Townsend

Richmond and Mary's first child Alex Bryant was born in Greene Co., Alabama. By then the family began their move towards Texas when the second child, Benjamin Franklin Townsend was born in Madison Co., Alabama in 1832. We know this young family was moving west as Elizabeth and her sister Julie were both born in Mississippi in 1836 and 1839. The remaining children were born in Texas by 1 November 1841. This coincides with Richmond receiving a land grant in Texas dated 26 December 1839

Richmond Townsend and Mary Bryant had the following children:

- **Alex Bryant Townsend**, born 1827, Alabama; married Elvira Brymer, 12 Jan 1854, Williamson Co., Texas and died aft 1900, Texas.

- **Benjamin Franklin Townsend**, born 1832, Madison Co., Alabama; married Lucy Ann Cartwright, 12 Nov 1863, Bastrop Co., Texas; died 9 Nov 1870, Elgin, Bastrop Co., Texas.

- **Elizabeth A. "Bettie" Townsend**, born Feb 1836, Mississippi; married William M. Gage, 17 May 1855, Bastrop Co., Texas; died 24 May 1904, Bastrop, Bastrop Co., Texas.

- **Julia Townsend**, born 12 Mar 1839, Mississippi; married John A. Garrett, 6 June 1866, Bastrop County, Texas.

- **Martha Townsend**, born 1 Nov 1841, Bastrop Co., Texas; married William Carlow, 21 Jan 1869, Bastrop Co., Texas; died 13 Apr 1927, Thorndale, Milam Co., Texas.

- **Mary Ann Townsend**, born 1 Nov 1841, Bastrop Co., Texas; married Elias J. Jones, 23 Nov 1854, Bastrop Co., Texas.

  Note: Martha and Mary were twins.

- **Andrew John Townsend**, born 6 Mar 1843, Bastrop Co., Texas; married Mary E Sides, 24 Nov 1870; died 31 Oct 1873, Williamson Co., Texas.

- **Lucy Townsend**, born 1845, Bastrop Co., Texas; married William E. Moore, 20 Jul 1870, Bastrop Co., Texas.

- **Henry B. Townsend**, born Mar 1847, Bastrop Co., Texas; married Nancy Dickey, 9 Mar 1873, Bastrop Co., Texas.

- **Emily Townsend**, born 1852, Bastrop Co. Texas; married J. Andrew Baker, 6 Oct 1866, Williamson Co., Texas.

- **Tabitha A Townsend**, born Feb 1853, Bastrop Co., Texas; married Thomas C Mayfield, 23 Apr 1867, Bastrop Co. Texas; died 31 Jan 1924, Hill Co., Texas.

Benjamin Franklin Townsend

He was a son of Richmond and Mary Bryant Townsend.

Ben fought in the Civil War as did his brother, Alex and brother-in-law William Gage.

Texas Land Record for Richmond Townsend

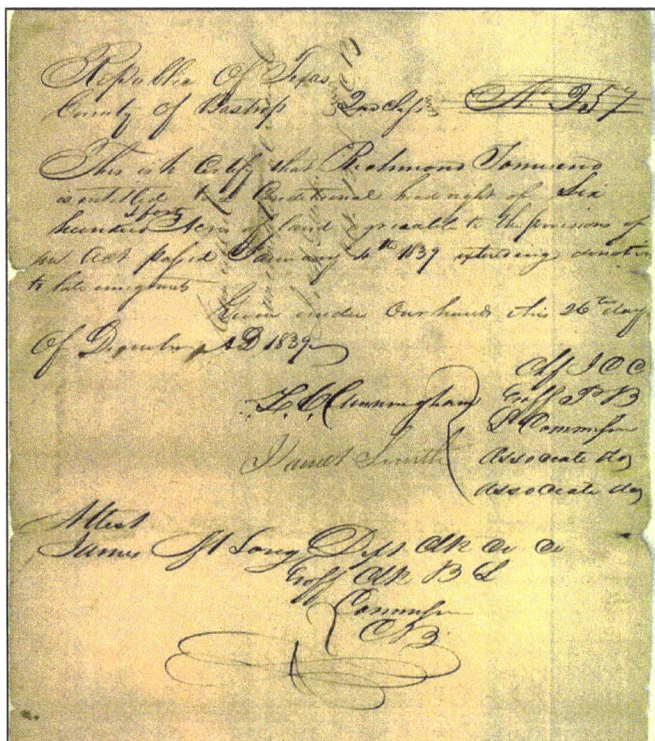

Republic of Texas
County of Bastrop, 2nd Class   No. 257
This is to certify that Richmond Townsend is entitled to a Centennial head right of Six hundred & forty Acres of land agreeable to the provisions of an Act passed January 4th 1839 extending donations to late immigrants.

      Given under our hand this 26^{th day} of December AD 1839.

                L C Cunningham, Clk ICC
                Daniel Smith, Eoff at P B
                L Commission
                    Associate "
                    Associate "
Attest
James H Long, Dept Clk C C
      Eoff Clk B L
      Commission, C B

The Third Class Headright Certificates

These were granted to heads of families and single men who immigrated to Texas after October 1, 1837, and before January 1, 1842.

Heads of families under this class were entitled to 640 acres of land and single men entitled to 320 acres.

Land was issued in the following manner: a board of land commissioners was appointed for each county by the combined houses of Congress. Headright claimants appeared before this board, and, if they produced satisfactory evidence of their eligibility, they were given certificates calling for the amount of land they were eligible to receive. Applicants engaged a surveyor who was authorized to locate and survey the land out of the unappropriated public domain. The surveyor usually received one-third of the land for his services and some of the early land barons amassed a fortune in this manner.

Printed first by CRUGER & WING, Printers

Austin: 1841

Document Issued for Service in Texas War with Mexico

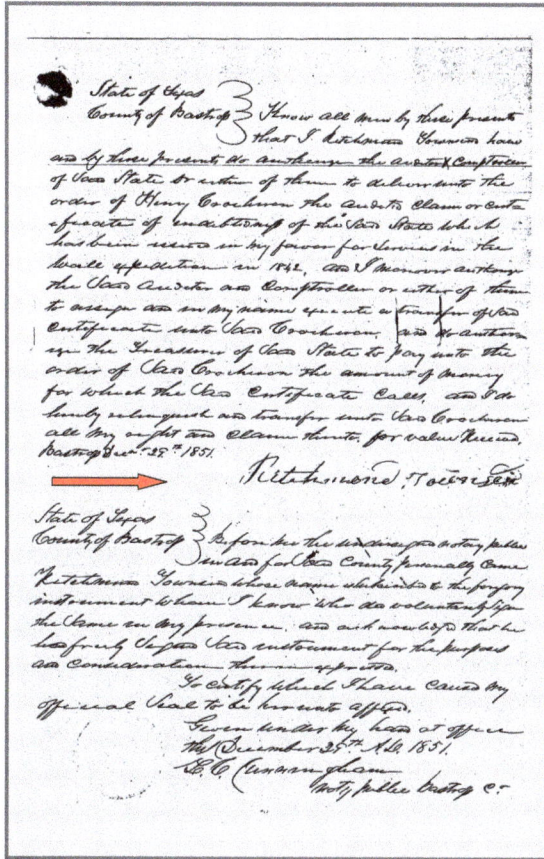

The above document has Richmond Townsend's signature and has been transcribed in the next column.

State of Texas \
County of Bastrop /

      Know all men by these present that I Ritchman Townsend have and by these present do authorize the auditor X comptroller of said state or either of them to deliver unto the order of Henry Crochran the audited claim or certificate of indebtness of the said state which has been issued in my favor for service in the Woll Expedition in 1842, and I moreover authorize the said auditor and comptroller or either of them to assign and in my name execute a transfer of said certificate unto said Crochran and do authorize the Treasurer of said state to pay unto the order of said Cochran the amount of money for which the said certificate calls, and I do hereby relinquish and transfer unto said Crochran all my right and claim hereunto for value received.

Bastrop, Dec 29, 1851

Ritchman Townsend

State of Texas, County of Bastrop

      Before me the undersigned notary public in and for the said county personally came Ritchman Townsend whose name is subscribed to the foregoing instrument whom I know who did voluntarily sign the same in my presence. And acknowledged that he has freely signed said instrument for the purpose and consideration herein approved.

      To certify which I have caused my official seal to be here unto affixed.

      Given under my hand at office
This December 29th A.D. 1851
G C Cunningham,

Republic of Texas Service & Claim

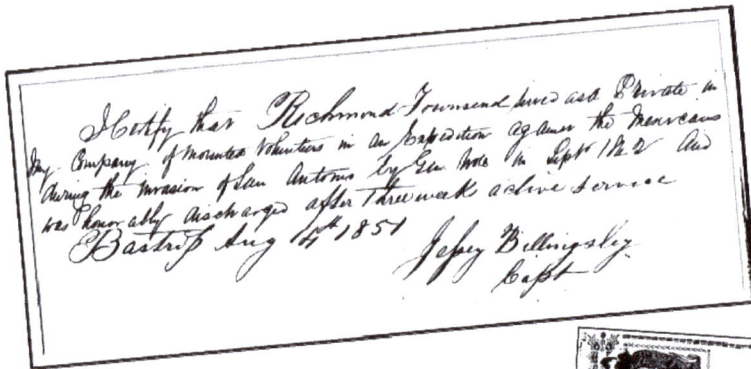

Certification of service in the War
With Mexico
&
Certificate of Debt owed to
Richmond Townsend

Information below is on the battle
Richmond was in against Adrian Woll

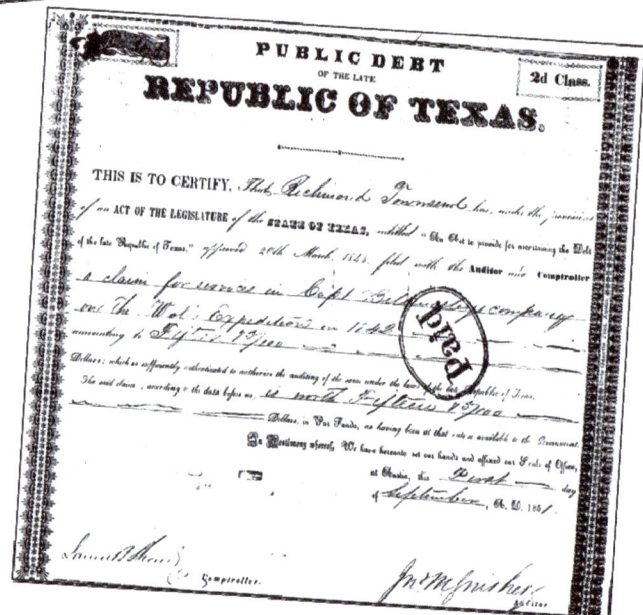

Adrián Woll (Dec. 2, 1795– February 1875) was a French soldier of fortune and mercenary who served as a general in the army of Mexico during the Texas Revolution and the Mexican-American War.

On September 11, 1842, Gen. Adrián Woll, with a force of 1,200 Mexicans, captured San Antonio. By September 17, 200 Texans had gathered on Cibolo Creek above Seguin and marched under Mathew Caldwell to Salado Creek six miles northeast of San Antonio. On September 18 Caldwell sent Hays and a company of scouts to draw the Mexicans into a fight; the battle of Salado Creek resulted. While the fight was going on, Capt. Nicholas M. Dawson approached from the east with a company of fifty-three men. These men were attacked a mile and a half from the scene of the battle and killed in what came to be known as the Dawson Massacre. Woll drew his men back to San Antonio and retreated to Mexico by September 20. The reinforced Texans pursued him for three days and then returned to San Antonio. By September 25 a large number of Texans had gathered at San Antonio, and plans were made for a punitive expedition, the Somervell expedition, which evolved into the Mier expedition.

David & Tabitha Thomas Townsend
Parents of Richmond Townsend

David was born about 1774 but the location is unknown, probably in North Carolina. He was a son of Solomon and Charity (last name unknown) and died in 1816 at the age of 42. He was buried in Sharon Cemetery, Richmond Co., North Carolina.

David Townsend and Tabitha Thomas were married about 1795 in Anson Co., North Carolina.

He signed a will on 15 Jul 1816 in Anson Co., North Carolina.

In the name of God, amen
I, David Townsend of the State of No Carolina, Anson County being weak in body but perfect in mind and memory desire to dispose of my worldly goods before I depart this life.
1st I will that my body be decently buried according to the customs of a Christian country.
2nd I will that all my estate real and personal be appraised by my Executors.
3rd I give and betroth the whole of my estate to my beloved wife Tabitha Townsend. During her natural life or widow hood and at her death or marriage to be by my executor equally divided between my sons and daughters Solomon Townsend, David Townsend, Richmond Townsend, Gilbert Townsend, Hamilton Townsend, Sherwood Townsend, Naomy Townsend, Susana Townsend, Charity Townsend and Malinda Townsend.
4th I will that what part of my goods and chattels my wife Tabitha Townsend may give to any of my above named sons or daughters when they shall have come of lawful age the valuation thereof according to appraisement be deducted from their part in the general division of my estate.
Also whatever she may spend for eather of their education to be deducted in like manner.
5th I do hereby constitute and appoint Benjamin Williams and John Harris sign my lawful executors to this my last will and testament,

and I do hereby declare this to be my last will and testament and all former will made by me are null and void in witness whereof I the said David Townsend here unto set my hand and seal the day and date above written.
David (X) Townsend
Witness: Wm Lewis, Page Azza (X) Harris
July (?) 1843

This the above will was proven in open Court by the oaths of John A McRus & Allen Carpenter, Esqrs. who proved the signature of Wm Lewis to be in his proven handwriting and the said has removed from this state and now resides beyond the limits of this state.
W.D. Boggan, MD

David and Tabitha Thomas Townsend had the following children:

- **Susan Townsend,** b. unknown
- **Belinda Townsend** b. unknown, married Benjamin Williams in 1833.
- **Sherwood Townsend**, b. unknown
- **Gilbert Townsend**, b. unknown
- **Solomon Townsend** was born on 11 Sep 1797. He died on 20 Jun 1873 at the age of 75 in Richmond Co., NC. He was married to Naomi Bostick in 1828.
- **David Townsend** was born on 24 Dec 1797 in Anson Co, North Carolina. He died on 16 Sep 1870 at the age of 72 in Lee Co. Mississippi. He married Elizabeth Williams before 1855.
- **Richmond Townsend**, born 1798, North Carolina; died after 1877, Bastrop Co., Texas and married Mary Bryant.
- **Charity Townsend** was born on 28 Sept 1808 and on the 8th of May, married Allen Gossett of Marshall Co., Mississippi.
- **Hamilton Townsend** was born on 8 Sept 1812 in Anson Co., North Carolina. He died in 1842 at the age of 30 in Anson Co., North Carolina.

Tabitha Thomas Townsend was born about 1775 but the location is not known but likely it was in North Carolina.

She was the daughter of Thomas Thomas, III and wife Avis Bostick. It was this deed that gives us this information: <u>15 October 1772, John Bostick to Avis Thomas, wife of Thomas Thomas, 294 acres, pr. by Chas. Robinson, Esq.</u>

Tabitha died about 1843 at the age of 68 in Anson Co., North Carolina. Her will was signed on 6 Apr 1843 in Anson Co, North Carolina.

In the name of God, Amen,

This is my last will and testament; I bequeath, will and give to my daughters Susan, Charity, and Belinda a note which I hold on my son Solomon Townsend for one hundred and eighty-two dollars, one horse now in my possession called Ned, one other horse called Cuff in the service of my son Sherwood Townsend, one ps. of land bought of my son Solomon joining the land on which I now live, Isaac W Hutchinson's land, and others containing more or less fourteen and one half acres, one yoke of oxen and cart, my household and kitchen furniture, whatever it may be (to wit), to beads, 2 bedsteads, and furniture, three chests, one sideboard, ten chairs and folding walnut table, one pie table, twelve dollars in money (??).

I will and bequeath unto my sons and daughters, <u>Solomon, David, Richmond, Hampton, Naomi, Susan, Charity, Belinda, and Sherwood</u> all my stock of cattle except the yoke of oxen and all my extra bead clothing, to be divided in that way and manner which may them all best, in this my last will and testament, it is my wish and desire that the first actually which I have bequeathed unto my three daughters, Susan, Charity and Belinda shall be divided equally between them.

It is further my will and desire that my stock of cattle as before named and extra bead clothing shall be equally divided between my sons and daughters Solomon, David, Richmond, Hampton, Naomi, Susan, Charity, Belinda and Sherwood.

Signed and Sealed this the 6th day of April in the year of our Lord one thousand eight hundred and forty-three in the presence of us.

Witnesses: J T Smith,
John W Hutchinson

Signed: Tabitha (/) Townsend (Seal)

Thomas Thomas (III) and Avis Bostick
Parents of Tabitha Thomas

The Thomas family is one of great antiquity in Wales. The surname has been borne by many who have been distinguished in all the various walks of life, civil and military.

We find our ancestor Tristram Thomas, leaving England and settling in Talbot Co., Maryland before May 1706. His wife Anne Coursey was born in 1633 in Sundridge, Kent. She married Tristam Thomas on May 20, 1652, in Talbot Co., Maryland. One of Tristram's and Ann's son was named Thomas, beginning our line of "Thomas Thomas" men.

Thomas Thomas, (I), was born ca 1659 and married Elizabeth about 1687 in Maryland. He became a planter and was a member of the Episcopal Church. His date of death is before 8 May 1706. Elizabeth, whose maiden name is unknown, was born before 1662, possibly in Maryland and died 25 November 1720 in Queen Anne's Co., Maryland.

Thomas and Elizabeth had a son, Thomas Thomas, (II) born before 1694 in Talbot Co., Maryland. He married Susannah, whose maiden name is unknown, about 1721 in Queen Anne's Co., Maryland. Thomas, Jr. died before 29 November 1770 and Susannah died before 3 December 1768, both in Queen Anne's County. Several of this family's children left Maryland and settled in North Carolina.

Thomas and Susannah had a son, Thomas Thomas, (III), born about 1732 in Queen Anne's County. Thomas III married Avis Bostick about 1753.

WILL OF THOMAS TOMAS (THOMAS)

In the name of God amen, I Thomas Tomas of the county of Anson and state of North Carolina being old with age and weak in bodily health and strength but sound in both mind and memory thanks be unto God for it.

Calling unto mind the mortality of my body and knowing that it is appointed for all men once to die do make and ordain this as my last will and testament. That is to say principally and first of all I give and recommend my soul into the hands of the almighty and my body I recommend to the earth to be buried in a decent Christian burial at the discretion of my Executors nothing doubting but in the general resurrection I shall receive the same again by the help of the almighty and as touching with worldly estate whereas it has pleased God to bless me with in this life I give dismiss and dispose of the same in the following manner and form.

Item*: I do give and bequeath unto my two sons namely John Tommas and James Tommas all the money that I shall leave due to me for the land that I sold to Simon Tommas on Catledgses Creek in Richmond County to be equally divided amongst them and David Townsen.*

*I do give and bequeath unto my sons John, James and my **daughter Tabitha** all my real and personal estate to be equally divided between them and their heirs forever.*

Item *I do give unto my daughter Susannah Tommas one dollar to be raised out of my estate and that for to be all that she is to have.*

Item *I do give and bequeath unto my sons Thomas Tommas the sum of one dollar to be raised as the above and that is to be his portion.*

Item *I do give unto my daughter Elizabeth Blewford the sum of one dollar and that is to be concluded her portion.*

Item *I do give and bequeath unto my daughter Mary Head the sum of one dollar and that is to be her portion.*

Item *I do hereby appoint Benjamin Williams and David Townsin the sole executors of this my last will and testament as witness my hand and seal this tenth day of January 1807.*

   Thomas (X) Tommas   *(Seal)*

Solomon Townsend and Wife Charity
Parents of David Townsend

Not a great deal is known about this Solomon Townsend and even less is known about Charity. A number of researchers have worked for years trying to find the parents of Solomon Townsend of Anson Co., North Carolina. The following is a synopsis of what some of us know about our Solomon Townsend.

We first find a Solomon Townsend in the Carolinas in 1747 and 1748 as a member of the New Topsail Company. This was a militia formed to protect Brunswick Towne during the Spanish Alarm from raids on coastal settlements. Brunswick Towne is located a few miles downstream from Wilmington, NC, on the Cape Fear River and is currently only a historic site. We have not been able to find any land, other courthouse or church records in the area for Solomon.

We next find a Solomon Townsend in 1755 acquiring land from Alexander Sherard by "lease and release" dated May 22nd and 23rd, 1755, in Craven County, Prince Frederick Parish on Maple Swamp. The current location would be near Dillon in Dillon Co., South Carolina. This document is on file at the South Carolina Archives, but we have not been able to find any information on the transfer or disposition of this tract.

We next find Solomon Townsend purchasing land in 1767 on the Long Branch of Jones Creek in the southern portion of current Anson Co., North Carolina.

Shortly after arriving in Anson County he began acquiring numerous tracts of land both by grant and purchase. Most of these tracts were in Anson County, but one was on Deep Creek in Craven Co., South Carolina, and one was in Sampson, now Duplin Co., North Carolina. The tract on Deep Creek in Craven County is just a few miles west of Chesterfield in current Chesterfield County, South Carolina, and a few miles below the North Carolina border and about ten miles from his original purchase on Jones

Creek in Anson County. The other was more than 100 miles southeast of his Anson County land. Considering the difficulty of travel at this time, one wonders why he would acquire land so far away. We know that this was our Solomon because his three sons sold this land after his death.

The wife of Solomon Townsend was Charity (last name unknown).

Solomon and Charity had three sons:

- **David Townsend** (1767-after 1822) m. Tabitha Thomas

- **Solomon Richardson Townsend** (1779-1854) m. Nancy Lyles

- **John William Townsend** (b. 1782-1865) m. Susannah T. McClendon.

Solomon's will was probated in Anson County in 1788. The only page remaining on file in the courthouse is a portion of his inventory.

After his death, his widow married Charles Weatherford and they moved to Jackson Co, Georgia. She took her youngest son, John W. with her and Solomon Richardson also moved to Georgia.

David Townsend continued to live in Anson County.

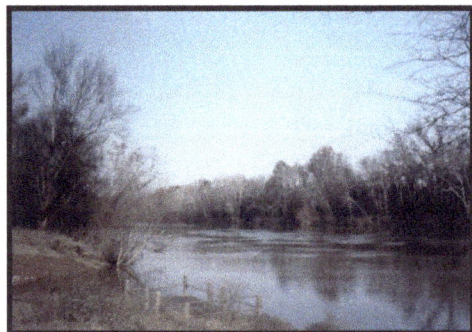

Pee Dee River
Anson County, North Carolina

A couple of surnames come down through the generations and they are Richardson and Sherwood. No one has been able to establish a connection to these names to date.

We are fortunate to have a member in our small research group who is a direct male Townsend descendent of Solomon of Anson Co., North Carolina. Tom Townsend, III, has a well-documented line back to Solomon of Anson County and submitted his DNA, which is posted on the Townsend Society of America DNA section. Tom's DNA is a perfect match with a number of researchers who trace their ancestry back to John Townsend of Snow Hill, Maryland. This match provides strong evidence that Solomon Townsend of Anson County is directly related to John Townsend of Snow Hill, Maryland. We were also able to get two more male Townsends directly related to Solomon through Richmond to DNA test and they are a match with Tom and others from John Townsend, who was born 1640 in Accomack, Virginia.

John Townsend of Accomack Co., Virginia, married and moved his family to Snow Hill, Somerset Co., Maryland. This family group is generally known as the Snow Hill Townsends,

which includes the Solomon Townsend family group of Anson Co., North Carolina.

Several years ago, Bennett Greenspan of FamilyTreeDNA in response to my question about the relationship between the Townsend men who DNA tested at that time wrote: "*There is no doubt that all of these men in this summary are closely related; especially the four who have 7's at DYS 459a. Of the nearly 20,000 people we have tested only .9 of 1% have a 7 at that position. Couple that together with the unusual 17 that all of these men have at DYS 19 and it drops to 7 men, 4 of whom are in this group (and 2 from a scientific study of Dr. Hammer)*".

Since Solomon has not been connected back to John Townsend through documentation, perhaps some descendant in the second, third or fourth generation left the Maryland area and researchers assume he died, or as a child was omitted or just simply slipped through unnoticed. Hopefully sometime in the future, documented proof will be found.

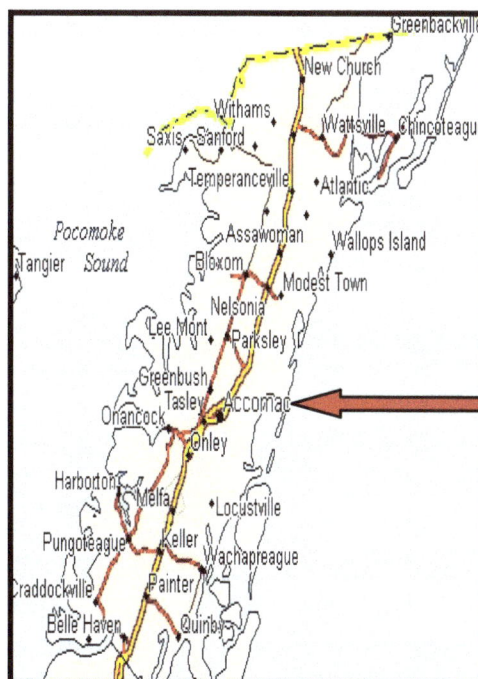

The John Townsend family settled near Hungar's Parish, Accomack Co., Virginia. This is a photo of the original **Hungar's Parish Church** – one of the oldest churches in America, built in 1645.

Alexander Bryant & Elizabeth Anderson

Parents of May Bryant Townsend

Elizabeth Cureton Anderson died on August 4, 1821 and Alexander died January 25, 1822. Mary lost both parents within six months. She and her siblings were placed under guardianship of four different men, Grandfather Benjamin Anderson, Wes Melton, Thomas Melton and Jeremiah Sanders. Mary was placed with her grandfather. There are extensive records in Greene County, Alabama settling the estate of Alexander and the caring of his orphaned children.

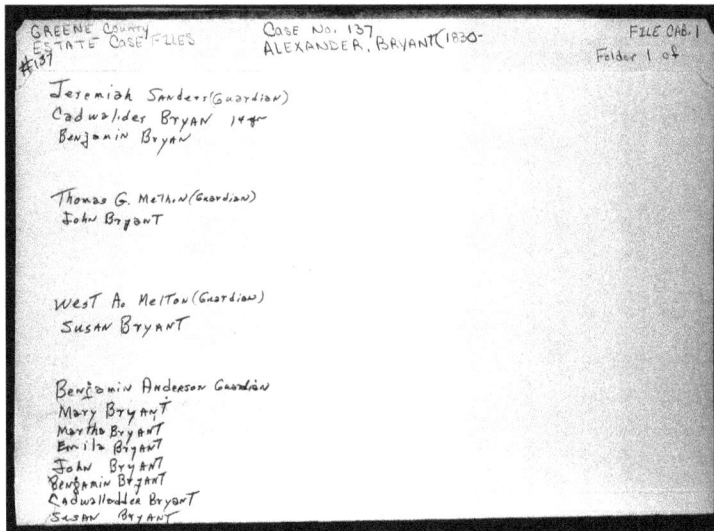

Guardianship Record for
the children of
Alexander & Elizabeth
Anderson Bryant

Greene County, Alabama

Alexander left a sizeable estate and it took many years to settle it. Perhaps it was because he had left his young children as orphans and they were to be provided for out of the proceeds. Alex had lost his wife on August 4, 1821. This left his family of seven children without their mother.

On 25 January, 1822, Alex died. It was thought to be an accident, but there has been no definitive answer to the cause. It was less than six months that these seven children lost both mother and father and became orphans.

Fortunately, Elizabeth's father, Benjamin Anderson lived nearby and could help. This could not have been an easy task as Benjamin had many small children of his own. The guardianship was divided between Benjamin and three other men.

Mary would have been about 13 years old when this tragedy occurred. She was the oldest of the children and Susannah/Susan would have been the youngest at only three months old. It was possibly the birth of Susan that eventually caused Elizabeth's death.

The task of caring and raising these orphan children would have been huge and was possibly the reason they were split up under three guardians.

Alexander Bryant's Estate
Page 1 of 3 of Estate Inventory

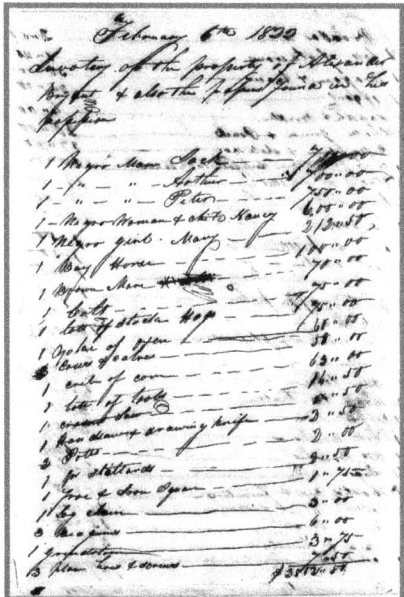

I have transcribed only page 1 of the 3 pages listing the inventory of Alexander Bryant's estate and total of all 3 pages. I have shown all three pages on the left.

February 6th 1822—Page 1

Inventory of the property of Alexander Bryant & also the property found in his possession:

1 negro man Jack	700.00
1 negro man Arthur	700.00
1 negro man Peter	750.00
1 negro woman & child Nancy	600.00
1 negro girl Mary	212.50
1 bay horse	100.00
1 brown horse	70.00
1 colt	75.00
1 lot of stock hogs	75.00
1 yoke of oxen	60.00
3 cows & calves	58.00
1 crib of corn	63.00
1 lott of tools	14.50
1 crosscut saw	3.50
1 hand saw & drawing knife	2.50
2 Potts	2.00
1 jar_____?____	2.50
1 fram & Iron Square	1.75
1 log chain	3.00
3____?_____	6.00
1 grip____?___	3.75
3 plow haws & screws	7.50
	$3512.50
Total from page 2	767.00
Total from page 3	94.62 1/2
Total of 3 pages	**$4374.12 1/2**

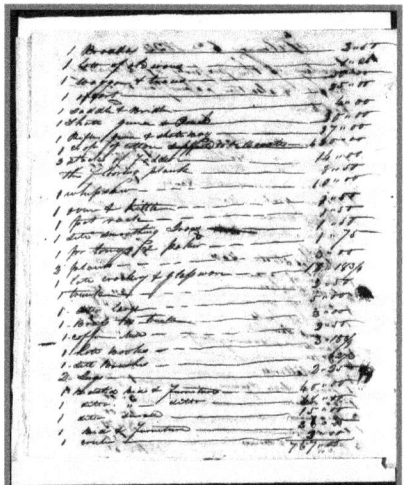

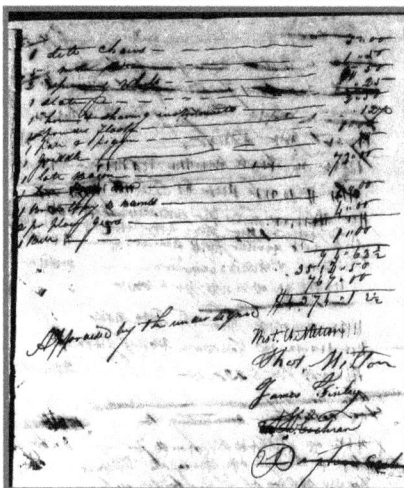

Benjamin Anderson and Rebecca Cureton
Parents of Elizabeth Anderson Bryant

Benjamin W. Anderson was born in 1751 in South Carolina and joined the Continental Army after the Tories killed his father. He first married Rebecca (Polly) Cureton and they had 9 children before she died. Benjamin next married Margaret Jane Williams and they had 16 children. He also served with the local militia during the Texas revolution.

Benjamin loved race horses and rode them until he broke a leg at the age of 96 during a horse race. He died September 14, 1853 and is buried in Blackjack-Attoyac Cemetery located 3.9 miles north of Chireno, Texas in Nacogdoches County. According to Clovis' book there are no markers on his grave, however there is a picture of it.

Benjamin was the son of Joshua Anderson (d: Mar. 8, 1769 in present day Newberry County, South Carolina) & his wife. Benjamin was their only son, and it is not presently known whether Benjamin had any sisters.

"Benjamin W. Anderson had a long, vigorous, interesting, and fruitful life. He and his wife, Margaret Jane Williams, came to Texas from Alabama in 1834 when he was well past three score and ten years of age, and spent a quarter century actively participating in the establishment and growth of the Republic and the young Lone Star State of Texas.

He was born in South Carolina, January 1751, and it was his boast that he never had a pair of shoes or a hat that wasn't made on the plantation until he was 16 years old. At that time his father, Joshua Anderson, who was fighting in the Revolutionary War, was killed by the Tories. Benjamin shouldered a gun and fought until the close of the war.

He received land from his grandfather, Abraham Anderson and also had land in Georgia.

Benjamin W. Anderson amassed a large fortune and had 25 children by two wives. He was a great traveler and visited all the adjacent states as well as Mexico. At almost 75 years of age he started to Texas with a colony composed almost entirely of his married sons and daughters, their children, his single children, and a large number of slaves. He also carried a large amount of gold. He headed his wagon train for San Augustine, Texas, arriving at his destination on Christmas Day, 1834.

For many years a large oak tree bore witness of this event. The bark was removed, a large slab of the trunk was smoothed and on it was carved the date of the Anderson colony and their pledge of allegiance to the Republic of Texas. This allegiance was later proved by the liberal contributions Benjamin Anderson and his sons made to help build up the defenses against the Indians as well as helping to organize, finance and outfit the militia. When Texas Independence was declared, six of his sons, four grandsons, and two sons-in-law were in the ranks as soldiers. On the memorial shaft at the San Jacinto battleground, the names to two sons and one son-in-law are inscribed as witness to their loyalty to Texas.

Friends and relatives from back home sometimes stopped by on their way to other parts of Texas. Strangers often dropped by and spent the night. A traveler judged a home by how well his horse was quartered and fed. One traveler who spent the night in the Anderson home was Mirabeau B. Lamar. "

In his diary, Lamar gives an account of spending the night at the Anderson place and humorously assailed Benjamin Anderson for "having so egregiously violated the Malthusian policy of population".

The diary contains Lamar's musings about the land and its inhabitants as he made the four-month journey from his home in Georgia to Texas in 1835.

Lamar writes of this lodging, "As I stretched my limbs on the floor to recruit my exhausted strength, there flocked all around in noisy confusion, a battalion of dogs and children; in which it was difficult to determine which were the more numerous or noisy."

To the last of his life Benjamin Anderson was an alert and vigorous man. He often staged horse races and wrestling matches in which he participated. The guests came from miles around and often stayed days and sometimes weeks. At the age of 96, Benjamin dared to enter a horse race. His horse fell and Benjamin's leg was broken - he said he had always been too impulsive and enthusiastic. However, he recovered and lived to over 100 years old, having lived wisely and well, to the honor and reverence of a large line of descendants in many parts of Texas. He died at his homeplace called Black Jack, near Chireno in Nacogdoches County.

The children of Benjamin W. Anderson and Rebecca Cureton, his first wife, were **Elizabeth**, *William C., Susannah, Joshua, Rebecca, James C., Oliver C., Martha and an infant who died. The children of Benjamin W. Anderson and Margaret Jane Williams were: Carolina,*

Margaret Anderson who married John P. Lawson; John W. married Elizabeth Briley; Mary/Polly married first, Capt. T.J. Shaw and second A. Webb; Benjamin W. who married Mary Ann Lee; Mitchell B.; Thomas Howard who married first Missouri Bailey and second Mrs. Harriett Lashing; George Washington married Bland Angelina Dameron; Margarett married Robert Emmitt Lindsey; Andrew Jackson married Sarah Ann Norris; Robert J.; Frances married James S.W. Merchant; Harriett married first Louis Spinks and second James Harrison; Napoleon Bonaparte (Dock) married first Callie Caldonia and second Rosalie Malone."

Information by Mrs. Robert S. Natusch, Sr. (Sandy) *Received from Lavelle Henderson who said it was from a newspaper article.*

Benjamin received a land grant from the state of Texas.

Benjamin left a considerable estate in Nacogdoches Co., Texas. Mary Bryant Townsend, along with her siblings, inherited a portion of his estate as an heir of their mother, Elizabeth Anderson Bryant.

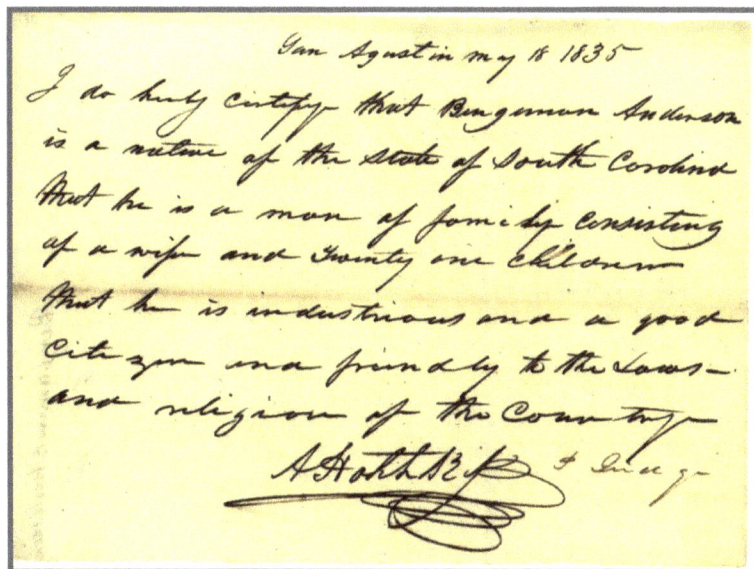

Transcribed:

San Augustin May 18, 1835

I do hereby certify that Benjamin Anderson is a native of the state of South Carolina that he is a man of family consisting of twenty one children

That he is industrious and a good citizen and friendly to the laws and religion of the country.

(Signature difficult to read)

"The Trip" by Bud and Terry Anderson

1832-34, From Western Alabama to East Texas"
Excerpted and paraphrased by Pamela Anderson Thompson

Sometime between 1832 and 1834 a small caravan crossed the Sabine River out of northwestern Louisiana and rolled slowly into Texas. It had been a long and wearing trip for the adults, the horde of children and probably a handful of slaves led by Benjamin W. Anderson, the patriarch in his mid 80's who was making his last great pilgrimage.

The people with him were his sons, daughters and their families. They carried all the possessions and necessities for the trip that they could load onto the wagons. There were approximately 33 members of the family who made the trip from Greene Co., Alabama to Texas. There were about eight adults, four teenagers and at least 18 children under 10 years old As many as five children were babies under a year old. Many of the women were pregnant. It is one thing for a large body of adults to make such a trek, but more than half of this party were children. This was a children's crusade lead by a handful of adults. If Benjamin and his tribe brought slaves, they were sorely needed, not only for the heavy work of driving livestock, driving the wagon and getting the wagons across fords, out of mud holes and up hills. Also, someone had to set up camp, prepare meals and keep the multitude of children out of trouble and accounted for.

The journey had begun months earlier in Greene County on the western edge of Alabama. The party followed a track through land that was primeval: dense forest, untamed rivers and streams. After heavy rains the rivers were largely not fordable. There were swamps to cross and hills that tested the strength of both man and beast. Although hunger should not have been a problem for a resourceful party, illness, injury and even death was a specter that walked with them every mile.

As far as we know, they all survived. ...In *"The Texas Republic"* William Ramsom Hogan pointed out that many immigrant families were practically self-sufficient enroute, for their carefully hoarded stocks of food were supplemented by game. Travelers were also advised to bring furniture, cooking utensils, wagons, farming implements, tools, and provisions of food and clothing with them in order to begin their new life with less hardship. This was a trek: 450-500 hard miles, day after day, walking into the unknown. It could be regarded as high adventure, although probably only the youngest considered it so.

This journey could not have taken less than two to three months under the best of conditions in the 1830s. It is also quite possible that the party spent some time visiting daughters Elizabeth and Susannah in Mississippi. We don't know the trail they followed, but today Interstate 20 runs a close appropriate path of least resistance through Alabama, Georgia, Mississippi and Louisiana, overlaying roadbeds and Native American trails. Almost certainly they would have had to cross the Mississippi on a ferry.

The most likely places are Vicksburg, Natchez or Baton Rouge. Vicksburg seems most appropriate because it is on the straight-line route from where they started the trip. This would also have pointed the party towards Natchitoches, Louisiana, an important trading center of the era.

There they could have rested and replenished supplies before heading southwest down a well-traveled road, corresponding approximately to today's State Highway 6 in Louisiana (Hwy 21 in Texas). And to Gaines Ferry across the Sabine River.

This road is an extension of the historic El Camino Real and traces of it can still be seen. The Anderson's would have entered Texas in Sabine County. There is some evidence that many remained in Sabine County before purchasing land in Nacogdoches County.

This passage from Eutaw, Alabama to Nacogdoches, Texas made use of trails and paths used for years by earlier travelers and takes advantage of established communities and trading centers. Even if they didn't buy or barter, it offered civility and relatively safe resting places.

There's no written record about their arrival, stepping off the ferry into Texas. Family lore has it that they arrived in December, 1834: old Ben, Jane, children, grandchildren and slaves. It would be romantic to call them pioneers, but they were farmers, people of their times. They moved with relative frequency on the heels of others who neutralized the most serious dangers of a new frontier.

The Andersons move in order to acquire land on the outskirts of the nation moving west. The size of the family dictated the relocation. Benjamin may have worried that he didn't have enough land to give all his children a suitable place to live. Also, cotton and corn deplete the soil and his crops may have been declining. Whatever the reason, Texas and its generous land policies under Mexican and Texas rule offered a great opportunity for farmers.

Abraham Anderson, Benjamin's grandfather accepted 200 acres on the Carolina coast in 1764 from King George III. They settled in Berkeley Co., South Carolina, and stayed until the threats of war from Spain were resolved and most of the Cherokee Indians had been removed by purchase and treaty.

They participated in a land rush to settle the Up country and the Piedmont. Benjamin stayed in South Carolina (probably on more free land) in

Newberry County in the Ninety-Sixth District, and then accepted 900 acres from the new state of Georgia on the Ocheegee River in Greene County late in the 1790s and then after 40 years in Alabama in Jones and Greene Counties.

Moving to Texas, he was eligible to receive a league and a labor for having settled prior to Texas becoming a republic in 1849. This time, however, Benjamin purchased land in Nacogdoches County in what was called Black Jack.

In his lifetime Benjamin Anderson moved halfway across the continent, from tidewater South Carolina to Georgia to Texas. He participated in one way or another in two major uprisings, the American Revolution in 1775-6 and the Texas Revolution in 1835-36. He moved always to the edge – a borderer. Whether by instinct or circumstances, this was his fate. He was born the subject of an English King and died a Texan.

At the age of 96, Benjamin dared to enter a horse race. His horse fell and Benjamin's leg was broken. Supposedly this was the scene.

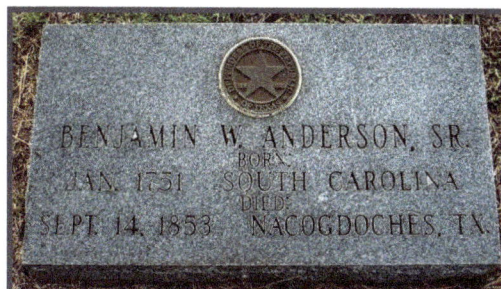

John Bryant and wife Judith Elizabeth Winfrey
Parents of Alexander Bryant

John Bryant was born on 5 Nov 1754 in Albemarle Co., Virginia. He served in the military during the Revolutionary War serving two tours when drafted into service. His last tour ended when he guarded prisoners at the surrender of Cornwallis. It was during the last tour of service that his regiment combined with George Washington's regiment.

John made pension application on 22 Feb 1838 at Open Court in Jackson Co., Alabama. Documentation exists of John Bryant's War of the Revolution pension papers, Application # 12299 issued in Jackson Co. Alabama in 1838. In his pension application he stated that after the war he lived in Lincoln Co., Kentucky, Lincoln Co., Tennessee, Jackson Co., Alabama, then back to Franklin Co., Tennessee and finally settling permanently in Jackson Co.,

Alabama. No reason was given for living in these various locations.

He married Judith Elizabeth Winfrey before 1781 and died on 29 Mar 1842 at the age of 87 in Carnes, Jackson Co., Alabama. Judith died September 22, 1842 also in Carnes, Jackson Co., AL.

John Bryant and Judy Elizabeth Winfrey had the following children:

Alexander, William, Benjamin, Randolph and James.

Alexander was born in Buckingham Co, VA. 1781. He married Elizabeth Anderson about 1800, most likely in Greene or Hancock County, Georgia.

The Winfrey & Turpin Families
Parents of Judith Elizabeth Winfrey

John Winfrey, father of Judith Elizabeth, married **Mary Turpin**. The source of information of the husband/wife relationship of John and Mary and birth date and name of their first child is found in the _Douglas Register_.

The basic information given in the _Douglas Register_ is: John Winfrey and Mary Turpin – first child to be born 13 February 1762, named Sally Winfrey. The source of this information is fully reliable to the last detail. It is noted that the date and place of the marriage of John and Mary is not given.

Israel Winfrey is the father of John. In a deed transferring land from Israel to Arthur Moseley, 5 June 1778, in Powhatan Co., Virginia, Israel states "which tract or parcel of land my son John Winfrey now liveth on".

Israel Winfrey and **Philip Turpin**, father of Mary, owned adjacent land on Swift Creek in Cumberland County (in 1777 this area became Powhatan County). Thus, they were neighbors, and Israel's young son, John, didn't have to go far to find Mary Turpin to court and later to marry.

Elizabeth Turpin, widow of Philip Turpin, in her Will names her daughter, Mary Winfrey.

William & Martha Baugh Cureton
Parents of Mary Rebecca, wife of Benjamin Anderson

William Cureton was born on 27 Mar 1737 in Prince George Co., Virginia. He signed a will on 11 May 1810 in Jackson Co., Georgia. He died in 1813 at the age of 76 in Jackson County, Georgia.

William Cureton served as Captain in the Militia, Newberry Co., South Carolina. He appears in the "Revolutionary Records of the State of Georgia", Vol. 1 page 32. He and his family moved to Wilkes Co. Georgia in 1766, living in Capt. Samuel Alexander's District where he signed a petition in 1774, as from the Parish of St. George, Burke County, south and west of Augusta. From there he moved his family to Jackson Co., Georgia where he is shown as paying taxes in 1809.

The 1994 edition of DAR Patriot Index Centennial Edition Part 1, page 732

- William Sr, born 3-27-1737, Virginia, d. 7-2-1810 GA. m. Martha Baugh, Lt. SC.

- William is mentioned in the Memorial Campaign against the Cherokee Indians by William Maybin, who served in General Andrew Williamson's command. Col. Maybin describes their participation in the "Ring Fight" against the Cherokees, and also their being with General Sumter on the Catawba River, in the Battle of Hanging Rock, South Carolina.

- William was a Justice of the Peace in Jackson Co. Georgia when he died.

- Granted bounty #622 for 450 acres of land in Washington Co., Georgia. "The "Georgia Revolutionary Roster" by Knight, page 379.

WILL OF WILLIAM CURETON
Georgia, Jackson County

I, William Cureton being in a low condition of body but of perfect mind and memory do make this my last will & testament hereby revoking all other will or wills by heretofore made.

1st. My will is that all of my last debts paid out of my estate by my executrix & executor to be by me hereafter appointed.

Item: *I give to my grandson Taylor Whatten one bed and furniture & two mares, one a bay with a blaze in her face, the other a bay & one cow & calf & one ewe and lamb, eight head of hogs now in his own Whatten one bed and furniture & two mares, one a bay with a blaze in her face, the other a bay & one cow & calf & one ewe and lamb, eight head of hogs now in his own*

Item: *I give to my well beloved wife Martha our negro woman Leth & one negro boy Mingo, & one cow & calf & two heifers & one bed & furniture & all my household & kitchen furniture & the legacy which due or coming to me in right of my wife, Martha out of the estate of her brother* <u>*William Baugh,*</u> *late of the State of Virginia deceased & all the balance of my flock of sheep to her & her heirs forever together with all my stock of hogs all of which property to be at the disposition of her my wife Martha at or before her death either by will or otherwise.*

Lastly: *I do hereby appoint my wife Martha my executrix & Hugh Montgomery my sole executor of this my last Will & Testament.*

Witness my hand & seal this 11th day of May 1810.   William Cureton, Sen (Seal)

In presence of Hannah (X her mark) Wallis
Wm McNeer, John Wallis

John Cureton & Frances Thweatt
Parents of William Cureton

William was the son of **John Cureton** and was born on 17 Jul 1687 in Virginia. John died in 1769 at the age of 82 in Virginia. His Cureton Bible Pages were located in the home of a descendant living in Alabama. Frances Thweatt and John Cureton were married in 1715 in Prince George Co., Virginia.

John was the son of **Thomas Cureton** who was born on 12 Jan 1660 in Grinshill, Shropshire, England. The Wem-Shropshire-Grinshill area is close to the Welsh border. He died on 13 May 1691 at the age of 31 in Wem, Shropshire, England.

Elizabeth Jane Price and Thomas Cureton were married in 1677 in Prees, Shropshire, England. **Elizabeth Jane Price** was born about 1660 in Prees, Shropshire, England.

Thomas bought land on the James River near City Point, Virginia in 1682, later returned to England and died at Myddle, Shropshire in 1724. In his will dated July 29, 1720 names sons Thomas and **John**, daughters Anne, Jane and Mary. Records taken from Myddle Parish Register.

Thomas, the son of **Richard Cureton** was born in 1642 in Grinshill, Shropshire, England. He immigrated in 1685 to Philadelphia, Pennsylvania. He died on 20 Jul 1699 at the age of 57 in Merion, Philadelphia, Pennsylvania.

Richard was buried in Friend's Burial Ground in Merion, Pennsylvania. Margaret Embry and Richard Cureton were married on 11 Feb 1681 in St. Mary's Church, Shrewbury, England. **Margaret Embry** was born in 1657 in St. Mary's Church, Shrewbury, England.

Frances Thweatt was born in 1697 in Prince George Co., Virginia. She died on 26 Sep 1747 at the age of 50 in Georgia.

Frances Thweatt was the daughter of **James Thweatt** and **Judith Soanes**. James was born in 1676 in Prince George Co., Virginia. Judith Soanes was born in 1678 in Virginia and died on 15 Jan 1758 at the age of 80 in Virginia. Judith Soanes and James Thweatt were married on 24 Nov 1701 in Virginia.

In 1703, he received two grants of land in Prince George - one for 234 acres and one for 223 acres. He also was a Justice of Prince George Co., Virginia (1712); and later was Sheriff of Prince George (1718/1719).

In Judith's father's will of 1714, William Soane of Henrico County mentioned "my daughter, Judith Thweatt."

This younger James Thweatt was attending the Prince George County court as a Justice on June 14, 1715. And on June 10, 1718, "James Thweatt having produced a commission from the Honorable Lieutenant Governor to be sheriff of this county, he accordingly took the usual oaths, etc." His bond was for £1,000 sterling.

Thomas Simmonds was sworn in as under-sheriff at the same time, taking the same oath. By 1719, Sheriff James Thweatt had a son James, Jr., who was of age. They witnessed many deeds and wills together from then until 1726.

James was a son of **James Thweatt and Mary Lee**. The elder James was born 28 February 1643 in in Bolton, Lancashire, England. Mary Lee and James Thweatt were married in 1670 in Virginia.

Mary Lee was born in 1647 in Virginia. She died on 4 Jan 1712 at the age of 65 in Virginia. James died in 1710 in Charles City, Charles Co., Virginia.

James Thweatt "of Bristol Parish" was an officer in the Virginia militia when he signed the loyalty oath in March, 1701/2. In 1704, Thweatt owned 750 acres, some on the south side of the Appomattox River which was in Bristol parish and some on the south side of the James River which was in Jordan's parish.

Prince George County interview of James Thweat, aged 64 years or thereabouts, sworn said that he had known the River now called the Nottoway River for the space of about 48 years or more and then it was called by the name of the Nottoway River and by no other name that the deponent knows or has heard. That when this deponent was first acquainted in those parts, the chief town of the Nottoway Indians was on the south side of the River where Major Wynne's Quarter now is, about three miles above the mouth of Monksneck Creek, and some few of them lived at Rowonte, which is about 4 miles up Monksneck creek; and two or three families of them at Tonnatora, which is on the north side of the River. And that they lived at some of these places, and at Cottashowrock, and there abouts, until about 25 or 26 years ago, and then they removed and settled their great town upon Atyamonsock Swamp at the place now called Old Town. That about 48 years ago the Meherrin Indians lived upon the Meherrin River at Cowochahawkon and some of them at Unote, and about 24 years ago they lived some of them at Unote and some at Taurara, but how long they lived there after that time, he cannot particularly remember. And further this deponent said not.

James Thweatt, November 12, 1707, sworn before us B Harrison, Jr.

James died in 1726 at the age of 50 in Prince George Co., Virginia.

JAMES BAUGH, III AND WIFE MARTHA
Parents of Martha Baugh Cureton

Not much is known about Martha Baugh Cureton. Her parents were James Baugh and wife Martha, last name unknown.

James was born in Prince George Co., Virginia, in 1713 to James Baugh and Elizabeth Moore. James married Margaret (Unknown) Baugh and had a child. He then married Sarah and had 2 children. After her death he then married Martha and had 5 children. He passed away on 1773 in Dinwiddie, Virginia, USA.

The Baugh family first shows up in Virginia about 1636. Early records show the Baugh family found in 1513 in Twining, England. The male line favored the given name of William and it was passed down for several generations until Martha's great grandfather, who was named James. James, designated as James, III was Martha's father.

MARTHA CURETON - WILL

Mrs. Martha Cureton, Nuncupative - April 13, 1813. Has died today and left no will. That she be buried by her husband at Mrs. Chandler's. Mr. James Rogers to preach her funeral. Her bed to Polly Wood, daughter of James Wood, dec'd. Some clothes to **Patsy Anderson** *and her little sisters. Feather bed to Taylor Whatley. That Hugh Montgomery to attend to all and get Mingo and keep him and Lett together as long as they live, if in his power. That her husband's grave be paled in with $2.00, Mr. McNess owes her.*

Signed Tabitha Chandler
Test. Thos. Niblack

Note: "Patsy" Anderson refers to **Martha "Patsy" Anderson**, daughter of Elizabeth Cureton Anderson, wife of Benjamin Anderson. Martha "Patsy" Anderson would have been named after her grandmother.

Will of Martha Baugh Cureton's brother, William: *Brunswick Co., Will Book 7, p. 238 (William Baugh)*

Testator: William Baugh (of Brunswick Co.) Date written: 1779 |1799 [looks more like 1779; no month/year given] Date proved: 28 Sep 1807

Witnesses: John Neal, Anthony Bennett, & James Harrison.

Executor(s): my two brothers James Baugh and Daniel Baugh

Description: —my whole estate . . . to be equally divided amongst my two brothers and two sisters namely James Baugh & Daniel Baugh, **Martha Cureton** and Elizabeth Eppes.

Record of Deed Book showing Martha Cureton was a sister of William Baugh.

Brunswick Co. Deed Book 20, page 525*

6 February 1809—John Epps and Elizabeth, his wife, of Newbury District, STATE OF SOUTH CAROLINA, and William Cureton and Martha, his wife, of JACKSON COUNTY, STATE OF GEORGIA (by their Power of Attorney to John Epps, aforesaid) sell to Hugh Love of County of Brunswick, State of Virginia, for 460 pds. 8 sh. One half of a tract of land in County of Brunswick, being the land William Baugh died possessed of and the above parties claim and sell as heirs and legatees of said William Baugh, dec'd, containing 704 acres, of which one-half is 352 acres. Recorded September 25, 1809.

William Soanes and Wife, Elizabeth

Judith Soane was the daughter of William Soane.

William was born in 1651 in Chesterfield Co., Virginia and died in 1714 Henrico Co., Virginia. He was married to Elizabeth, whose last name is unknown.

William was the son of **Henry Soane**, described as a "gentleman" in the records, owned a good deal of property in James City Co., Virginia. Henry (died 1661) was a Virginia politician and landowner. He immigrated to Virginia around 1651, settling in James City County along the Chickahominy River. He served in the House of Burgesses 1652–55, 1658, and 1660–61, and was its Speaker in 1661.

He began with a land patent for 297 acres on the east side of the Chickahominy River (Hoggs Island) in November 1651, which he had obtained for the transporting of six persons, including himself, his wife, his father, and his mother. Five years later, he purchased 2,200 acres on the northeastern side of that river. In 1662 he added 500 acres at the head of the river for having transported 10 persons and 500 more on the northeast side for having brought over another dozen persons.

At first it seems that Henry Soane's widow, Judith, continued the land purchases after his death: she acquired 450 acres in March 1666 on the north side of the James River near the Chickahominy River. It turns out, however, that Henry had claimed this land in return for transporting nine persons but did not take possession of it, and so Virginia's government granted the land to his widow after her petition.

RECORDS & PATENTS OF HENRY SOANE

24 Nov 1651 - Henry was granted 297 acres on the east side called Hoggs Island for transporting 6 all members of his family or his wife's (James City County Patent Book 2, p. 351)

3 June 1652 - 450 acres and marsh on the south side of the Rappahannock for transporting 9 (Virginia Patent Book 3, p. 191)

10 April 1653 - 200 acres on the northeast side of the Mattaponi River (Ibid, p. 27)

10 April 1653 - 1200 acres on the northeast side of the Mattaponi River (Ibid p, 26)

31 July 1653 - 700 acres on the easternmost side of the Mattaponi River (Ibid, p. 213)

25 Mar 1656 - 2800 acres in New Kent County on the north side of the Mattaponi River for Transporting 2 (Virginia Patent Book 4, p. 60)

10 Dec 1656 - 2200 acres on the north and east side of the Chickahominy River called Rickohocke from Edward Diggs (James City Patent Book 4, p. 80)

10 Nov 1656 - 300 acres on the north side of the Wallingford River alias Chickahominy Adjacent his own land for transporting 6 (Ibid p. 23)

1655 - Received permission to employee 2 Indians (Minutes of the General Court)

Henry Soane (1622-1642), son of Henry Soane (of the Soanes of Rottindean and Litlington) and Elizabeth Worger (of the Worgers of Brighton, East Sussex in England).

Henry's wife was Judith Fuller (b. about 1620 - died post 1695), who descended from the Fullers of Heathfield and Hellingly in Sussex and the Brabons of Hastings in East Sussex.

The Anderson, Jans/Kip & OpDyck Families

Jochem Andries – born about 1570-1576, possibly in Friesland, Netherlands; probably died before 1632, possibly in Leeuwarden, Friesland, Netherlands.

Marriage – Grietje/Gryet [Margaretha?] Paulus/Pauwels/Pouwels

Jochem's son Andries Jochemszen was born about 1607 in Leeuwarden, Friesland, Netherlands; married Celitje Fredericks on January 11, 1632, in Amsterdam; died in New York after 1674.

Dictionary of New Jersey stated as follows: ***20 Dec 1631***: *publishing of the banns of Andries Jochemsz, born at Leeuwarden, seaman (varentsgezel), 24 years old, living in the Lindestraat, assisted by Grietie Pouwels; and Celitge Frerix, born in Amsterdam, 22 years old, parents dead, assisted by Celytgie Willems, her grandmother, living in the Boomstraat. He signs with cross. She signs: Seletien Fredericks.*

11 Jan 1632: *marriage in the New Church in Amsterdam (Reformed).*
Seaman Andries Jochemszen and his wife Celitje Fredericks migrated to this small Dutch colony in New Netherlands sometime between May 20 and September 18, 1650

Andries' son was Jochem Andrieszen, born about 1635-1640 in Amsterdam, Netherlands; died 1674/75 in Elizabethtown, New Jersey. He married Emmetje Jans, in New Amsterdam about 1664.

Emmetje Jans was the daughter of Jan Janszen (Wanshaer) and Baertje Kip. Emmetje was born in 1640 in New Amsterdam, New Netherland and was a sister of Hendrick Wanshaer and Carel Wanshaer. She died in 1674 in New Amsterdam, New Netherlands.

"Her father, Jan Jansen Wanshaer, the first and only person to come to America, by that name, reached New Amsterdam about 1642 at about 26 years of age. He was born in Cadzand-Bad, Holland, in the province of Zeeland in 1621.The name Wanshaer is probably patronymic derived from the Frisian name Wanse or Wanne.[Frisian is a West Germanic language, which is spoken by about 400,000 people in the province of Friesland in the Netherlands.] It is closely related to Dutch but also shows a number of striking similarities to English.

Jan Wanshaer was not known to use his surname until after his marriage. The reason for this is unknown but nicknames were common in his time. Wanshaer was named in various recordings as the following names: Jan Jansen Van St.Cubis, Van St. Ubis, Van St. Obyn, Jan Van Sam, Jan Van Sam, Jan Wanshaar, Van St. Berres, Jan Wanshaer and Jan De Caper (meaning Jan the sailor in English). He certainly was a sailor, because as early as 1644 he was a ship pilot in New Amsterdam.

He had formed a partnership with Anthony Carol, Christopher Pieterson, and Abraham Philip in purchasing the frigate La Grace. This was a good sized ship, larger than a sloop or brig, probably with batteries on two decks and likely carried from 28 to 60 guns. Two years later in 1646 Jan sold his interest in the La Grace.

Jan Wanshaer *was wed to **Baertje Hendricks Kip from** Amsterdam in 1649 at about age 33. Baertje was the daughter of a prominent citizen of New Amsterdam named **Hendrick Henderson Kip** who was one of the most influential men of his time. Kip was one of the nine select men of the colony sending delegates to Holland.*

Jan and Baertje married in the Dutch Reform Church that was organized in New Amsterdam in 1626. It had held regular meetings since 1633.

The marriage of Jan and Baertje produced 12 children, 10 sons and two daughters, all the names of which were recorded by the church baptismal records.

In 1657 Jan is recorded as being one of the 204 residents of New Amsterdam.

The Wanshaer family lived on Brouwer Street that is today known as Stone Street. It was among the first streets in New Amsterdam to be built and was the first road to be laid out along the East River. Ancient grants refer to it as "the road" and was spoken of as "east of the fort". The name Brouwer Street, or Brewers Street came from the fact that two breweries were built on it. It was the first street on Manhattan Island to be paved with stone. After 1657 it was re-named Stone Street. It was the street of the wealthy and was the broadway of the town. Residents on this street had a clear view of the East River and no doubt anchored their crafts there.

The Jan Wanshaer family appears to have been quite prosperous being able to live in this neighborhood beside both his Kip brothers-in-law Isaac and Jacob. By 1662 Jan had been appointed by Governor Peter Stuyvesant to be

the first naval officer of America whose duty was to protect the city of New Amsterdam.

Hostilities between the English and the Dutch grew to the point that the English forced the Dutch to give up their rights to New Amsterdam and New Holland. This occurred August 29, 1664. On or about October 25, 1664, Jan took the oath of allegiance to the English conquerors else he would have been expelled and lost all his property. A legal record shows that on August 12, 1670, Jan Wanshaer's name had been Anglicized to "John Wants hair", and started a name changing process that will end in the various variations in his surname that we know today.

Jan Jansen Wanshaer appears to have died in his early 50's prior to April 101674, for among the 16 sloop captains mentioned in the records, his name does not appear on the tax roll. Perhaps Skipper Kip, who was Jan's brother-in-law, had taken over his business. In 1677 records refer to Baertje as "widow Wansart" who remarries. One more name in the evolution of our family name to Wanzor."

(Information from research by James W. Clark.)

Joshua Anderson

Jochem's son was Josua (Joshua) born in Elizabethtown, New Jersey, baptized February 30 [sic], 1667, in New York City; married Engeltie (Angel) OpDyck; died 1730 in Maidenhead, Hunterdon County, New Jersey.

Joshua Andrieszen name gradually morphed into **Joshua Anderson**. The witness at his baptism was his grandmother, Celitje Fredericks.

Joshua was actually 28 years old when he married **Engeltie (Angel) OpDyck** on June 23, 1695, as recorded in the Dutch Reformed Church of New York City. The record indicated both of them were living in Newtown at the time.

After their marriage in 1695, in the 1690's two more New York church records showed Joshua and Engeltie participating in the normal Dutch life of the times. On March 18, 1696, their son, Joshua, was baptized in New York City.

On December 3, 1730, Joshua Anderson wrote his will and probably died shortly after that. An inventory of his property was done on January 5, 1731, so he was certainly dead by then. He was about 63 years old.

Joshua's will is posted in the *Calendar of New Jersey Wills, Vol. II, 1730 - 1750* as follows:

3 Dec 1730; **Joshua Anderson** *"of Maidenhead," Hunterdon County, Es Qr (Esquire), will of: Wife Anjel, his dwelling and plantation. Eldest sons – Joshua and John, land in Hopewell adjoining land of William Briant. Sons Benjamin, Isaac, Jacob, Abraham. Daughter Catharine and her children. Daughter Hannah. Cedar swamp in Maryland is to be divided among eight then living and they are to discharge debt in the Loan Office. Executors -- wife, son Abraham and neighbor Theophilus Philips. Witnesses -- Jasper Smith, Enoch Andrus, and Giles Worth. Codicil of same date directing sale of house and plantation if wife see cause.*
Proved October 28, 1731. Lib. 3, page 163.
1730-31, January 5. Inventory of personal estate (of Joshua Anderson Sen'r)
£749. 15. 7., including debts of William Landers, Thomas Coleman, Daniel Biles and Thos. Brodreet; made by Jasper Smith and Jas. McKinly.

ENGELTIE OPDYCK. (Daughter of Johannes, Son of Louris)

Engeltie Opdyck and Joshua Anderson were "ingeschrieben" (inscribed) 22 June, and "getrouwt" (married) 23 June, 1695, in the New York City Dutch church, "Beide wonende tot Nieuwthuyn" (both living at Newtown).

They brought their first-born, Joshua, to be baptized in the same church 18 March 1696. Again, Joshua Anderson and Engeltie Opdyck brought their daughter Anna to be baptized at Hopewell, New Jersey., by Rev. Paulus van Vleq in 1712, as stated in his record before mentioned.

In both these Dutch baptisms the full maiden name of "Engeltie Opdyck" is given. Engeltie's husband Joshua himself had been baptized 30 Feb 1667 by his father Jochem Andriesen in the New York Dutch church, where also appear the baptisms of four brothers of Joshua, Elias, Cornelius, Andries and Benjamin.

Tryntie's husband Enoch must have been another brother of Joshua, for reasons already stated, and because he named his first son Jochem, the Dutch usually naming the eldest for the grandfather.

In 1697 Joshua with his wife and child joined in that patriarchal migration of Johannes Opdyck, his sons and daughters, sons-in-law, daughters-in-law, and grandchildren, from Newtown on Long Island to the wilderness of Maidenhead in New Jersey, where they were soon followed by many of their old Newtown neighbors.

The next year Joshua appears as one of the trustees of the Maidenhead 100 acre church-farm, with Johannes and Lawrence Opdyck, Enoch and Cornelius Anderson. In 1699 he signs the road survey through land of his father-in-law, and in 1703 he joins with his father-in-law in signing the land agreement at house of Ralph Hunt in Maidenhead.

Joshua and Engeltie's land was in the Maidenhead Township. There they raised their children and participated in building a community.

In 1731 Joshua died in Maidenhead, leaving his will on record, bequeathing to his wife *"Anjell"* (Engeltie) his dwelling house, plantation, and all personal property; to his sons Joshua and John 500 acres in Hopewell adjoining the Province Line on the east; to his sons, Benjamin, Isaac. Jacob, and Abraham, and to his daughters Catharine and Hannah, 100 Pounds each and his "cedar swamp in Maryland" to all the eight children.

Joshua's homestead must have long been the most central and prominent in Maidenhead, as the town meeting was held there in 1719, and from 1721 continuously until his death; thereafter it was " held at ye house of ye widow *Angel Anderson* " every year from 1733 to 1741. She also appears upon the Maidenhead town records in 1734 recording stock, and on the Hunterdon records in 1741 bringing suit as executrix of Joshua.

Of her sons, Joshua Anderson Jr. filled almost all of the township offices of Maidenhead from 1734 until 1756, and was Freeholder in 1752; John was Collector in 1727 and filled other offices at Maidenhead; Isaac and Benjamin voted from Hopewell in 1738; Jacob may have been the Jacob Anderson that became Sheriff of Hunterdon, Judge of Common Pleas, and Commissary with the rank of Captain in the Revolution.

In 1709 son Abraham witnesses the deed from Johannes to Enoch for land on Assanpink, adjoining his own which he bought in 1707 out of the original Mahlon Stacy tract and sold in 1722 to his brother Enoch.

From later records, it appears that Abraham's own children were being born in the mid to late 1730's and into the 1740's, so it is possible that he was living at home and not yet married at the time of his father's death.

Although he served responsibly as an executor of his father's estate, by the 1740's Abraham Anderson began to attain notoriety in his home colony of New Jersey. By that time he was married to Susanna and had started a family, but the last name of his wife remains unknown.

He lived in Hunterdon County, somewhere in the Maidenhead Township, and became involved in the land disputes which were sweeping New Jersey and causing great unrest. These land disputes were common in many colonies but reached the point in New Jersey that violence broke out and the colony's government almost collapsed.

Briefly, land purchased originally from the Indians or from others who claimed ownership was subsequently claimed as belonging to the King of England, who in turn granted various tracts of land to friends and relatives. These gentlemen proprietors would send envoys to the colonies and require that the land be repurchased or the settler would face a lawsuit for trespass and eventual eviction

In 1710 Abraham is joined with Lawrence and Albert Opdyck, Enoch and Cornelius Anderson, as trustee of the Lawrenceville church-plot in Maidenhead. In 1712 he subscribes with Johannes and Lawrence Opdyck and Enoch Anderson at Maidenhead town-meeting to the expenses of setting off Hunterdon County.

Maidenhead Township elected him in 1706 Overseer of Highways, in 1712 Overseer of the Poor and an auditor of the Treasurer's accounts, 1718 Assessor, 1722 Overseer of Highways, 1724-5 Collector and 1728-9 Town Clerk. He was Commissioner of Hunterdon in 1722-5; and was appointed Justice of Peace by George I. in 1725, the royal commission on heavy parchment with large seal being still preserved in the office of the County Clerk at Flemington. He continued to act as Justice until he was elected County Clerk.

While Joshua was sitting as Justice, there was brought before him an amusing indictment against Jacob and Isaac Anderson, doubtless his own sons, "for Stealing a Book entitled the *New Testament*, belonging to John Titus"; the defendants were duly tried by jury and acquitted.

Johannes Laurenssen Op Dyck & Wife Catrian/Tryntjye

Parents of Engeltie Opdyck Anderson

Johannes was a planter at Dutch Kills, Long Island, and in Maidenhead and Hopewell, New Jersey. By 1675 he had married Catrian (Tryntjye) whose surname has not been found at this time, and had a daughter. He named his first daughter *Tryntie*.

Johannes cares for his farm, and appears again upon the census in 1683 as a large cultivator. He is careful to record the ear-mark of his stock; he buys "a ball face horse with one white foot behind," "at an outcry;" he is interested in orchards, where the far-famed Newtown pippin originated; he has his last purchases of land surveyed; he is one of the grantees under the Dongan patent; he joins with his old another person in an agreement to purchase 88 more acres; he receives another town lot.

On his farm Johannes raised wheat, peas, rye, corn, flax, and especially tobacco. His orchard produced in abundance apples, pears and peaches. As he cleared new land, he made the wood into pine-staves, a common article of export, for which Newtown elected two inspectors.

There was also a town inspector of meat and fish barreled for exportation; and Johannes' residence on the creek, near the river islands and Hellegat, would "supply him with fish before he could leave off the recreation."

His eldest son Lawrence, (named in true Dutch style for the grandfather), could easily bring down, with his gun, a fat deer. The second son, Albert, could furnish the house with stores, of wild fowl, or amuse himself with spearing and trapping the valuable beaver.

The daughters, **Tryntie, Engeltie and Annetie**, would readily find in the woods an oversupply of strawberries, raspberries, mulberries, huckleberries, cranberries, plums and grapes for the table. The garden furnished melons and any vegetable one chose to plant, with all the fruitfulness of a virgin soil." You shall scarce see a house but the south side is begirt with hives of bees which increase after an incredible manner," wrote Denton in 1670

Surplus products he exchanged by barter, for currency was scarce; we find one man buying a house and farm with "600 lbs. of tobacco, 1,000 clapboards and half a fat of strong beer;" another exchanging "a negro boy" for land. Prices were: beef 2d, pork 3d, butter 6d per pound; wheat 5s, rye 2s 6d, corn 2s per bushel; victuals 6d per meal, labor 2s 6d per day, lodgings 2d per night, board 5s per week, beer 2d per mug.

The census of 1683 showed, that Johannes had more cultivated acres and stock than was the average of his fellow townsmen. Newtown then contained about 500 population, one eighth as many as New York, for that now mighty city could boast that year only 4,000 people.

 The time arrives when Johannes is blessed" with a large family of children; two of his daughters are married, and three infantile voices call him grandfather.

Dutch Kills was too small for his household and herds. His sons and sons-in-law want more room. Restless spirits are talking of the Jerseys as a very paradise for climate and soil, how its government is liberal, taxes low, land plentiful and cheap.

Letters are read, and experienced men are quoted, that between the Raritan and the Delaware is a rich rolling country where clear streams are crossed with every mile of travel, "where you shall meet with no inhabitants but a few friendly Indians, where there are stately oaks whose broad-branched tops have no other use but to keep off the sun's heat from the wild beasts of the wilderness, where is grass as high as a man's middle, that serves for no other end except to maintain the elks and deer, who never devour a hundredth part of it, then to be burnt every Spring to make way for new.

In May or June the whole family moved from Dutch Kills in wagons, and in carts, with horses and oxen, furniture and farming utensils, their herds of stock in the rear doubtless driven by a negro slave or two, who formed part of the establishment of every prosperous planter in those days.

Their route lay through Flatbush to a ferry at the Narrows, across Staten Island, and up the Raritan to its lowest fording-place, Indian's Ferry.

Here they were perhaps joined by the women and children who had come in the easier way by boat on the Bay. Thence they followed the old Indian trail, then called "the King's highway," across the State, in recent days the turnpike from New Brunswick through Princeton to Trenton, none of which towns were even contemplated at the   period we are describing.

In the party were Enoch, Joshua and Cornelius Anderson, husbands of Tryntie, Engeltie and Annetie. We can faintly imagine the delight of all at the far rolling views, the ever-varying scenery of hill and dale, the richness of the vegetation, and the beauty of the babbling brooks by whose sides they encamped and ate of the fish, game and fruit of the untrodden forest.

On went Johannes and his family across Mill-stone River and Stony Brook, to the Eight Mile Run of the Assanpink, six miles east of the Delaware River, close to what is now Lawrenceville of Lawrence Township in Mercer County. It was then Burlington County of West Jersey, up to the New York State line; and the whole unsettled country north of the Assanpink, from the Delaware to the old province line, was called *Maidenhead* after a castle in England.

There is a well-preserved tradition among the descendants that the carts, of the Opdyck settlers were turned up at night to shelter the women and children until a few days work with axes and stout arms had prepared the first log-houses, into which the family moved with sensations   of which perhaps we in our days have no conception.

Food was abundant; it was from the mouth of the Assanpink that Mahlon Stacy wrote a short time before: "*I have seen peaches in such plenty that some people took their carts a peach gathering. I could not but smile at the conceit of it. They are a very delicate fruit and hang almost like onions that are tied on ropes.*

*My brother Robert had as many cherries this year as would have loaded several carts. It is my judgment by what I have observed, that fruit trees in this country destroy themselves by the very weight of their fruit. As for venison and owls we have great plenty. We have brought home to our houses by the Indians seven or eight fat bucks of a day; and sometimes put by as many, having no occasion for them and fish in their season very plenteous. *There is plenty of beef and pork and good sheep, and cheap. *The common grass of the country feeds beef very fat.*
* *In Burlington there are eight or nine fat oxen and cows in a market day and very fat.*"

 Trenton then "contained scarcely a house;" and in a private dwelling there was held the new Hunterdon County Court from 1714 to 1719, and alternately at the church meeting-house in Maidenhead. In 1721 Johannes was 70 years of age, yet some evil-doer in Hunterdon County stood in such terror of the old man's physical vigor as to apply to the Court for protection.

The early records of Hopewell Township are lost, as are those of the Presbyterian churches of Maidenhead and Hopewell.

A Dutch Clergyman from Bucks County, Pennsylvania, baptized in Hopewell six children of Annetie, Tryntie, and Engeltie in 1710 and 1712; Lawrence baptized a son in the Dutch church of the Raritan in 1704. The records of the Dutch churches are in the language of Holland, as was their preaching; we know therefore that Johannes and his children still clung to the Dutch religion and language even in the Jersey wilderness.

Joshua's homestead must have long been the most central and prominent in Maidenhead, as the town meeting was held there in 1719, and from 1721 continuously until his death; thereafter it was " held at ye house of ye widow *Angel Anderson* " every year from 1733 to 1741. She also appears upon the Maidenhead town records in 1734 recording stock, and on the Hunterdon records in 1741 bringing suit as executrix of Joshua.

Feb. 12, 1729, at the age of 78 years, Johannes Opdyck made his will in Hopewell. His wife was already dead. In the touching formula and quaint spelling of the day, he left his property to be equally divided among his eight children then living, and appointed his son Lawrence and grandson Eliakim, son of Annetie, his executors. Two months later he died and the will was admitted to probate by Governor Montgomery; it is now preserved in the vaults of the State House at Trenton.

The burial place of Johannes and his wife is unknown. The graveyards of the Old Dutch Church at Harlingen and of the Presbyterian churches of Lawrenceville and Ewing contain many tombstones of sufficient antiquity, but their inscriptions are now illegible.

Charles Wilson Opdyke in his book, "*Op Dyke Genealogy*" also wrote this: "Let us revere the name of our sturdy ancestor, who in two States met the savage, the wild beast and the wilderness, and left in their stead the farm, the mill, the school, the organization of township and county, the determined Dutch love of freedom under just and equal law. It was a long stride in civilization. His descendants have inherited the benefits of his life as unconsciously as they have many of the traits of his character"

104

Joshua Anderson, Jr. was concerned in an interesting episode related at length in Dr. Cooley's communications to the Trenton State Gazette for 1842-3, and in Snell's History of Hunterdon and Somerset Counties. In 1744 he, Benjamin Stevens (son-in-law of Tryntie Opdyck and Enoch Andrus), and the Rev. William Tennent were away on a visit in Pennsylvania with the Rev. John Rowland, when the latter was personated by some vagrant, who took advantage of his striking resemblance to Rowland to commit theft and burglary. The reverend doctor was arrested on his return and was acquitted through the testimony of the companions of his journey.

Public belief in the identity however was so strong that the witnesses were tried for perjury. Joshua was convicted, and sentenced to stand one hour on the steps of the Trenton Court House, with a placard on his breast, --- "*This is for Willful Perjury*;" while his companions were saved only by the timely arrival of a farmer and his wife from Pennsylvania, with whom they had all lodged the night of the burglary, and who had been warned in a dream to hasten to New Jersey to give testimony in the case.

Abraham Anderson & Susanna
Parents of Joshua Anderson

Abraham Anderson was born 1700-1709 in Maidenhead, Burlington Co., New Jersey; married two wives, Susannah, last name unknown, second was a widow, Ruth Gordon. He was buried October 7, 1764 in Newberry Co., South Carolina.

Abraham was probably the youngest of Joshua and Engeltie Anderson's six sons. He was named one of the executors in his father's will of 1730, so he was probably at least 21 years old by that time.

Sometime in late 1746, Abraham Anderson was arrested and thrown into the Somerset County jail, likely as a continuation of the "Debt & Trespass" suit, which had started against him in 1739.

This event was extremely worrying to those in power in New Jersey. These Daring Disturbers of the Public Peace interpreted the incident as follows:
"The arrest of Hunterdon anti-proprietor leader Abraham Anderson at the end of 1746 set off a chain of events that brought the government to the brink of complete collapse within a year. When a crowd drawing strength from Essex, Somerset, and Hunterdon counties arrived to free Anderson from the Somerset County jail in December 1746, the great gentry realized the period of quiet had been only a respite. The coalition had developed a well-organized striking arm capable of coordinating men from different counties in direct action miles away from their homes."

With the collapse of colonial governmental authority, other incidents of law-breaking occurred. A wave of counterfeiting broke out in New Jersey during the 1740's with both coins and bills being illegally produced. At some point, Abraham Anderson became involved in this practice, and at a Court of Oyer and Terminer in Hunterdon County in June of 1748, he was indicted along with Houghton Mershon, Job Rosell, and Robert Wild for counterfeiting Spanish cobs. Cobs were silver coins from Spanish America that circulated in the colonies as valid money.

The *New Jersey Supreme Court Case 20341 The King vs. Abraham Anderson et al* for counterfeiting and treason accused the men of *"wickedly and Designedly Contriving...Craftily and Subtly to deceive, Cheat and Defraud [with] diverse and sundry pieces of money Composed of Copper and other Base and Mixt Metalls in the likeness and Similitude of good silver Forreign Coin of the Kingdom of Spain commonly called Spanish Cobbs..."*

An act had been passed in New Jersey in the preceding year which allowed pardon for counterfeiters who gave themselves up and made a full confession.

Spanish Cob

It seems all too likely that Abraham did not avail himself of that process, because a warrant for his arrest was issued to bring him to the Supreme Court in March, 1749.

Leaving the New Jersey area, Abraham and wife Susanna, traveled through Maryland and stayed near relatives before moving on to Virginia and from Virginia the family migrated to South Carolina.

Abraham Anderson, his seven sons and possibly three daughters and a wife, found empty land in the frontier area of Berkley County, South Carolina by 1753. The portion where they settled eventually split off to become Newberry County. The first land record in the South Carolina Archives for Abraham Anderson was a land grant of 600 acres surrounded by vacant, unclaimed land on Indian Creek in Berkley County in 1754. At that time a petitioner for land could receive 50 acres for each member of his household.

On November 25, 1753, Abraham Anderson wrote the South Carolina Council:

"The petitioner having 12 persons in Family humbly prays to prove his Right before His Excell'y and that in order may issue to the Surveyor General to lay out 600 acres on Indian Creek between Broad and Saludee Rivers so that he may obtain a grant for the same."

Due to Indian unrest, Abraham and his sons were active in fighting the Cherokee War of 1760-61. Because of continued Indian unrest, by the early 1760's, the white settlers were building block houses and forts for protection. These private forts sprang up across the South

Carolina frontier when several attacks occurred from about 1760 to 1763.

Settlers who got to the forts seemed to survive fairly well, although life inside these enclosures must have been uncomfortable at best. Settlers who tried to load their possessions onto wagons in an attempt to outrun the war parties were caught and killed, as at nearby Long Canes Creek where about fifty people were killed or captured. Fear of Indian attacks severely disrupted the growing of crops and left many families in bad shape economically.

According to the books **Descendants of Capt. Henry Anderson, Sr.** by Lucien L. McNees and **Gordons of the Deep South** by Erminie Northcutt Marshall, this fort is where Abraham Anderson met Ruth Gordon. Since each had lost a spouse by this time, it would have been a typical marriage of the period between a widow and a widower.

Abraham did not live too many years longer. He died in 1764 being either in his late fifties or early sixties. Just before his death, he applied for another land grant of 200 acres, due to his newly enlarged family through the marriage to Ruth Gordon. The combined family of Anderson children and Gordon children was mentioned in Abraham Anderson's will, written July 11, 1763. The will was proved in court on Jan. 5, 1765.

The **Register of St. Philip's Parish 1754-1810**, by Smith & Salley, gives Abraham's burial date as October 7, 1764. His will was proved Jan. 5, 1765. South Carolina Will Book QQ 1760-1767, p. 446

Being sick and weak, willed to my loving wife RUTH all household furniture, her riding horse and saddle, two best work horses, six cows and calves and the privilege of killing the stock any she thinks necessary before the division, excepting two beds and their furniture, also all my negro slaves and my homestead place during her life or widowhood. Gives JACOB BROWN (husband of RUTH GORDON BROWN) one negro girl Nann after the decease of my wife. Gives to WILLIAM GORDON one negro boy Babb, gives to GOVIN and GEORGE GORDON jointly one negro Chloe. Gives dwelling plantation to be equally divided between my four youngest sons, LEVY, HENRY, ABRAHAM, and JACOB. My son Jacob is to have my homestead place after my wife's decease. The residue of Estate lands to be divided so that all my children and my wife's children have an equal part only, William Gordon, Jacob Brown, Govin Gordon, George Gordon to have one half part, with the rest in consideration of their legacies mentioned before.

On September 25, 1765, almost a year after his death, three of Abraham's neighbors conducted an inventory of his estate. It looks as if either the Andersons had escaped serious monetary harm during the Cherokee war or perhaps Ruth Gordon had brought wealth to this marriage. Certain things stand out as indicators of this wealth, such as slaves, horses, and silver.

The actual number of slaves is not entirely clear but at least six are listed by name in the various records: Nann, Babb, and Chloe from the will (given to Gordon children), Toney from the inventory, Patt and Philip from the memorandum of sale. Toney, an adult male, was valued at 300 British pounds.

There were eleven different horses listed on the inventory: one stone (?) horse and one brown horse valued together at 85 pounds, one roan, one bay, a brown colt and a black colt, one bay mare and two colts, and two grays. Since horse racing was a favorite colonial pastime, it is possible the most valuable horses were used for that purpose.

Gazette on June 19, 1762. This advertisement was for a Doctor Anderson in the forks of the Broad and Saluda Rivers who could *"cure consumption, cancker and inward imposthumes."*

Listed on the 1765 inventory are doctors' drugs, one brass kittle [sic], bottles, and a portmantua [sic]. Even though Abraham Sr. was not formally trained in medicine, he owned the equipage of a

traveling doctor or purveyor of patent medicine. Would this be how he had replenished his wealth after fleeing New Jersey?

The silver articles included a silver watch and five silver spoons valued at 34 pounds and ten shillings, a pair of silver knee buckles and a pair of silver clasps. A case of pistols, a sword, tea ware, tea kettle, dishes, plates, spoons, knives, forks, tin ware, pewter, brass kettles, a looking glass, multiple candlesticks, and books all indicate a comfortable 18th century lifestyle.

Other items on the inventory are of prime interest because they prove that our ancestor, Abraham Anderson Sr., was indeed the person who had advertised in the South Carolina Gazette on June 19, 1762. This advertisement was for a Doctor Anderson in the forks of the Broad and Saluda Rivers who could *"cure consumption, cancker and inward imposthumes."*

Listed on the 1765 inventory are doctors' drugs, one brass kittle [sic], bottles, and a portmantua [sic].

A gift of land from Abraham Sr.'s estate to one of the three older sons, Gabriel Anderson was recorded in 1771 as follows:

Ruth Anderson and others to Gabriel Anderson, Renunciation Deed Gift*: To all Christian people to whom these presents may come, We, Ruth Anderson and others, to Gabriel Anderson, of Berkley County for in consideration of the love, good will and affection which we have and do bear towards our loving brother Gabriel Anderson of the same province and county aforesaid have given and by these presents do freely give and grant unto the said Gabriel Anderson a certain tract of land on Beaverdam Creek containing two hundred acres.*

Ruth Anderson (her mark), Abel Anderson, Levy Anderson, Henry Anderson, Jacob Anderson, Thomas Gordon, William Gordon, Govin Gordon, George Gordon, Ruth Gordon Brown Witnesses: Abraham Anderson [Jr.], James Caldwell, John Valentine.

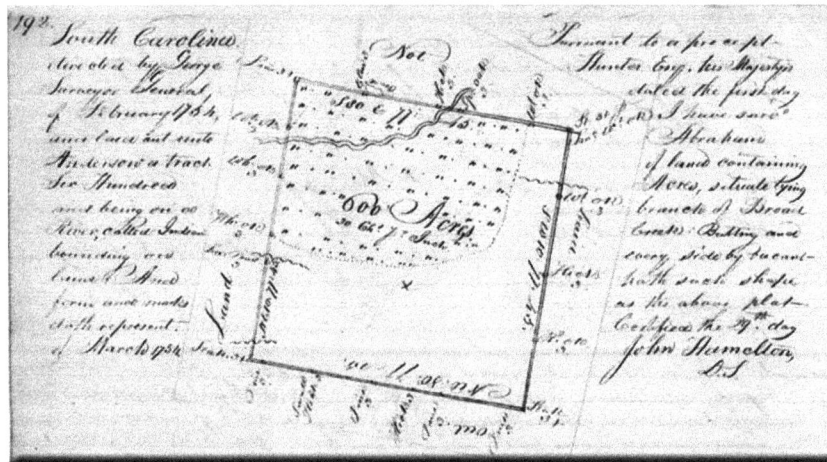

Land acquired by Abraham Anderson consisting of 600 acres situate on a branch of Broad River called Indian Creek, South Carolina, Certificated dated 29 March 1754.

Abraham & wife Susanna had the following children: Joshua, Able, Sr., Gabriel, Levi, Henry, Abraham, Jr. & Jacob. There were unnamed daughters, one of whom married William Gordon.

Joshua Anderson, born before 1741, likely before 1737, in Hunterdon County, New Jersey; died in 1769 in Newberry County, South Carolina; shoemaker and beekeeper; unknown wife likely died in childbirth; only known child Benjamin, who moved to Green County, Georgia then Texas and reputedly sired 25 children. It is thought that Joshua married Rebecca Gordon, but to date that documentation has not been found.

South Carolina Militia List of Colonel John Chevillette's Battalion in the Cherokee Expedition Pay Roll of Captain Edward Musgrove's Company Private Abel Anderson. Also listed are **Pvt Joshua Anderson** and Pvt Abraham Anderson.

Joshua Anderson served in Col. Roebuck's regiment before and after the fall of Charleston. A.A. (Audited Accounts in the SC Archives) 117.

Joshua's only son was Benjamin Anderson. Joshua is said to have been killed by Tories.

*"Mar 1769 Gabriel Anderson and Thomas Gordon to administer on the estate of Joshua **Anderson** late of Enoree River as nearest of kin 8 Mar 1769 Friday, 10th Mar 1769."*

Note: The Anderson information was researched by Cindy Anderson Cochran, who granted me permission to use. Her information is copy write entitled, *"An Anderson History: 300 Years from Friesland to Oklahoma"*. I have copied only the portions of her work that apply to our Anderson ancestors. Our Andersons have been proven to be part of this Dutch family through the DNA testing of Cindy's Anderson brother.

Joshua's estate information is on the following pages.

An Inventory of the Sale of the goods and chattels belonging to the estate of <u>Joshua Anderson</u>, deceased, sold at publick (sic) Vandue (sic) by Gabriel Anderson and Thomas Gordon, Exors .

Page 2

Qty	Article	To Whom Sold	Price £sd
1	Feather bed & furniture	Thomas Gordon	16..
1	Quantity of pewter	Thomas Gordon	10..
1	Suit of clothes & hat	Levi Anderson	20..
1	Pair shoes & silver buckles	Gabriel Anderson	3.10
1	Whip San	Wm Vardeman	3.15
2	Rasor & stone	Charles King	2..
1	Parcel of Tin Ware	Rebecca Walentine	2.10
1	Warming Pan	Able Anderson	2.10
1	Broad Ax	Wm Hendricks	1.12
1	Pair of seales & weights & ax	Coll Thos Fletchall	1.15
1	Ax	Charles King	2..
2	Wedge 3 Rings	James Caldwell	..16..
2	Weeding Hoes	John Caldwell	3..15..
1	Drawing knife gouge 1 Chissel	Wm Murray	1..18..
1	Wedge	Gabriel Anderson	..19..
1	Grind stone	Eg Morgan	..15..
1	Saddle True & Hammor	Charles King	..8..
1	Parcel of Old Iron & other Articles	Able Anderson	1..5..
1	Box of old iron	John Caldwell	1..15..
1	Set of shoe makers tools	Wm Dickson	2..10..
1	Box of Money Seales	Wm Dickson	3..
1	Rifle gun & pouch	John Johnston	1..11..
1	Box some books	Wm Gordon	2..5..
1	Truck	Wm Murray	2..3..
1	Box from Iron Heaters & glass	Henry Anderson	1..15..
2	Doz pewte spoons	Thomas Gordon	1..15..
1	Chest	Margaret Parks	2..15..
1	Hams	Anthony Parks	2..15..
1	Churn pails & Tub	Nicholas Dickson	..16..
1	Saddle & Bridle	Thomas Gordon	6..
1	Pot & hooks	Gabriel Anderson	10..5..
1	Pot & hooks	James Caldwell	3..10..
1	Pot & hooks	James Hughes	3..5..
1	Bed & furniture	Wm Wardeman	2..5..
1	Bed & furniture	Doctor T more	15..17..6
1	Quantity of plank	Lawrence Kerrel	37..10..6
1	Quantity of corn	Gabriel Anderson	6..10..
1		John Odell	3..
1	Bed and Blanket	Robert Bishop	2..
1	Jug	William Dickson	..2
1	Parcel of Cotton	Able Anderson	2..
1	Bee Hive	John Caldwell	1..7..
1	Bee Hive	John Johnston	1..8..
1	Bee Hive	Henry Anderson	1..5..

An Inventory of the Sale of the goods and chattels belonging to the estate of <u>Joshua Anderson</u>, deceased, sold at publick (sic) Vandue (sic) by Gabriel Anderson and Thomas Gordon, Exors .

Page 2

1	Bee Hive	James Caldwell	1..11..
1	Bee Hive	William Cooper	1..8..
1	Bee Hive	William Dickson	1..8..
1	Quantity of Bacon	Henry Anderson	26..
1	Plough and Furniture	James Sheepherd	9..11..
1	Hatchet and some forks	Thomas Gordon	2..10..
1	Bag of Wool	Joseph Kelley	3..
1	Still	Martin Livinston	77..
1	Cow & Calf	Joseph Whitman	15..5..
1	Cow & Calf	Edward Riley	15..
1	Cow & Calf	Abraham Anderson	12..10
1	Cow & Calf	John Lindsey	13..5..
1	Cow & Calf	George Little	12.15..
1	Corn	Mrs Ruth Anderson	10..10..
1	Heifer	William Harmon	7..5..
1	Heifer	Joseph Whiteman	7..
1	Cow & Calf	John Reid	13..
2	Yearlings	Wm Murray	6..8..
1	Heifer	John Reid	5..10..
1	Cow	Wm Cotter	13.15..
10	Hogs	Jesse Chandler	17..
9	Sheep	Robert Bishop	30..
1	Horse	John Robison	36..5..
1	Horse	Enoch Pearson	65..10..
1	Mare & Colt	James Caldwell	31..10..
1	Mare, Colt & Bull	Thomas Davis	34..5..
1	Negro Wench	Wm Vardeman	210..
1	Negro Boy	Gabriel Anderson	141..
1	Loom	John Reid	3..2..
1	Parcel of Flax	Eg Virgin	5..5..
1	Trunk	Thomas Bead	..11..
1	Bull	John Caldwell	1..
1	Bull	James Hughes	1..19..
1	Horse	Robert Wilson	20..15..
1	Brass Cock	John Davis	..8..
1	Parcel of Rye	Gabriel Anderson	1..
1	Bull	Thomas Gordon	..5..
	Total Sum of Sales		**£ 1039.2.6**

Estate Records taken from Charleston District, South Carolina Estate Inventories, Fold 3, pages 175, 176 & 177.

Note: Money is shown in £ (pounds) shillings, and pence. The symbols **£sd** were to become a convenient abbreviation for the pre-decimal system of currency used in Britain up to 1971.

Pearson Families

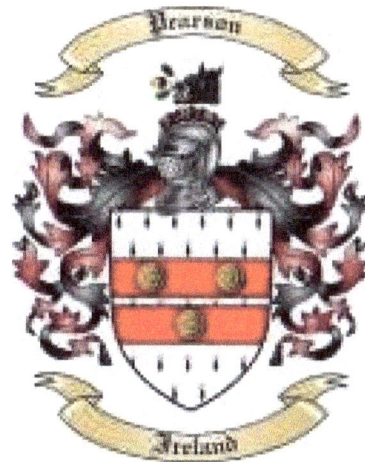

Charles M Pearson & Elizabeth Longley Pearson
Parents of Nancy Lee Pearson

Charles' Tombstone Inscription
Charles M Pearson
Born Apr 2, 1833
Died Mar 5, 1893

"A loved Father has gone from our circle of earth we shall meet him no more. He has gone to his home in heaven and all his afflictions are over."

Elizabeth' Tombstone Inscription

Elizabeth Pearson
Born Feb 3, 1833
Died Sep 19, 1889

"A place is vacant in our Home which can never be filled."

Millerville Cemetery, located in Erath County near Hico, Texas.

PEARSON FAMILY

I am quoting almost verbatim from "The Beavers, Their Roots and Branches", written by Lois Beaver Smith, 10500 Academy, N.E. #223, Albuquerque, N.M. 87111, and printed in 1986. Lois' mother, Samantha Adeline (Minnie) Pearson Beaver was the youngest child Charles and Elizabeth Pearson.

"Charles Pearson was born 2 Apr. 1833 in Tennessee. He married Elizabeth Longley in 1853. She was born 3 Feb. 1833, in Tennessee. They had three sons and four daughters, the first six were born in Tennessee** but the youngest, my mother, was born in Missouri. They were all members of the Methodist Church, and one son, Doc Pearson became an ordained Methodist minister.

Sometime between 1866 and 1870 the Pearson family migrated to Missouri and settled in Bates County. They were friends and neighbors of the John Wilsons and Joseph Beavers. Accordingly, they joined the wagon train that migrated to Texas in the fall of 1874. My mother, the youngest of the Pearson children, was four years old in December of 1874, and could not recall much about the trip. Most of the information about the six week's trek has come to us from the Wilson and Beaver ancestors.

After they all moved to Erath Co., Texas, their children grew up, married, and settled in surrounding towns and communities. Mama told us that her father became blind while she was still living at home. At the time, she was engaged to my dad who was a staunch believer in the Church of Christ, and had discussed certain scriptures with her many times.

Her father would have her read the Bible to him almost daily. Sometimes she would read a verse or two that Dad had quoted to her, and she would say to Grandpa, " Pa that is Campbellite doctrine". She said he would immediately answer, "hush, hush".

Grandma Pearson died 19 Sept. 1889, at the age of 56. Grandpa Pearson died 5 Mar. 1893, at the age of 60, just 4 years after Mama and Dad married. They are buried in the Millerville cemetery with markers at their graves. "

The remainder of this Pearson history is from Lois Reba Edwards Carter's, Hamilton Co. Cemetery book and other research sources.

"The wagon train from Bates Co. Mo. went first to Travis Co. Tex. The Wilsons and Beavers came on to Erath Co. in the fall of 1876.

It is not known when Charles and Elizabeth Pearson came to Erath Co. They were not in the 1880 Erath Co. census, which does not prove anything, because there are always families who are missed. However, their daughter Nancy (Nannie) was said to have married at her home in Lanham, Hamilton Co., to W. E. Pointer, 2 Jan 1881. So they probably spent some time there before settling in Erath Co."

NOTE by Jean McCullough: I have copied the above information from the book, *"Early Settlers of the Millerville Community, Erath County, Texas"*, by Marilyn Giesecke Mills Evers, Stephenville, Texas, Dated 1992, revised August 1993, September 1994 and later March/ April 1998.

**Comment: Nancy Pearson Pointer was born in Alabama as later proved by the 1860 Jackson Co., Alabama Federal Census Record.

Children of Charles Mastin & Elizabeth Longley Pearson Charles

Pearson's Bible Page

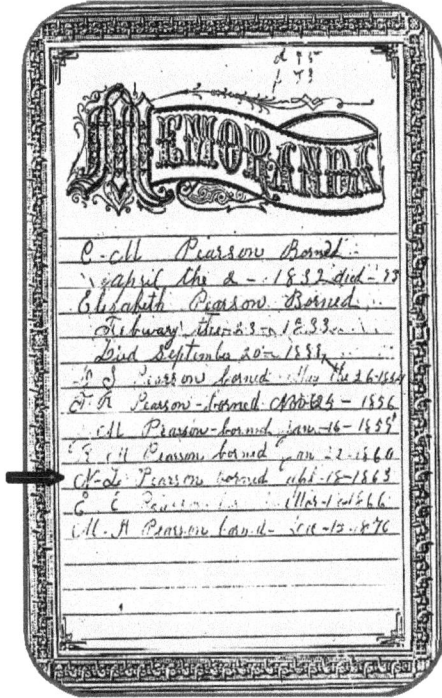

Sons
Francis R (Frank), Doctor S Pearson
J M Pearson (died young)

Daughters

Rebecca Matilda Pearson Jones,
Ella Elizabeth Pearson Hovey
Nancy Lee Pearson Pointer
Samantha Azeline [Minnie] Pearson Beaver

Doctor S Pearson and Sisters
Front Row: Doctor S Pearson, Nancy Pearson Pointer,
Ella Elizabeth Pearson Hovey, Henry Francis Hovey
Back Row: Martha Bell Clements Pearson and Willaim E Pointer

Charles and his family lived in Jackson Co., Alabama at the time but enlisted in Tennessee to serve in the Civil War. He served in the following regiment during the war.

The 34th Regiment, Tennessee Infantry (4th Confederate Infantry), *also called 1st Mountain Rifle Regiment, was organized during September, 1861, at Camp Smartt, near McMinnville, Tennessee. On April 26, 1865, it surrendered.*

Company G - Captains Philip H. Roberts, Davis H. Barnes - "The Overton Rifles." **Men from Jackson County, Alabama**.

Overview: 34th Infantry Regiment, formerly the 4th Confederate (Tennessee) Regiment, was organized at Camp Sneed, Knoxville, Tennessee, in August 1861. Its members were from the counties of Hardin, Knox, Moore, Jackson, Davidson, Shelby, and Coffee. Companies A and G contained men from Alabama. After serving at Knoxville and Cumberland Gap, the unit was assigned to General Maney's Brigade and during the spring of 1864 consolidated with the 24th Sharpshooters Battalion. It fought with the Army of Tennessee from Murfreesboro to Atlanta, was part of Hood's winter operations, and ended the war in North Carolina attached in Palmer's command. In September, 1861, it had 654 officers and men fit for duty and during January 1862, while at Cumberland Gap, there were 521 present. It lost fifteen percent of the 371 engaged at Murfreesboro and forty percent of the 163 at Chickamauga. During December 1863, the regiment totaled 165 men and 105 arms. Few were included in the surrender on April 26, 1865. The field officers were Colonels William M. Churchwell, Robert N. Lewis, and James A. McMurry; Lieutenant Colonel Oliver A. Bradshaw; and Major Joseph Bostick.

Doctor Pearson & Lovey (Unknown)
Parents of Charles Mastin Pearson

There is not a lot known about Doctor Pearson. What is known through his father Sherwood Pearson's Bible, is that his given name was "Doctor". So far there has been no information as to why this son was given that name. He was one of eleven children of Sherwood and Elizabeth Ligon Pearson. He was the sixth of nine sons and two daughters.

We first find documentation of Doctor Pearson marrying Phoebe Rives Brown on Oct 3, 1814 in Franklin Co., Virginia. Phoebe was the daughter of John Brown and Sarah (Sally) Rives Brown.

Marriage Bonds of Franklin CO. VA 1786-1858 by Wingfield: *Pearson, Doctor and Phoebe R. Brown, dau. John, Oct 3, 1814. Sur. Joseph Rives.*

Doctor and Phoebe R Brown Pearson had one child, a daughter Phoebe E.W. Pearson born about 1815. Sherwood Pearson's Bible gives us the date of Phoebe's death which was recorded as 16 March 1816.

Doctor is found still living in Franklin County on the 1820 census but by 1830 he is living in Tennessee. The 1830 census record shows him living in McMinn County being 43 years of age, with a son under 5 years of age, a wife between 20 and 29 years of age with one daughter under 5 years, three daughters between the ages of 5 thru 9, one daughter between the age of 10—14 and another daughter between the age of 15—19. We know that he had a son, Charles Mastin born on 2 April 1832. Doctor died the following year at the age of 46 leaving his wife Lovice (Lovey) to raise these small children.

To date a marriage record for Doctor and Lovey has not been found. We do know from census records she was born in 1808 in North Carolina. Several records indicate a connection between John and Chrisley Foster, but none of the known records establish a relationship.

Lovey is found on the 1860 census living with daughter Rebecca Stamper and her family in Jackson Co., Alabama and again living with her on the 1870 Bates Co., Missouri census. Nothing more is found on her after that date. Rebecca moved on to the Oklahoma Territory and is found on the 1880 Optima, Beaver Co., Oklahoma census living with her son Isaac and his family. Rebecca is no longer living by 1910.

- **Phoebe E. W. Pearson**, born about 1815, Franklin Co., Virginia; married Smith L. Morris, 6 Nov 1834.

- **Elizabeth\Eliza Pearson**, born about 1822, Franklin Co., Virginia; married George Monroe, 25 April 1840; died 6 February 1854, McMinn Co., Tennessee.

- **Sherwood W. Pearson**, born 8 November 1824, Tennessee; married Angeline Mashburn, about 1852; died 27 December 1906, Boone Township, Maries Co., Missouri.

- **Lucinda Pearson** was born in 1826 in McMinn Co., Tennessee.

- **Nancy Pearson**, born 1827, McMinn Co., Tennessee; married James Ellis, 28 August 1846, McMinn Co., Tennessee.

- **Gizelda Pearson**, born 25 July 1829, McMinn Co., Tennessee; married Nathan Lowe, 30 June 1853, Tennessee; died 18 May 1886, Johnson Co., Texas.

- **Rebecca E. Pearson**, born 1830, Tennessee; married William Stamper, about 1849, Tennessee; died before 1910, Oklahoma.

- **Charles Mastin Pearson**, born 2 April 1832; married Elizabeth Longley, 1853, Tennessee; died 5 March 1893 and buried in Millerville Cemetery, Erath Co., Texas.

War of 1812 Record for Doctor Pearson (Pierson)

There was a list showing Doctor Pearson had served in the War of 1812 but until I found his pay record, I could not document his service. I was used to seeing the surname spelled as "Peerson" but this was the first time I came across "Pierson".

According to Stuart Lee Butler's, *A Guide to Virginia Militia Units in the War of 1812,* the 110th Militia Regiment was from Franklin Co., Virginia and that the militia companies of the 42nd and 110th regiments participated in the defense of Richmond and Norfolk in 1813 and 1814.

Located in the Library of Virginia is the following information:

<u>Pierson, Doctor.</u>

Gen. note	**Muster Rolls, p.640**
Note	**Part of index to: Pay Rolls of Militia Entitled to Land Bounty Under the Act of Congress of Sept. 28, 1850 (Richmond, 1851) and: Muster Rolls of the Virginia Militia in the War of 1812 (Richmond, 1852) which supplements Pay Rolls. This collection is also available on microfilm.**
Note	**War of 1812 pay rolls and muster rolls**

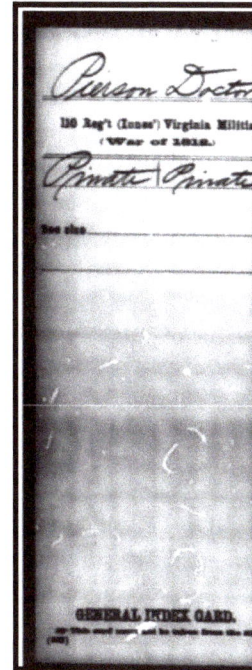

The **War of 1812** was a military conflict, lasting for two and a half years, fought by the United States of America against the United Kingdom of Great Britain and Ireland. The war resolved many issues which remained from the American Revolutionary War but involved no boundary changes. The United States declared war on June 18, 1812 for several reasons, including trade restrictions brought about by the British war with France, the impressment of American merchant sailors into the Royal Navy, British support of Indian tribes against American expansion, outrage over insults to national honor after humiliations on the high seas, and possible American interest in annexing British territory in modern-day Canada.

Franklin County is where Doctor's first wife, Phoebe Rives Brown's family lived and where Doctor and Phoebe were married in October 1814. It would seem that Doctor and Phoebe married shortly after his service in the war ended.

Doctor is also found on the 1820 Franklin County census record. After that I was unable to trace his movements until he showed up in McMinn Co., Tennessee.

There is no record of Doctor receiving a bounty land grant in Tennessee; however, it is documented that he owned land in Roane and McMinn Counties. McMinn County court house had a fire in 1964 which caused a huge loss for researchers.

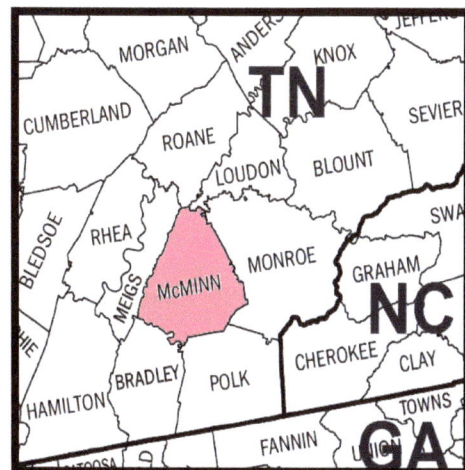

WILL OF DOCTOR PEARSON

WILL FILED: McMinn County, Tennessee Will Book B, Sept. 1830 to Mar 1838 and also Wills & Estate Records of McMinn County, Tennessee 1820-1870. (Transcribed record of Doctor's will.)

Doctor Pearson Will, page 123- 124, Inventory page 135

I, Doctor Pearson, being of sound mind and memory do make and publish this my last will and testament in manner and form following.
First, *I wish all my just debts paid out of my personal property that is to say out of my cattle and horses should there be a stock sufficient to discharge my debts to be lawfully sold by my Executors hereafter to be mentioned and should it be insufficient to satisfy the demands against my estate any other articles or articles that my family can best spare until all is satisfied.* ***Secondly***, *I wish all the remainder part of my personal property to be kept together until my youngest son* <u>Charles Maston Pearson</u> *arrives to the age of twenty one years and then to be equally distributed share and share alike to all my lawfull heirs.* ***Thirdly***, *as to my real estate that is to say my land, I leave it for the support of my helpless family until the above mentioned Charles Maston Pearson arrives to the aforesaid age of twenty one years and then for my heirs to make an equal division betwixt themselves, share and share alike. Each one to have and to hold their equal share forever.* ***Fourthly***, *I appoint my beloved Lovey Pearson and John Foster, my executors to this my last will and testament. Hereby revoking all former will or wills by me.*
In witness thereof, I set unto with my hand and seal this 4th day of September in the year of our Lord one thousand eighteen hundred and thirty three.
Doctor Pearson
In the presence of us, test—Wm. Dotson, J. M. Pearson

March Count 1832— **An inventory Of the estate of Doctor Pearson, deceased.**

Note James Rutherford & Joel Jones note	21.31 ¼
James M Montgomery & John D London note	39.62 ½
John Bell & Alvis ____ note	32.00
Wm Aikson and Thomas Maldin note	7.56 ½
John Cook Sr. & John Cook note	3.70 ½
C Foster & Wm Foster note	34.00
Isaac Redding & Rebecca Redding note	37.68 ¼
Thomas Vernon & Wm A Witten note	17.10
John Smith & James Kenedy note	65.86 ¼
Money paid by Wm Dodson & Others	31.18 ¼
George Montgomery & Grace Redding note	<u>3.25</u>
Due the Estate by Book account of Doctor Pearson	
	$293.24 ½
James Tate	3.75
Joel James	.50
John Kirkpatrick	.20
Beesoir Fields	.20
William Aikson	1.00
James Roberts	1.00
Wm. Moreland	8.75
John Field	<u>1.65</u>
Supposed to be debts	**$ 12.65**
Moreland	.50
David Hersildson	,40
Jospeh Pain	1.00
Thomas Taylor	.50
Wm Parmen	.10
Thomas Moreland	1.50
Jarvis McCully	.70
Thomas Hardin & John Bile	<u>.85</u>
This whole amount that is paid and due by note	**$ 18.20**
and book accounts to the Estate	**$ 311.44 1/2**

Sherwood Pearson and Elizabeth Ligon

Parents of Doctor Pearson

Sherwood Pearson was a son of Charles Pearson and Rebecca Walton. [1] He married Elizabeth Ligon, daughter of Thomas Ligon in Charlotte Co., Virginia on 3 September 1770. [2] Their children were Mastin, Richmond, Hal, Joseph, Thomas, Doctor, Charles, William, Sherwood, Elizabeth and Polly. [3]

Per a letter written by Miss Nell Peerson, descendant of Sherwood & Elizabeth Ligon Peerson (Pearson) in 1970, she visited the graves of Sherwood and Elizabeth. They are buried in a family plot on their home about 12 miles outside of Danville, Virginia.

A direct quote from her letter says, *"Some distance from the house in the back under a very old walnut tree is the cemetery. Time has worn the old stone markers so that Elizabeth and Sherwood's names are barely legible as are those of Rachel Hutson and Mastin Peerson. Many others are unmarked. It is gratifying that several hundred acres of the original place are still owned by members of the family.*

Alfred Douglas is working on his book, "The Camp Branch Peersons". Turkey Cocke Creek borders one side and Camp Branch Creek flows through the place. The house stands on a high point overlooking the pretty farmland. Tobacco seems to have always been the main crop. Some log barns still stand with furnace inside for curing the tobacco leaves which are hung there." [4]

George Walton was Sherwood's guardian after the death of Sherwood's father. *"George Walton sold 200 acres of land in Charlotte County to Sherwood, who was living in Prince Edward County in 1767. After moving to Charlotte County, Sherwood married Elizabeth Ligon in 1770. When this family moved into Pittsylvania County is not certain, but they were still in Charlotte County on the 1782 tax list, but by 1788 he was selling land in Pittsylvania County".* [5]

References:

1. St. Peter's Parish Register, by G. C. Chamberlayne, pages 497-498 shows birth of children of Robert and Frances Walton. Rebecca's birth, date is recorded as 20 April 1720.

2. The record is shown as Sherwood <u>Purson</u> and Elizabeth Ligon, daughter of Thomas Ligon, Charlotte County Marriages, by Knorr, page 68. Bible record located in the Library of Virginia Archives

3. Pearson Family, compiled for Miss Nell Pearson by Charles Hughes Hamlin, C.G, 8 June 1968

4. Lunenburg County VA Order Books 1754-1759, Order Book 5, p.1A - November Court 1757

5. In 1788, John Muse purchased 359 acres on Turkey Cock Creek from Sherwood Pearson in 1789 (D. B. 8, p. 436).

Sherwood Peerson orphan of Charles Pierson dec'd came into Court, and (being of lawfull age for that purpose) made choice of George Walton to be his guardian who is accordingly appointed, he giving Bond and security, whereupon he together with Henry Jubell his Security, enter into and acknowledged their Bond for that Purpose.

This record would indicate that Sherwood would have been at least 14 years old as that was the legal age a child had to be to choose their guardian. Choosing George Walton as his guardian is significant as Sherwood's mother was Rebecca Walton, sister to George. Their parents were Robert Walton and wife Frances Sherwood.

We know that records of Sherwood are found in several counties in Virginia: Lunenburg, Pittsylvania and Charlotte. Perhaps one of the most important records found for Sherwood is his family Bible which is stored in the Library of Virginia.

Several pages of that Bible revealed information of his family. Another important document is the marriage bond between Sherwood & Thomas Ligon, father of Elizabeth.

A land document between Sherwood and Thomas Ligon states:

"*February 4, 1771, Thomas Ligon of Charlotte County in consideration of sixty pounds sold Sherwood Pearson of same county, one hundred and fifty-three acres in the county of Charlotte on the branches of Little Roanoke River. Recorded Charlotte County, February 4, 1771.*"

[The same information is included on page 673, in "*The Ligon Family and Connections*", Vol. I. book]

There are other instances of Sherwood Pearson named in court documents and the spelling of his surname was either Peerson or Pearson.

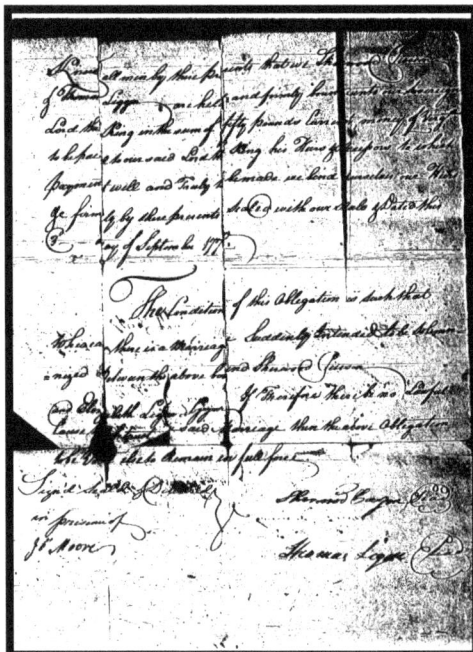

Transcribed Marriage Bond
Charlotte County, Virginia Court

Know all men by these presents that we Sherwood Peerson & Thomas Liggon are held and firmly bound unto our Sovereign Lord the King in the sum of fifty pounds Current money of Virginia to be paid to our said Lord the King his Heirs & successors to which payment will and Truly be made we bind ourselves our Heirs & firmly by these presents Sealed with our seals & Dated this 3rd day of September 1770.

The Condition of the Obligation is such that Whereas there is a Marriage Suddenly Intended to be Solemnized between the above bound Sherwood Peerson and Elizabeth Ligon Liggon. If Therefore there be no Lawful Cause to obstruct said Marriage then the above Obligation to be Void else to Remain in full force.

In the presence of J E Moore

Sherwood Pearson (seal)

Thomas Ligon   (seal)

In researching Sherwood Pearson, I found his bible located in the Library of Virginia. The pages are difficult to read but legible. Being able to document his family and dates, has been extremely helpful. It is incredible that these pages are well over 200 years old. Shown below are the pages giving us the family births and deaths.

The names shown on the "Birth" page are:

Sherwood Pearson his wife Elizabeth married (illegible) day of September 1770

Richmond L Pearson was born (illegible)

Hall Peerson was born August 2 (illegible)

Joe Pearson was born January (illegible)

Sherwood Pearson was born September 22, 177_ (illegible)

Mastin Peerson was born June 6 (illegible)

Thomas Peerson was born January 2 17_ _ (illegible)

Doctor Peerson was born April 17 17_ _ (illegible)

Betsy W Peerson was born May 9 177_

Charles Peerson was born April 8 179 _

Polly Peerson was born November 9 179_

William L Peerson was born August 19 1799

The page showing the deaths of Sherwood and Elizabeth's family is somewhat more legible but overlapping pages appear to cut off some of this page. What is shown is:

Hall & Joe Pearson died of December 1807

Sherwood Pearson, Jr died 29 February 1808

Sherwood Pearson, Sr died 28 October 1816

Phoebe R Pearson died the 16th of March 1816

Elizabeth Pearson died the 25 October 1826

William S Pearson was kild the 17 of June 1864

Henry A Hankins died the 15 of March 1866

Mastin Pearson died the 27 of December 1869

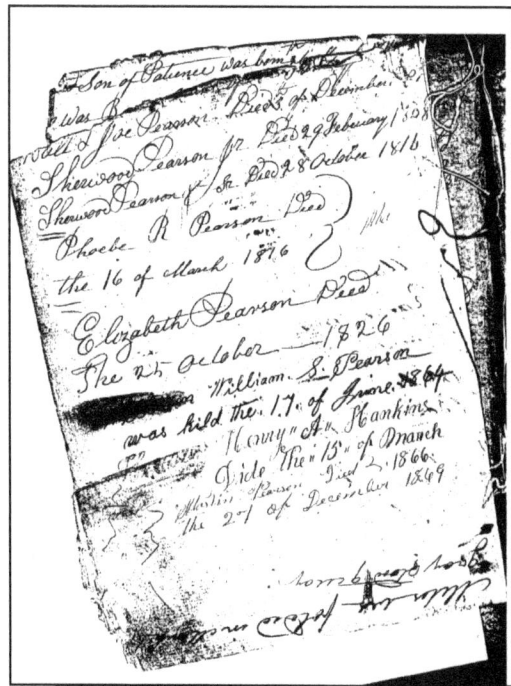

Note: A copy of Sherwood's original will is in my possession but it is too large and contains several pages as is shown in the following transcription. Sherwood was a person of considerable material possessions.

LAST WILL & TESTAMENT OF SHERWOOD PEERSON (PEARSON)

In the name of God Amen, I Sherwood Peerson of Pittsylvania County and State of Virginia being of perfect health of body of perfect mind and memory thanks be given unto God, calling unto man the mortality of my body and knowing it is appointed for all men once to die, do make and ordain this my last will & testament. (That is to say) principally and first of all I give and recommend my soul into the hand of Almighty God, who gave it, and my body I recommend to the earth to be buried in a decent custom (like [this word was stricken out]) burial at the discretion of my Executors and touching such worldly Estate wherewith it hath pleased God to bless me in this life. I give and devise and dispose of the same in the following manner and form. First my will &desire is that all my just debts be paid.

Item I give and bequeath to my son RICHMOND PEERSON a Negro man Solomon, also a tract of land lying in the State of Kentucky, Green County supposed to contain three hundred Acres, by the same more or less to him and his heirs forever.

Item I give to my son MASTIN PEERSON one negro named Peter to him and his heirs forever also ninety dollars to be paid in money which sum is now due to him for services formerly rendered.

Item I give to my son THOMAS PEERSON one negro boy named Abram to him and his heirs forever.

Item I give to my son DOCTOR PEERSON one negro boy named Yorrick to him and his heirs forever.

Item I give to son CHARLES PEERSON one negro boy named Randolph to him and his heirs

forever.

Item I lend to my daughter ELIZABETH LACY the following slaves

VIZ. One negro girl named Ailey, one Negro girl named Marie and one Negro man named Jesse and their increase to his and her heirs forever. And it is my will & desire that the said negros, Ailey, Marie, Jesse and their increase shall never be sold from my said daughter Elizabeth and the lawfull heirs of her body moreover I request and impower my Executors or any of them that if at any time the above named Negroes or their increase should be about to be sold or eliminated under what pretence soever or by whomsoever that in that case my Executors or any of them shall take the Negro or negroes into his or their possession in trust for the use and benefit of my said daughter and her heirs.

Item I give to my daughter POLLEY PEERSON and the lawfull heirs of her body forever one negro woman named Amey and her child Hero and their increase forever and it is my will and desire that the said negroes and their increase shall never be sold under what (unclear word) forever or by whomsoever that is that case my Executors or any of them shall take the said Negro or negroes into his or their possession in trust for the use and benefit for my said daughter Polley and her heirs. I also give to my daughter Polley Peerson two cows and calves, one young horse or mare, one bed and furniture and one small table.

Item I give to my son WILLIAM PEERSON one negro boy named George and a girl named Milley and their increase to him and his heirs forever.

Item I give to my granddaughter ELIZA PEERSON two hundred dollars to be received when of age or married and to be paid either in money or property as my Executors shall think most advisable.

Item Considering that I have given my son SHERWOOD PEERSON, Dec'd, his full portion of my Estate in land, stock, a Negro and other property,

It is also my will and desire that if any or any either of my children as before named should die before a general division takes place without a lawfull heir of his, her or their body that the Negro or negroes that was given to him her or them Shall return into the general stock to be hereafter named and shall remain there until a division takes place when it shall be equally divided among my living sons or if one or more of or negroes that I have given away to any of my children shall die before the child or children to whom him, she or they were given has become of lawfull age or had received him or her or them into his, her or their possession that one of equal value shall be taken from the general stock and given to him, her so that has sustained the loss or losses under the above mentioned circumstances.

__Item__ I lend to my well beloved wife ELIZABETH PEERSON during her natural life, under the agency and management of Mastin Peerson the tract of land whereon I now live together with the plantation, utensils, household & kitchen furniture & all my stock of every description whatsoever with the following slaves Viz. Easther, Miner, Isaac, Squire, Lucy, Jug, Patience, Lidia, Luris, Seney & Dick for a general stock to be managed by Mastin Peerson as aforesaid for the maintenance of my wife and the youngest children and should my wife Elizabeth Peerson die before my youngest son William becomes of age the above property is still to be held by Mastin Peerson until my son William becomes of lawfull age for the purposes above mentioned. When a general division is to take place and all the property consisting of negroes and stock to be divided as hereafter proscribed Viz. to all of the property that I have hereafter lent unto my wife together with its increase be equally divided amongst my sons Vis: RICHMOND, MASTIN, THOMAS, DOCTOR, CHARLES, & WILLIAM PEERSON making deduction with those who have here before to received stock of any kind.

__Item__ it is my request that my son William shall be sent to school until he is capable of working interests.

__Item__ it is my will and desire that upon a general division that the tract of land whereon I now live estimated at five hundred and forty nine acres be the same more or less be equally divided Viz: according to quality and quantity between my sons, Mastin, Thomas, Charles and William for them and their heirs forever,

It is my will and desire that in case my daughter Polley should not marry before a general division takes place that my sons Thomas, Mastin, Charles & William should attend to her welfare together with the welfare of her property suffering her to continue with them or either of them which she has cause and enjoin it an them to maintain her decently with the assistance of her property during her natural life unless she should sooner marry.

*__Item__ it is my wish that after my decease no more restraint may be laid on my negro woman Easter and she suffered to live with either of my children which she may think most proper** And lastly I do hereby constitute and appoint my wife Elizabeth Peerson Executor and Mastin Peerson, Thomas Peerson, Charles Peerson and William Peerson Executors of this my last will & Testament revoking all wills by me formerly made and acknowledging this duty to be my last will & Testament. In Testimony whereof I have hereunto let my hand and seal this twenty eight day of March One Thousand eight hundred and fourteen."*

Signed, Sealed and published Interlined, before signed

In the presence of Sherwood Peerson
(Seal)

Jabez Smith, John Smith, Junr, Allen X (his mark) Wray, James Thomas

At a court held for Pittsylvania County the 17th Day of January 1817,the within last will & Testament of Sherwood Peerson, Dec'd was presented in Court and proved by the Oaths of Jabez Smith, John Smith, Junr and James Thomas, three subscribing witnesses thereto and ordered to be recorded, to be recorded and upon the motion of Mastin Peerson and Thomas Peerson two of the Executors named in said will who made Oath thereto according to law and together with Jabez Smith, John Smith, Jnr and Samuel Call and their securities entered into and acknowledged their bond in the penalty of twenty thousand dollars conditioned as the law directs. Certificate is granted them for obtaining a probate of said will in due form and leave reserved to the other Executors named in said will to join in the probate thereof whom they shall think proper.

Note: As is specifically directed in Sherwood's will, he wanted special care given

to a particular "slave", Easter. It is also interesting to bring attention to Sherwood's concern regarding the division of the "slaves" and how they were to be treated after his death. Another comment about this will is that by the time it was probated, Doctor was living in Franklin County, a short distance away from Pittsylvania County and was fighting in the War of 1812 and later in 1816 was dealing with the death of his wife, who left him with a small daughter.

Sherwood did remember this grandchild in his will:

"*Item I give to my granddaughter ELIZA PEERSON two hundred dollars to be received when of age or married and to be paid either in money or property as my Executors shall think most advisable.*"

Perhaps because of the loss of Doctor's wife Sherwood did not assign any responsibilities to him regarding the care of Elizabeth, William and Polly.

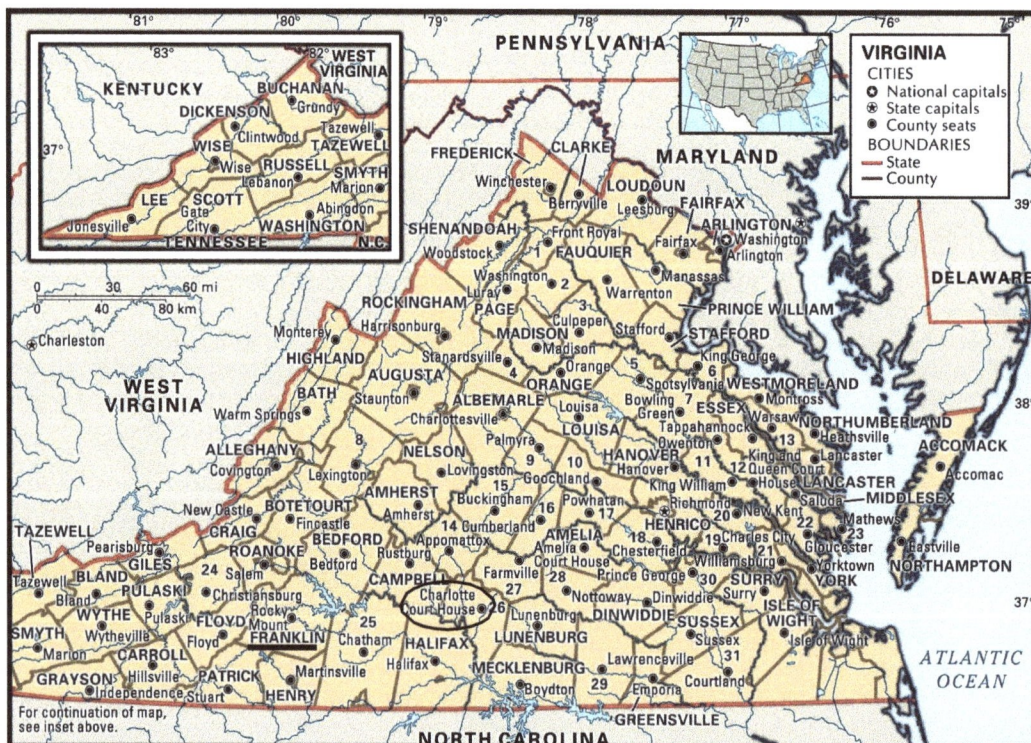

Ligon/Lygon & Harris

Related Families

Anderson, Sherwood, Walton, Worsham

Thomas Ligon and Ann (Unknown)
Parents of Elizabeth Ligon Pearson

Not a great deal is known about **Thomas Ligon**, father of Elizabeth Ligon Pearson. There is a baptismal record of Thomas, son of Matthew and Elizabeth found in the Bristol Parish Register, pages 56 and 57. It is again listed in *"The Ligon Connections"* by William Ligon.

"Thomas son of Matthew and Elizabeth Ligon born Feb 7 1724".

Genealogically this fits the time frame for Elizabeth's father and naming her after his mother is again in line with the naming pattern of that time.

We find Thomas in Lunenburg County, Virginia on the Court Ordered Road Orders.

8 March 1758, Page 39— On the Petition of sundry the inhabitants of Little Roanoak River for a Bridle Way to be Cleared the best and Convenienced way from the Mosing ford on the said Little Roanoak River to the Plantation of the Reverend Mr. William Kay, Deceased. It is ordered that David Caldwell, Joseph Perrin, and Thomas Ligan, being first sworn do View and Examine.

4 May 1762, Page 27—Thomas Leigon is appointed Surveyor of the Road Whereof David Gwin was late Surveyor.

By 1764 Thomas Ligon is now in Charlotte County. Charlotte County was created 26 May 1764 from Lunenburg County.

"Charlotte County Virginia was founded in 1765, as provided by an act of the General Assembly. The ancestry of Charlotte can be traced down from Charles City County, Prince George County, Brunswick County and Lunenburg County. Early Charlotte County names are found in the Vestry Book of Cumberland Parish until the formation of Cornwall Parish in 1757."

-- December 18, 1760, Robert Jones of the Parish of Raleigh in County of Amelia, in consideration of £25 sold **Thomas Ligon of Parish of Cornwall in County of Lunenburg**, land lying within the aforesaid parish of Cornwall in County of Lunenburg on the lower side of Twitty's creek and adjoining the said creek also to the dwelling plantation of the said Thomas Ligon, his part of a tract held by the said Jones on the said Twitty's creek to the line between the said Jones' land and the land of William Perrins. Witnesses: David Gwin, Thomas Bedford, Jack Townes, George Gwin. Recorded, Lunenburg County, March 30, 1761. Teste: Clement Read, C.L.C. Charlotte Co., Virginia.

-- **Deed Book 1, p. 82**: May 7, 1765, Joseph Perrin and **Thomas Ligon of the County of Charlotte,** in consideration of six pounds, sold Josephus Perrin of the same county 150 acres lying in the County of Charlotte, beginning at a beach on Twitty's Creek and adjoining widow Moseley's line, thence to Thomas Ligon's line, being part of the tract whereon the said Josephus Perrin and Thomas Ligon now dwell. Witnesses: Thomas Bedford, William Read, P. Carrington, Thomas Stuart.
Recorded, Charlotte County, May 6, 1765.
Teste: Samuel Cobbs, Clerk. Truly recorded, Thomas Read, Deputy Clerk.

-- **Deed Book 3, p. 180**: January 1, 1771, **Thomas Ligon of Charlotte County** sold Sherwood Pearson of same county eighty acres in said county. Recorded, January 4, 1773.

Deed Book 3, p. 181: Know all men by these presents that I, **Thomas Ligon of the Parish of Cornwall in the County of Charlotte**, for the love I bear towards my friend John Bridges of the Parish and County aforesaid (in obeyance of his marrying my daughter Mary) do give and grant to him the said John Bridges, two negro girls named Annaha and Suckey, also two negro boys named Tom and Peter. Dated November 4, 1772.
Witnesses: William Rose, Thomas Williams, Thomas Chardwick.
This deed of gift was recorded Charlotte County, January 4, 1773. Teste: Thomas Read, Clerk.

Deed Book 3, p. 519: December 27, 1774, **Thomas Liggon of the Parish of Cornwall, in the County of Charlotte**, in consideration of seventeen pounds sold Josephus Perrin of same parish and county seventeen acres beginning at a poplar in the said Perrin's corner, etc.
Witnesses: Sherwood Walton, William Sullivant, Thomas Bedford. Recorded, Charlotte County, June 5, 1775. Teste: Thomas Read, C.C.

Deed Book 4, p. 162: October 13, 1779, **Thomas Ligon of the County of Charlotte**, in consideration of 140 pounds sold James Hamlett of same county thirty-four acres in the county aforesaid beginning where Mr. James Hamlett's line crosses Twitty's Creek, thence on said Ligon's line to Mr. Jacob Mosby's corner line, thence on his line to Mr. Josephus Perrin's Line, etc.
Witnesses: Diggs Bumpass, George Perrin, Robert Bedford. Recorded, Charlotte County, November 1, 1779. Teste: Thomas Read, Clerk.

Deed Book 5, p. 198: September 3,1787, **Thomas Ligon, Sr. and his wife, Ann, of Charlotte County** in consideration of sixty-one pounds, sold Thomas Bedford of same county all that tract of land where on they now live, containing 122 acres lying on Twitty's Creek joining Littlebery Bedford's line.
Recorded: Charlotte County, September 3, 1787.

Thomas and Ann had the following children. It is not known at this time the exact birth order of these children so they are just listed as shown:

- **Thomas Ligon**, (Jr.) married Frances Bumpas in Charlotte County, 13 December 1780. Thomas died in Charlotte County (will dated 19 July 1799, proved 7 April 1800). Both nominated executors, Paul Carrington and Joseph Ligon, renounced executorship.

  Note: Records indicate that Frances Bumpas was the daughter of Charles Pearson and Rebecca Walton. She married first Stephen Bedford, second Diggs Bumpas and third Thomas Ligon. She was a sister of Sherwood Pearson.

- **Elizabeth Ligon** married Sherwood Purson (Pearson) in Charlotte County 3 September (bond) 1770.

- **Joseph Ligon** married Mary Church, daughter of Richard Church, in 1778. He and his family later moved to Georgia. Mary died in Oglethorpe County in 1827 (will dated 24 July 1827, proved Sept. 1827).

- **Mary Ligon** married John Bridges in Charlotte County 5 May (bond) 1772. They left Virginia and settled in Kentucky.

- **Obedience Ligon** married John Owen in Lunenburg County 11 March 1784.

To document this Ligon line, shown below are the descendants from Thomas Ligon and Mary Harris to Elizabeth Ligon Pearson.

Thomas Ligon & wife Mary Harris

Thomas Lygon, *Gent, did by will appoint his wife Mary to be his executrix, and this is confirmed. 16 March 1675.*

200 acres at Curls—Deeds p. 231 Mary Ligon, Sr. of Henrico Co. for love & affection to my **sons** <u>Richard Ligon</u> and Hugh Ligon of same, 200 acres at Curls, being part of a grant to Capt. Thomas Harris, dec'd, and given by his will to said Mary Ligon, his daughter.

Son, Richard & wife Mary Worsham

Richard was born about 1657 in Henrico Co., Virginia. He married Mary Worsham in Henrico County between 1678 and 1681. Mary was the daughter of William Worsham and his wife, Elizabeth, whose surname is thought to be Littleberry.

William Ligon and Richard Ligon, [brothers] have agreed to divide the land equally between said William Ligon and **Matthew Ligon, son of above Richard;** the lower half to William and upper to Matthew.

Richard, called the 'Indian Fighter,' passed away in 1724. Surviving court records show his executor and son, <u>Matthew Ligon</u>, presented Richard's will 2 March 1723/4, but the original will was destroyed along with other wills and deeds of Henrico County of this period. Abraham Womack Sr., Robert Elam, and John Knibb appraised Richard's estate for £30:3:3.

Son, Matthew & wife Elizabeth Anderson

Matthew Ligon was born between 1681 and 1685 in Henrico County, Virginia. He signed a will on 21 April 1764 in Cumberland County, Virginia. Will of Matthew Ligon of Southam Parish, date (?) April 1764, Proven 24 September 1764. Son, James Ligon; son, Richard Ligon. Exrs: son, Richard-sole executor. Wit: **Thomas Ligon**, William Ligon, Frances Ligon. He died between 21 April 1764 and 24 Sept 1764 in Cumberland County, Virginia.

Elizabeth Anderson, was the daughter of James Anderson. Her brother, Matthew Anderson, Jr left a will 25 February 1717/18 date 10 June 1718 and proven Prince George Co. Book 1713-1728, Part II, Page 232. Legates to Brother William, Brother James, and **Sister Elizabeth Liggon**. Wit. James Thweat and Buller Herbert. This will gives us the siblings and children of James Anderson They were Matthew, William, James and Elizabeth. Unfortunately little else is known about this James Anderson because he lived during a period for which most of the county records have been destroyed.

Note: From the Bristol Parish register:

"**<u>Thomas</u> son of Matthew and Elizabeth Ligon born Feb 7 1724**".

Son, <u>Thomas Ligon</u> & wife Ann (last name unknown)
Daughter, <u>Elizabeth Ligon</u> & husband Sherwood Pearson

Charles & Rebecca Walton Pearson
Parents of Sherwood Pearson

The first record of our Pearson family is found in New Kent Co., Virginia in The Vestry Book and Parish Register of St. Peter's Parish New Kent and James City Counties, Virginia, 1684-1786,' transcribed and edited by C. G. Chamberlayne, published by the Library of Virginia, Richmond, Virginia. 3d reprinted edition, 1997. p. 386,

Charles son of [   ] Pirson baptized August 8th, 1714.
Frances Walton, daughter of Charles & Rebecca Pearson, (born) July 2, 1739, baptized Aug 13.

Charles is thought to have died before 1757. This date is further supported by the record of son Sherwood's court record selecting as his guardian, George Walton.

There are records in the Vestry Book and Register of St Peter's Parish of New Kent and James City County's indicating Charles Pearson was paid 400 # tobo (tobacco) for keeping Andrew Furnea in 1751 and again in 1752 he was allowed 200# tobo for keeping Andrew Furnea for 6 months. The Vestry Book had no further entries for Charles after 1752.

Rebecca Walton's birth is recorded in *The Vestry Book and Parish Register of St. Peter's Parish New Kent and James City Counties, Virginia, 1684-1786*, page 142.

"Rebecca, daugh of Robt and ffrans:: Walton born Jan'ry 7th 1717/18."

Possible children of Charles and Rebecca:
- John
- Charles

Proven children are:
- Frances Walton
- Sherwood
- Joseph
- Richmond

Robert & Frances Sherwood Walton
Parents of Rebecca Walton

ROBERT WALTON was born circa 1692/4, and died 5 Mar 1733/1734 in New Kent Co., Virginia. It is possible that Robert was the son of Edward Jr. and Elizabeth Walton. He is listed as Robert Walton "Jr." in the St. Peter's Parish records of New Kent County, where he served as Clerk of the Vestry from 1723 to 1734. The designation "Jr." does not necessarily mean that his father was named Robert, but that a Robert Walton older than he was living in the same locality.

It is believed that Robert "Jr." lived and died in New Kent County, where he, as eldest son, would have inherited his father's estate in 1720. William and Thomas Walton, alleged younger brothers of Robert "Jr.," resettled in an area of Goochland County that became, in 1749, Cumberland County. Two children of Robert, George and Robert "III" Walton, settled in the same vicinity of Goochland and/or Cumberland County, as evidenced by land records and other courthouse documents.

Robert "Jr." married **Frances Sherwood** (approximately 1715). He was born on Jan. 17, 1697 and died on March 10, 1780." Their children were born in New Kent Co., Virginia.

Robert Walton and Frances Sherwood's children were:
- **Robert Walton**, b.7 Jan 1717/1718, Prince Edward Co., Virginia
- **Rebecca Walton**, b.20 Apr 1720, New Kent Co., Virginia d.1789) m Charles Pearson
- **Joseph Walton**, b.10 Feb 1721/1722, New Kent, Co., Virginia
- **George Walton**, b.17 Feb 1723/1724, Prince Edward Co., Virginia
- **Frances Walton**, b.14 Jan 1726/1727, New Kent Co., Virginia
- **Sherwood Walton**, b.10 Jul 1728, New Kent
- Co., Virginia
- **Sally Walton**, b.1730, New Kent Co., Virginia

LT. Col. Thomas Lygon and Mary Harris Ligon
Parents of Richard Ligon

Thomas Ligon was born in 1623, Stowe, War-wickshire, England and died in 1675. He married Mary Harris daughter of Thomas Harris.

The couple had six children:
- William, born in 1650
- Thomas, born 1651
- Johan (a daughter), born in 1653
- Richard, born in 1657
- Matthew, born in 1659
- Hugh, born in 1661
- Mary, born in 1663

Lt. Col. Thomas Lygon, after accepting his share of his father's estate in England, came to Jamestown, Virginia in 1641 with his second cousin, Sir William Berkeley, Royal Governor of Virginia. Their kinship stems from the marriage of Sir Henry Berkeley, grandfather of Sir William, to Margaret Lygon, aunt of Thomas Lygon.

Colonel Lygon, whose name spelling change to Ligon at some time in his life, was appointed surveyor of Henrico County and surveyed, among other locations, Malvern Hills. He was also a Justice of the Peace for Charles City County in 1657 and a Lieutenant Colonel of the County. He was a member of the House of Burgesses (Virginia Congress) from Henrico County in 1655 and 1656.

On April 18, 1644 the Indians made a sudden attack against the settlements in Virginia and massacred 300 settlers before being repulsed. While this famous attack was in progress Col. Thomas Ligon who happened to be passing the residence of Dr. John Woodson, helped Sara Woodson defend her home against the Indians. Sara was alone in the house and the only weapon they had was an old gun which Col. Ligon handled with deadly effect. With his first shot he killed 3 Indians, his 2nd shot killed 2 more and his 3rd shot killed 2 more for a total of seven Indians killed by him that day. The old gun which rendered such valuable service was made in England and today it is now in the

possession of and on display by the Virginia Historical Society in Richmond, Virginia. To commemorate this historic occasion, the name Ligon was crudely carved upon the stock of the Woodson rifle.

Governor's recorded in Charles City County (Book 1655-65, P. 144, Va. Mag. 41, P. 194).

"Sir:
I shall desire you to send the account what tobbo you received the last yeare and what is behind, for I have given Mr. Price order to pay you what remaines. I will not dispute whether the tobbo MR. LIGON paid you for the two servants were part of this debt, but leave it to yourselfe who can best Judge of itt, Sir if your boate comes downe I would desire you to send the Salt-Sellers with itt. Pray present my service to your Lady.
Your humble servant
William Berkeley
For my honoured Friend
Mr. Thomas Stegge
(Rec. May 21, 1658).

The destruction of the Henrico records prior to 1677 prevents us from obtaining very much information about Thomas Lygon. In 1657 Thomas Lygon bought a tract of land from Col. Wm. Byrd (Byrd's Reports). He was a member of the House of Burgesses from Henrico in 1655 and 1656. He was also a Justice in Henrico and Lieutenant Colonel as evidenced by the following:

Ambler Papers, Congressional Library
(Va. Mag. Vol. 12, p. 205)
Henrico County Court, Feb. 1669
Present
Hon. Coll. Thos. Stegge, Esqr.
Mr. Wm. Baugh, LIEUT. COLL. THOMAS LIGON, Maj. Wm. Farrar, Capt. Frances Eppes, Comrs.

He and Capt. Wm. Farrar patented 335 acres in 1664 (Book 5 P. 417) and as "Colonel" Thomas Lygon he patented 1468 acres in 1672 (Book 6 P. 425). As Thomas Ligon, senior, he was granted 340 acres in 1672 (Book 6 P. 447).
Col. Ligon made his will the 10th day of January 1675. This perished in the destruction of the Henrico records. We know the date because of a law suit instituted against his grandson William in 1740 (Tyler Vol. I, P. 118). This suit states that his eldest son was William, second son Richard, other two Thomas and Hugh.
He married Mary, daughter of Captain Thomas Harris of Henrico, for in 1691 Mrs. Mary Lygon, Sr. conveyed to her sons, Richard and Hugh, 200 acres in Curles, formerly granted to her father Captain Thomas Harris and devised to her. The Harris connection is further proven by the fact that Thomas Harris, brother of Mrs. Mary Harris Lygon, Sr., in his will June 2, 1679, bequeathed horses and colts to his "cozen" (nephew) Richard Lygon. Also on November 1, 1679 Mrs. Mary Lygon, Sr. deposed that she and her brother Harris had agreed that Harris should hold the surveyor's place until her son came of age. Mrs. Mary Lygon, according to a deposition, was born in 1625. Her will was probated in Henrico Feb. 1st, 1703-04, as follows:

Henrico Book 1697-1704 Page 365-7.
Probated February 1, 1703-04.
(Extract from will).

501

K 203
COLONEL
THOMAS LYGON

Colonel Thomas Lygon, who came to the Virginia colony in the early 1640s from Worcestershire, England, patented several large parcels of land on the north bank of the Appomattox River in an area known as The Cowpens, near Mount My Lady, which was then part of Henrico County. It is likely that he lived in this area with his wife Mary Harris and their five children. Lygon served in the House of Burgesses from Henrico County in 1656, as a colonel in the county militia, and as surveyor of the county until his death in 1675.

Lygon/Ligon

This Lygon line connects back to:
the Kings of France
the Kings of Spain
the Kings of Portugal
Charlemagne, the first Holy Roman Emperor
The Merovingian Dynasty, which preceded Charlemagne
and the Kings of most other European nations

Birth-Death	Lygon Ancestors
1623-1675	Lt. Col. Thomas Ligon's father was Thomas Lygon, who married Elizabeth Pratt
1560-1626	His father was Thomas Lygon of Elliston, who married Frances Dennis
1508-1567	His father, William Lygon of Madresfield, Esquire, married Eleanor Dennis
1474-Unknown	Her father, Sir William Dennis, married Anne Berkeley
ca 1497-1562	Her father, Sir Maurice 3rd Lord Berkeley, married Isabel Meade
Abt 1396-1452	His father, Sir James "The Just" de Berkeley, 1st Lord Berkeley, married Isabel Mowbray
1366-1399	Her father, Sir Thomas Mowbray, 1st Duke of Norfolk, married Elizabeth FitzAlan
1338-1375	His father, John 4th Lord Mowbray, married Elizabeth de Segrave
1315-1353/1320-1399	Her father, John 4th Baron de Segrave, married Margaret Plantagenet, Duchess of Norfolk
1300-1338	Her father, Thomas of Brotherton, Prince of England, Earl of Norfolk, married Alice Hayles
1239-1307/1279-1317	His father was Edward I, (Longshanks) King of England, who married Princess Marguerite (daughter of Philippe III, King of France)
1207-1272	His father was Henry III, King of England, who married Eleanor of Provence
1199-1216	His father was John I, King of England, who married Isabella d'Angoulême.
1133-1189	His father was Henry II, King of England, who married Eleanor Duchess of Aquitaine.
1152-1212/1102-1167	His father was Geoffrey Plantagenet, Duke of Normandy, Count of Anjou & Maine, who married Matilda (Maud) Empress Of Germany. Her grandparents were **William the Conqueror** and his wife Matilda of Flanders and **King Malcolm III** of Scotland and **Margaret of Atheling.**
1100-1135/1080-1118	Her father was Henry I, King of England (son of William the Conqueror, the 1st Norman King of England), who married Edith of Scotland(she changed her name from Edith to Matilda)
1031-1093/ca1045-1093	Her father was Malcom III Canmore, King of Scotland, who married Margaret of Atheling of Scotland.
1018-1057	Her father was Edward "Atheling", who married Agatha of Kiev
Reigned April – Nov 1016 -	His father was Edmund II "Ironside", King of England, last King of the Saxon House of Wessex, who married Ealdgyth

7 Generations from Charles Mastin Pearson to Thomas Ligon

Generation 1

Charles Mastin Pearson: born 2 Apr 1832; died 5 Mar 1893. Buried in Millerville Cemetery, Erath Co., Texas.

Generation 2 (Parents)

Doctor Pearson: born 17 Apr 1787; married abt 1821; died abt 1833 in McMinn Co., Tennessee.
Lovice\Lovey (maiden name unknown): born 1808 in North Carolina.

Generation 3 (Grandparents)

Sherwood Pearson: born abt 1743 in Virginia; married 3 Sep 1770 in Charlotte Co., Virginia; died 28 Oct 1816 in Pittsylvania Co., Virginia.
Elizabeth Ligon: born abt 1749 in Charlotte Co., Virginia; died 25 Oct 1826 in Pittsylvania Co., Virginia.

Generation 4 (Great Grandparents)

Charles Pearson: born 8 Aug 1714 in New Kent Co., Virginia; married 1737; died bef Nov 1758.
Rebecca Walton: born 20 May 1720 in New Kent Co., Virginia; died 1789.

Thomas Ligon: born 7 Feb 1725 in Bristol Parish, Henrico Co., Virginia; died aft 1787 in Charlotte Co., Virginia.
Ann (maiden name unknown)

Generation 5 (2nd Great Grandparents)

Unknown Pearson and wife

Robert Walton: born abt 1690 in York Co, Virginia; married 1715 in Essex Co, Virginia; died before 5 Mar 1733/4 in New Kent Co., Virginia.

Francis Sherwood: born 1697 in Essex County, Virginia; died 10 Mar 1780 in New Kent Co., Virginia.

Matthew Ligon: born 1682 in Henrico Co., Virginia; married 1710 in Virginia; died abt 1764 in Virginia.
Elizabeth Anderson: born bef 1689 in Charles City Co., Virginia; died abt 1740 in Virginia.

Generation 6 (3rd Great Grandparents)

Edward Walton: born 1645 in York Co., Virginia; married 20 Oct 1672; died bef 1737 in New Kent Co., Virginia.

Unknown

Mr. Sherwood: born 20 Mar 1667/8 39.
Mrs. Sherwood: born 6 Aug 1672; died 7 Nov 1746.

Richard Ligon: born abt 1657 in Henrico Co., Virginia; married 1679 in Henrico Co., Virginia; died 1724 in Henrico Co., Virginia.
Mary Worsham: born abt 1659.

James Anderson: born bet 1663 and 1668 in Charles City Co., Virginia.
Elizabeth (surname thought to be Thweat)

Generation 7 (4th Great Grandparents)

Thomas Ligon: born 11 Jan 1623/4 in Sowe, England; married 1650 in Henrico Co., Virginia; died 16 Mar 1675/6 in Henrico Co., Virginia.
Mary Harris: born 1620 in Henrico Co., Virginia; died 1703/4 in Henrico Co., Virginia.

William Worsham: born in 1619 in England. He married Elizabeth Littlebury in Charles City Co., Virginia. He died in 1661 in Henrico Co., Virginia.
Elizabeth Littleberry: born in 1623 in Henrico Co., Virginia. She died on 9/23/1678 in the Bermuda Hundred, Henrico Co., Virginia.

Reynard Anderson: born abt 1640; married 1662 in Charles City Co., Virginia.
Elizabeth Skiffen: born abt 1640; died abt 1694 in Charles City Co., Virginia.

Lygon Ancestral Family Home

Shown below is the castle belonging to the Lygon Family called Madresfield. The original Great Hall, built in the 12th century, stands at the core of this building. In 1593 Madresfield Court was rebuilt, replacing a 15th-century medieval building. It was again remodeled in the 19th century to resemble a moated Elizabethan house, with the result that it contains 136 rooms. The chapel was designed by the architect Philip Charles Hardwick and sumptuously decorated in the Arts and Crafts style by Birmingham Group artists including Henry Payne, William Bidlake and Charles March Gere.

Distinguished collections of furniture, art, and porcelain are housed at Madresfield, which was rated by Sir Simon Jenkins among the 50 best in his book on 1,000 historic houses. The house is managed by the Elmley Foundation, a British registered charity.

*Colonel Ligon's land was situated near **Malvern Hills**, where one of the famous battles of the Civil War was fought. He gave this name to the Hills, as the noted **Malvern Hills** of England was near Madresfield, Worcestershire".*

Colonel Thomas Ligon was the Royal Surveyor of Henrico Co., VA and a Lt Colonel in the British Army. He came to this country around 1640 with his kinsman William Lord Berkeley, the Royal Governor of Virginia. It should be noted that in England the surname of Ligon is spelled Lygon.

Malvern Hills

Of England

superscribed
ffor my honoured ffriend
Mr. Thomas Stegge.
(Recorded May 21, 1658)."

It is without doubt that Col. Thomas Lygon, the founder of the Ligon family in the new world, came over to Virginia with Governor Berkeley in 1641/2. The close association of the Lygons and Berkeleys in England was continued in Virginia. Richard[10] Lygon, brother of Thomas[10], in his will in 1662 leaves his property to his cousin, Edward Berkeley, because he had stood security for his debts to Henry Killegrew.

Governor Berkeley not only appointed Colonel Thomas[10] Lygon, County Lieutenant, but he also made him surveyor of Henrico County, a lucrative office in that day and time.

Thomas Lygon, died April 10, 1507.

Sir William Lygon, 1501-1567.

Lady Eleanor (Dennis) Lygon,
wife of Sir William Lygon.

Photos shown are from "*The Ligon Family & Connections*" Book

Thomas Harris and Adri (Gurgany*)

Parents of Mary Harris Ligon

Thomas Harris was born about 1586 in England. He came to America in 1611 aboard the ship "Prosperous" with Sir Thomas Dale. He no doubt participated in establishing the settlement of Henricus, named for Henry, Prince of Wales, the eldest son of King James I of England. Thomas Harris served in the militia and was promoted to Captain during the Indian uprising of 1622. He served in the House of Burgesses in 1623, 1624 and 1647. His land ownership was in excess of 2,500 acres.

Thomas Harris was a Captain in the Charles City regiment in 1623, against the Indians, and was second in command to Captain Thomas Osborne in an expedition in 1627. He served as a member of the House of Burgesses from Charles City County in 1623-24, and again from Henrico in 1639-47. A Captain Nathaniel Butler wrote a pamphlet entitled *"The Unmasking of Virginia"* and presented same to the King. This pamphlet reflected upon the officials of the King's administration in Virginia. The House of Burgesses undertook to reply to it, and presented a document entitled, *"'The Answer to an Information Presented unto your Majesty',* by Captain Nathaniel Butler entitled 'The Unmasking of Virginia'." Thirty-four members of the House Burgesses signed it, and among them was Thomas Harris, who spelled his name "Harries." (Burgess Journals, Vol. 1)

He received a grant of 750 acres in Henrico, "within Diggs Hundred, November 11, 1635 (Nugent's Abstracts, p. 304), Southward upon land of Edward Gurgany, Northward upon land of Joane Harris, his wife, West upon the river and East into the woods." This land was re-granted to him with the addition of 70 acres for the adventure of his first wife Adria, as her name does not appear in the first grant. This grant was as follows: "Capt. Thomas Harris 820 acres, Henrico Co., February 25, 1638, (Nugent's Abstracts, p. 615), commonly known as the Long Field, beg at a creek over against Capt. Martin, E.S.E towards Bremo, W.N.W. upon the main river. Due as follows: 100 acres for his own personal adventure, 100 acres for personal adventure of his first wife Adry, as being Ancient Planters in the time of Sir Thomas Dale, and 620 acres for the transportation of William Purnell, John Godfrey, John Searle, Thomas Kean, Richard Mascall, Nath. Moore, John Edwards, Ann Ridley, William Jones, Thomas Morgan, Wm. Jones and 2 Negroes.

He received another grant of 400 acres, which was bequeathed by Anne Gurganey, widow of Edward Gurganey (*Gourgainy) who came to Virginia in 1608, ahead of his family, in order to prepare a home for them. He was listed among the gentlemen, and one of Argall's associates in settling Argall's Gift or Town, which he and Thomas Pawlett represented in the Convention and Assembly of 1619, as did his wife, as shown in a patent to Captain Thomas Harris as follows: "Same to Capt. Thomas Harris, July 12, 1637, (Nugent's Abstracts, p. 438). Confirmation. *'Due unto the sd. Capt. Harris as followeth: 400 acres being granted to Edward Gurganey by order of Court, bearing date October 1, 1617, from the late Treasurer and Company and bequeathed by Anne Gurganey widdowe and relict of the said Edward Gurganey to the said Thomas Harris, as by her last Will, bearing the date the 11th of February A.D. 1619-20, appeareth."*

Curles Neck Plantation—Curles Neck Farm

In November of 1635, a year after the formal designation of Henrico County as one of 8 shires (or counties) in the Virginia Colony, a land patent for 750 acres (3.0 km^2) was granted to Captain Thomas Harris, who had apparently served under Sir Thomas Dale. The tobacco farm was referred to by early settlers as "Longfield", but soon thereafter became known as Curles Neck. Captain Harris served in the House of Burgesses at Jamestown as a Burgess for Curles Neck.

Curles Neck Plantation (also known as **Curles Neck Farm**) is located between State Route 5 and the north bank of the James River in the Varina District of Henrico Co., Virginia. One of the great James River Plantations, Curles Neck has remained in active use for almost 400 years and remains a privately owned working farm which is not currently open to the public.

As "Curles Neck Farm", a 5600 acre property was listed on the U.S. National Register of Historic Places in 2009.

"Of particular interest are the ruins found during the excavations at Curles Neck in eastern Henrico along the James. Archaeologists uncovered the Thomas Harris house foundation, one of the oldest homes found in Virginia dating between 1635-1654. Thomas Harris served as Burgess for Curles Neck. The archaeologists noted that the framing posts of this house sat in the full basement and some were enclosed by bricks which was unique in the Chesapeake area. A large centrally located chimney suggests that there was a lobby entrance. Built later in the early 1700's, adjacent to this structure, was the home of Nathaniel Bacon, the leader of the rebellion against the English authorities. Landscape features include intricate terraces and traces of underground tunnels down to the James River which could be used as an escape route from potential Indian invasions." *(Inventory of Early Architecture County of Henrico, Virginia)*

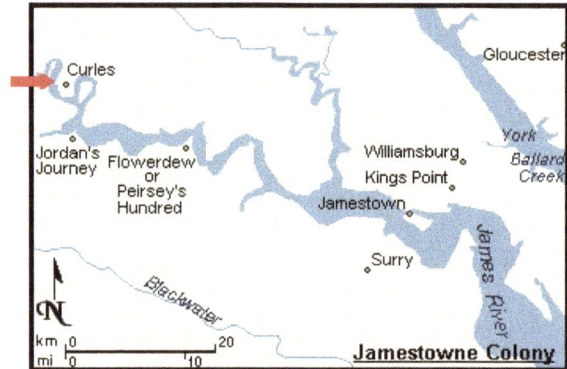

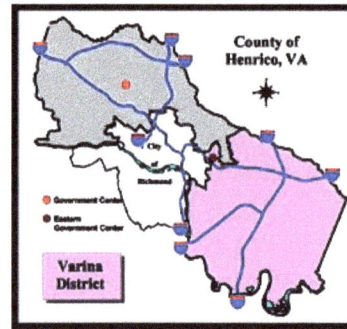

Below is a "Muster" list of the early inhabitants of Virginia, showing Thomas Harris, age 38 having arrived in Virginia with wife Adria, age 23 and kinswoman, Ann Woodlase, age 7 in 1620.

MUSTERS OF THE INHABITANTS IN VIRGINIA. 203

Neck-of-Land
Charles Cittie   The MUSTER of THOMAS HARRIS

THOMAS HARRIS aged 38 yeares in the *Prosperous* in May
ADRIA his wife aged 23 yeares in the *Marmaduke* in November 1621
ANN WOODLASE theire kinswoman aged 7 yeares
                    Servant's
ELIZABETH   aged 15 yeares in the *Margrett & John* 1620

The MUSTER of JOHN PRICE

JOHN PRICE aged 40 yeares in the *Starr* in May
ANN his wife aged 21 yeares in the *Francis Bonaventure* August 1620
MARY a Child aged 3 Months

The MUSTER of HUGH HILTON.

HUGH HILTON aged 36 yeares in the *Edwine* in May 1619

The MUSTER of RICHARD TAYLOᴿ

RICHARD TAYLOR aged 50 yeares in the *Mary Margrett* September 1608
DOROTHY his wife aged 21 yeares in the *London Marchant* May 1620
MARY theire Child aged 3 months.
                Servant's
CHRISTOPHER BROWNE aged 18 yeares in the *Dutie* in May 1620

COL THOMAS LIGON

He was born in England and came to Virginia about. 1641. He died in 1675. He married **Mary Harris, daughter of Thomas Harris. Mary is descended from Edward III, King of England, and thus from William the Conqueror, through Lionel Plantagenet, Duke of Clarence** and his daughter **Phillippe**, who **married. Edward Mortimer**, *Earl of March, and their daughter* **Elizabeth**, who **married Sir Henry Percy**, the famous Hotspur of Shakespeare's "Henry IV".

We descended through the Percy and later the Harris lines for 12 generations.

Still, when you read of Hotspur, or Robert Spencer, or Maude of Pembroke, or even **poor King Richard**, *to whom we are related through Dorothy Walgrove and Hugh Dudley, it makes history a little more personal in that these were real people who had an important part in bringing you here. That is the main purpose of this discussion of the Harris Branch of the family.* **Note**: Above was taken from *"The Ligon Family & Connections"*.

CHART VI. PERCY — HARRIS — LIGON.

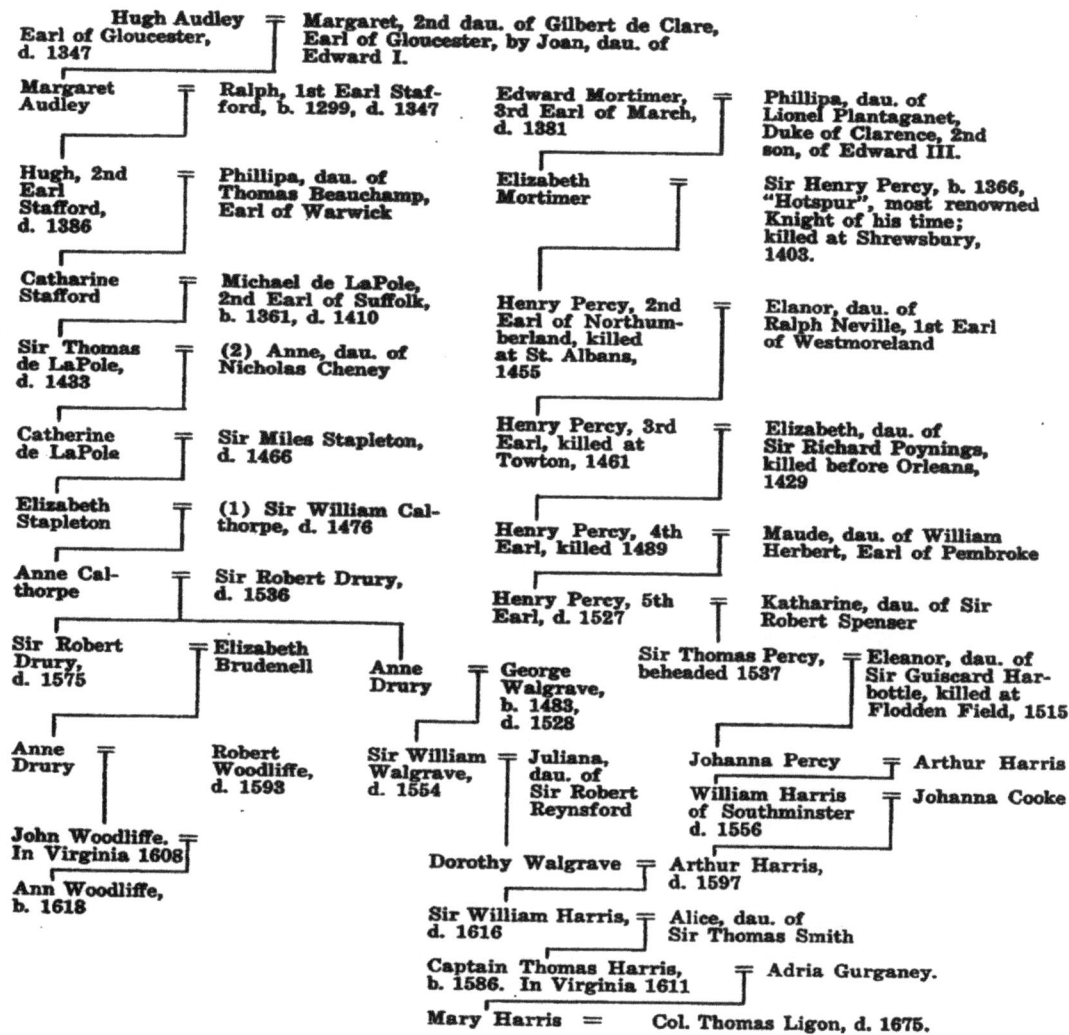

Hugh Audley Earl of Gloucester, d. 1347 = Margaret, 2nd dau. of Gilbert de Clare, Earl of Gloucester, by Joan, dau. of Edward I.

Margaret Audley = Ralph, 1st Earl Stafford, b. 1299, d. 1347

Edward Mortimer, 3rd Earl of March, d. 1381 = Phillipa, dau. of Lionel Plantaganet, Duke of Clarence, 2nd son, of Edward III.

Hugh, 2nd Earl Stafford, d. 1386 = Phillipa, dau. of Thomas Beauchamp, Earl of Warwick

Elizabeth Mortimer = Sir Henry Percy, b. 1366, "Hotspur", most renowned Knight of his time; killed at Shrewsbury, 1403.

Catharine Stafford = Michael de LaPole, 2nd Earl of Suffolk, b. 1361, d. 1410

Sir Thomas de LaPole, d. 1433 = (2) Anne, dau. of Nicholas Cheney

Henry Percy, 2nd Earl of Northumberland, killed at St. Albans, 1455 = Elanor, dau. of Ralph Neville, 1st Earl of Westmoreland

Catherine de LaPole = Sir Miles Stapleton, d. 1466

Henry Percy, 3rd Earl, killed at Towton, 1461 = Elizabeth, dau. of Sir Richard Poynings, killed before Orleans, 1429

Elizabeth Stapleton = (1) Sir William Calthorpe, d. 1476

Henry Percy, 4th Earl, killed 1489 = Maude, dau. of William Herbert, Earl of Pembroke

Anne Calthorpe = Sir Robert Drury, d. 1536

Henry Percy, 5th Earl, d. 1527 = Katharine, dau. of Sir Robert Spenser

Sir Robert Drury, d. 1575 = Elizabeth Brudenell

Anne Drury = George Walgrave, b. 1483, d. 1528

Sir Thomas Percy, beheaded 1537 = Eleanor, dau. of Sir Guiscard Harbottle, killed at Flodden Field, 1515

Anne Drury = Robert Woodliffe, d. 1593

Sir William Walgrave, d. 1554 = Juliana, dau. of Sir Robert Reynsford

Johanna Percy = Arthur Harris

William Harris of Southminster d. 1556 = Johanna Cooke

John Woodliffe. In Virginia 1608

Ann Woodliffe, b. 1618

Dorothy Walgrave = Arthur Harris, d. 1597

Sir William Harris, d. 1616 = Alice, dau. of Sir Thomas Smith

Captain Thomas Harris, b. 1586. In Virginia 1611 = Adria Gurganey.

Mary Harris = Col. Thomas Ligon, d. 1675.

137

Longley, Campbell and Bodine Families

LONGLEY FAMILY

Campbell

Le Boudin

Joel Longley and Nancy Bodine Longley
Parents of Elizabeth Longley Pearson

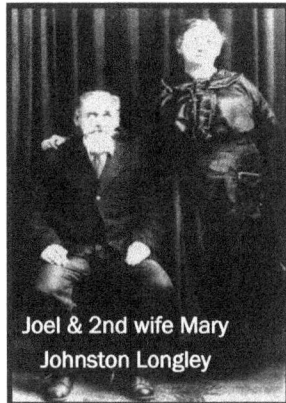

Joel & 2nd wife Mary Johnston Longley

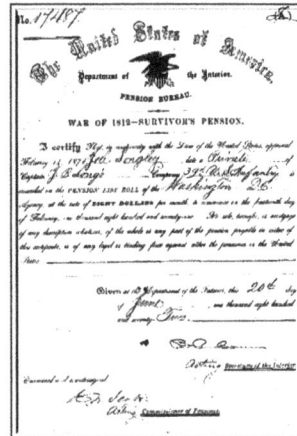

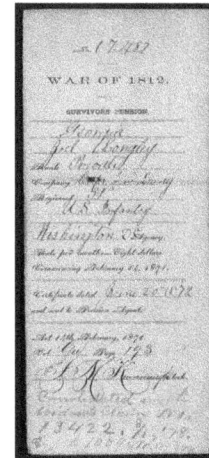

JOEL LONGLEY was a son of William and Mary Ann Bodine Longley.

Joel was born on 1 Sep 1791 at Rockbridge, Rockbridge Co., Virginia; he was referred to in his mother's widow Revolutionary War pension application as "2nd son," and states the date as 22 Nov 1845 in his sworn statement in Polk Co., Tennessee.

He married Nancy Bodine, daughter of Francis Bodine and Winifred (Young?) Bodine, on 26 December 1815 at Sentreville, Fairfax Co., Virginia. His first wife Nancy's name, date, and place of marriage is in his War of 1812 Pension application. Sentreville (Centerville) is now in Fairfax Co., Virginia.

He married Mary "Polly" Johnston in December 1835. His second wife and date of marriage was also stated in War of 1812 pension application.

He married Jane P. Lovelady on 13 Dec 1871 in Catoosa Co., Georgia; his third wife's name was taken from a Daughters of the American Revolution application. Joel died on 23 Feb 1877 at Ringgold, Catoosa Co., GA, at age 85.

Joel and Nancy Bodine were Baptist church members included 1818, as Joel Langley and Nancy Langley. They were members of the Forks

of the Little Pigeon Baptist Church in Sevier Co., Tennessee before 1823. The minutes of this Church show that both had apparently been removed from fellowship, but they subsequently joined another church and were restored to fellowship and given letters of dismission: Nancy in June 1823 and Joel in November of 1824.

The family was recorded in the 1830 Census of McMinn County, Tennessee on November 28, 1839, in Polk County, Tennessee. Polk was created from McMinn and Bradley Counties. Joel appears there in the census of the following year as he does in 1850. By 1860, he had relocated to Catoosa County, Georgia. That is where he found his third wife. He had two daughters by his second marriage. Following his death, his widow filed for a widow's pension. She furnished information on Joel's previous marriages from the family bible. His widow, Jane Lovelady, was still living there in 1880.

Joel and Nancy had the following children: Hannah, Joel Young, Elizabeth and Andrew William

Joel and Mary Johnston his second wife had the following children: Matilda and Nancy.

139

Joel began military service in 1813 in the War of 1812 as a private in Captain John B. Long's Company, 39th U. S. Infantry Regiment.

He enlisted on 18 November 1813 at Jennen's Creek, Jackson County, TN as a private along with his brother Joseph. Joel witnessed Joseph's death and gave his statement to that effect in his War of 1812 pension declaration. He ended military service on 17 Nov 1814 at Fort Montgomery, Mississippi Territory; honorably discharged, according to statement in Joseph Longley's bounty warrant application.

*The **39th United States Infantry** was a regiment of the regular Army. It was authorized on January 29, 1813 and recruited in East by Col. Williams Tennessee. It was commanded by Colonel John Williams, who had previously led the Mounted Volunteers of East Tennessee. On December 31, 1813 Major-General Thomas Pinckney ordered the regiment to join Andrew Jackson's force countermanding orders that had been sent from General Flournoy at New Orleans who wanted them there, thus providing a disciplined core and strategic resupply for his command which was down to about 75 men eating roots and acorns. The historian Henry Adams speculated that, without this regiment, Jackson would have fared no better in 1814 than he had the previous year. At the Battle of Horseshoe Bend, Jackson placed the regiment, (because they were the best-trained soldiers he had) in the center of his assault force. Consequently, the 39th suffered significant casualties, 20 killed and 52 wounded, and those figures are disputed. Col. Williams reported to Secretary of War Armstrong that "one half of the officers and one sixth of the troops of the 39th engaged in the battle of Tohopeka are among the killed and wounded. The officers remaining with the regiment fit for duty are insufficient for ordinary camp duty." *War information taken from:* "Regimental Histories of Tennessee Units during the War of 1812" and "Lineage And Honors Information, 7th Infantry (Cottonbalers)".

United States Army Center of Military History.

NANCY BODINE was born about 1797, Manassas, Loudoun/Fairfax Co., Virginia. She died September 13, 1835, McMinn Co., Tennessee.

Her parents were Francis Bodine and wife Winifred, last name unknown. She was married December 26 1815, in Centerville, Fairfax Co., Virginia, to Joel Longley (son of William Longley and Mary Ann Bodine).

She was given one dollar per her father's will. Her married name is given as Langly, but it should have been Longley. There is a marriage record where she and Joel Longley were married. Nancy's mother was Joel's first wife Winifred (last name unknown, but thought to be Young).

The basis for consideration of Winifred's surname is due to the Bible of Catherine Longley, wife of Joel Young Longley, brother of were the children of Francis and first wife,

Nancy Bodine

Elizabeth Longley Pearson. Joel and Elizabeth Longley, whose mother was Winifred.

Joel and Catherine had only one son, James Walton, who was born 29 December 1861. James died 24 June 1882 and his father, Joel Young Longley died 23 July 1888.

Catherine was left in Sand Mountain, Alabama with no family. I was contacted by the daughter of a neighbor who had stored Catherine's Bible. The family, who were neighbors, had been given it after Catherine's death. This family had continued to keep the Bible for many, many years. The daughter contacted me and as I was the only distant relative she could locate mailed it to me. The Bible is old and worn. It was given to Catherine as a Christmas gift from her son in 1878 and I'm sure was very precious to her.

William C Longley and Mary Ann Bodine Longley
Parents of Joel Longley

William was the son of Joseph Longley and unknown wife. He was born between 1761 and 1764 in the New Jersey Colonies. He served in the American Revolutionary War under General Layette in Yorktown and served as a prison guard.

William was in Sevier Co., Tennessee in 1800 and listed in the 1840 Polk Co., TN census.

Not much is known about Mary, but research has shown her to be the daughter of James Bodine.

Mary and Francis Bodine, Nancy's father, were siblings thus making Mary both mother-in-law and aunt to Nancy Bodine Longley.

William received a pension for his service in the Revolutionary War.

William Longley was a blacksmith and gunsmith. He received permission to go into the Cherokee Nation to set up his business of smithy and to "tarry in the said Nation for the term of three months 25 June 1803 Tennessee.

William Longley was born in the state of New Jersey, in the year 1761, the names of his parents are not stated.

While residing in Loudoun County, Virginia, with his father, William Longley enlisted sometime in October, 1780 and served as a private in Captain Thomas Humphries' company, under Major Armsted, Colonels Niswonger, George Eskridge and Summers, with the Virginia troops. He was in the battles of Burrells Ferry, Williamsburg and at the siege of Yorktown, and was discharged in February, 1782.

After the Revolution he lived a short while in Loudoun County, then lived in Shenandoah, Rockbridge and Washington Counties, Virginia, and in 1800 moved to Sevier County, Tennessee.

William Longley was allowed pension on his application executed June 3, 1833, then a resident of McMinn County, Tennessee.

The soldier, William Longley, married September 1, 1784 in Loudoun County, Virginia, Mary, her maiden name not stated. He died November 7, 1841 in Polk County, Tennessee, and his widow, Mary, died June 7 or 9, 1844 in Polk County, then aged about seventy-eight years.

The following children survived their mother—Jonathan born in 1788; Joel born September 1, 1791; James, Mercy, and Abigail, their ages not shown; and John C. born in 1806.

John C. Longley was living in Polk County, Tennessee in 1844 and then stated that he was the youngest child of William and Mary Longley. William T. Patterson and his wife, Abigail (formerly Abigail Longley), were in Catoosa County, Georgia in 1854. Mrs. Etha Burk, sister of the widow, Mary Longley, was seventy-three years of age in 1854, at that time in Catoosa County, Georgia.

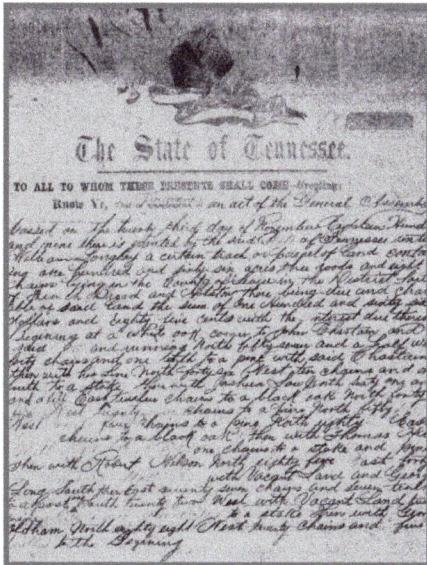

The State of Tennessee.

TO ALL TO WHOM THESE PRESENTS SHALL COME

Land grant No. 1040 issued to William Longley containing 166 acres in Sevier Co., Tennessee. Granted to him on 23 November 1809 and recorded on 12 May 1810. This land was given to him for his service in the Revolutionary War.

William Longley home in Sevier County, Tennessee before it was torn down

Revolutionary Pension Application of William Longley

Declaration In Order to Obtain the Benefit of the Act of Congress Passed June 7, 1832— State of Tennessee, County of McMinn on the 3rd Day of June_Personally Appeared in Open Court, Before the Justice of the County Court of said County, William Longley, A Resident of said County and State Aged About seventy-two Years, Who Being First Duly Sworn According to Law, Doth, On His Oath, Make the Following Declaration, in Order to Obtain the Benefit of the Act of Congress, Passed June 7, 1832. That He Entered the Service of the United States Under the Following Named Officers, and Served as Herein Stated.

He entered the service as a drafted man, in the militia of the State of Virginia, in the month of October, 1780, as well as he now recollects, in Loudoun County in said State, where he then resided with his father, -- under the siege of Major Armstead -- whose Christian name is not recollected -- Captain Thomas Humphries, Lieutenant John Bartlett. There were about 700 troops from said County of whom declarant was one, and he thinks they were called light infantry. There soldiers were marched from Loudoun County to Williamsburg in Virginia where they were stationed in the barracks for several months, and from whence portion of our men were detached to hold the British forces under Arnold, in check.

After being stationed here some months -- declarant does not recollect the precise time -- the British forces, landed at Burrell's ferry, at the mouth of James River, where about 200 of our men and declarant one of them, were stationed. We stood our ground and fired upon the enemy until our cartridges were exhausted, each man of us having fired near 30 rounds, when we were so far outnumbered that we had to retreat. We retreated to Williamsburg, 6 miles from the above named ferry, and on reaching there all our troops marched in and occupied our barracks that night. We had retreated only a mile or two into the woods from whence after night set in we marched back to town and attacked the enemy, drove in their pickets, and fired on them until outnumbered and drove from the field.

Next morning we were marched for Richmond, and on the same day the enemy left Williamsburg, crossed James River at Jamestown, and marched up the country. Near the same time that we got to Richmond the enemy arrived at Manchester on the opposite side of the river, and commenced destroying property and burning the large quantity of Tobacco stored there. We were stationed on Chuck's Hill. When the British appeared a part of our men were stationed on the bank of the river to prevent them crossing, and if they had attempted it they would have met with a warm reception as we were very hungry and greatly incensed at them. We had but one field piece, a six pounder, and it was placed on the hill before mentioned, and leveled against the enemy, and its effects told so well amongst them that they were quickly induced to leave off their depredations and quit the place. The enemy left Manchester and pursued their course still further up the country, and after some time turned their course and marched to Yorktown.

Declarant and his comrades were stationed at Richmond, as he thinks, about six weeks, when they were marched from thence and joined the army under Gnl. Lafayette at Yorktown on the Gloucester side of the river. About this time or shortly after, the siege was formed, as the army under Washington shortly arrived. Declarant was at this time constantly engaged in working on the entrenchments and other works that were going on.

During the siege declarant was in several skirmishes with portion of the enemy. On one occasion after night, 500 of the Virginia troops, declarant one of them, with 500 of the French under the command of Lafayette were marched to make a breach through the enemy's works on the Gloucester side, another detachment having made an attack on the other side. Declarant recollects getting so near the enemy's works that he put his hand upon them, and looking up saw the tar barrels placed on the breast works to be lighted in the event of an attack.

The firing having ceased on the York side, we were ----------, the enemy having discovered us, and opened their guns upon us as they fought but their balls went far above our heads.

Declarant was one of the troops forming the hollow square into which the prisoners were marched when Cornwallis surrendered. The prisoners taken on the Gloucester side were marched to Winchester in Virginia, declarant being one of their guard. These prisoners were guarded at Winchester three months, as declarant thinks, when they were marched to Fredericks town in Maryland, where declarant was discharged in February, as well as he recollects, 1782. Declarant cannot recollect the precise time he served; he will set it down at fifteen months, as he is confident he served that long.

Declarant was <u>born in the State of New Jersey in the year 1761</u>, as he was informed by his parents -- has no record of his age, nor has he ever seen one as well as he recollects. He resided in Loudoun County a short time after the war, then in Shenandoah, then in Rockbridge; then in Washington all in Virginia, whence he removed to Sevier County Tennessee in 1800, where he resided until he came to the county of McMinn Tennessee, where he now resides. He received a written discharge from the service in Shepherdstown, Va. from Col. Niswonger but it is lost, and he knows not where it is. James D. Sewell, a clergyman; John Grisham, George Long & Jackson Smith, are some of his present neighbors who can testify as to his veracity, and their belief of his services as a soldier of the Revolution. He hereby relinquishes every claim whatever to a pension or annuity except the present, and declares that his name is not on the Pension Roll of the Agency of any state.

Sworn to and subscribed the 3d day of June 1833
A. R. Turk, Clerk
William Longley

We James D. Sewell a clergyman residing in the county and state aforesaid, and John Grisham residing as aforesaid, hereby certify that we are well acquainted with William Longley who has subscribed and sworn to the above declaration; and we believe him to be 72 years of age; that he is reputed and believed in the neighborhood where he resides, to have been a soldier of the Revolution, and that we concur in that opinion. Sworn to and subscribed the 3d day of June 1833.

STATE OF TENNESSEE, POLK COUNTY, personally appeared before me, Andres R. Stephenson, an acting Justice of the Peace in and for the said county, **Joel Longley** and makes oath in due form of Law, that he is the Son of William and Mary Longley, deceased, late of Polk County, Tennessee, that his Said Father, was a Revolutionary pensioner up to the day of his death. Deponent further states that he was born on the first day of September (1791) Seventeen hundred and ninety-one. And ever since his first recollection his Said father and mother, William and Mary Longley, lived together as husband and wife up to the day of his death – Deponent further states that he is the Second Son of the Said William and Mary Longley, deceased and that Jonathan Longley is his eldest brother and that his Said parents William and Mary Longley always told the deponent that his Said brother Jonathan was Two years and Two months older than deponent.

Sworn to and subscribed before me this 22nd day of November 1845.
Joel Longley (S E A L)
A. P. Stephenson, Justice of the peace for Polk County.

STATE OF TENNESSEE, POLK COUNTY
I, James Parks Clerk of the County Court of Polk County, do certify that A. R. Stephenson Esquire whose signature appears to the foregoing certificate is and was at the time of signing the same an acting Justice of the peace for my county, duly commissioned and qualified according to Law.
Given under my hand and Seal of office in Benton this 22 day of November 1845.
James Parks, Clk.

Joseph Longley, Jr. and Wife
(Parents of William Longley)

Joseph was born about 1725 and died by 1810.

Information about Joseph Longley, Jr is very limited. We know from records where he lived, but not who he married.

Various documents give us a small time frame for Joseph:

- Joseph Longley, Jr. 'lives in Hopewell and was a soldier in the Jersey Regiment'. (1756)

- Joseph Longley, Jr and father, Joseph, Sr. 'lived in Pennsylvania'.(1763)

- They 'lived near Newman's Ferry - gone to Virginia. (1764)

We have learned from the Revolutionary War Pension Application of William Longley, son of Joseph, Jr., that from 1779 to 1781 William and his father were living in Loudoun Co. VA and were on the tax list in Cameron Parish. As of Oct 1780, Joseph was still in Loudoun Co., VA.

Joseph Langley/Longley, Sr. and Wife Mary Campbell
Parents of Joseph Longley, Jr.

Joseph, Sr. lived in Hunterdon Co., New Jersey, and was married by 1732 to Mary Campbell, who came from Monmouth Co. New Jersey. Their son Joseph Jr. and his son William Longley (Revolutionary soldier) were in Loudoun Co., Virginia, by 1764. Joseph Sr. was apparently the son of Thomas Langley, born 1686 of Gloucester Co., New Jersey, and Frances Woodward, and had moved from Gloucester Co. to Hunterdon Co. Thomas Langley, born 1686 was apparently the son of John Langley, born 1640 and died 1699 in Gloucester Co., New Jersey, leaving widow Susannah to sell the land he bought in 1687. No record to prove his children is found.

Joseph was a cordwainer (shoemaker), a genteel trade in a shop with 8-10 employees who each specialized in a different step of the shoemaking process. Shoes were both custom-made and ready-made imported from England until the Revolution cut off overseas trade. 'The founding steps of the earliest colony can be traced back to shoes. Captain John Smith's Jamestown settlement explorations were partly funded by the Worshipful Company of Cordwainers, London's shoemakers' guild,' Colonial Williamsburg's D. A. Shaguto says, 'The prestige of shoemakers only grew with the expanding colonies; every town needed accomplished cordwainers and they were heavily recruited in 17th century Virginia. In fact, in most 18th-century Colonial towns, shoe making and tailoring were the two largest shop keeping professions. Shoemaking was considered then a genteel trade. It didn't smell bad or make horrible noises.

Thomas Langley/Longley and Mary Chew
Parents of Joseph Longley

Thomas married Mary Chew about 1735. Mary was the daughter of Richard Chew and wife Frances Woodward. The Chew family is covered on page 158.

Frances Woodward was the daughter of Nathaniel Woodward and Margaret Jackson. She was apparently born about 1657, in Queens, Province of New York. Her date of death is uncertain, however she was still living in 1700 when a census was taken of the town of Flushing in Queens County.

John Campbell and Wife Charity (Last Name Unknown)
Parents of Mary Campbell

Joseph Longley, son of Thomas Langley and Mary Chew, married Mary Campbell. The closest date for their marriage is sometime before 1722. Mary was the daughter of John Campbell and wife Charity, last name unknown.

John Campbell was born about 1664 in Kintyre, Argyll, Scotland and Charity, was born about 1679 in Scotland. Argyll, Scotland was the seat of the Campbell clan.

The exact date and place of the birth of Charity his wife, has not been documented at this time. By 1716, John and Charity were married. Her name does not appear on any early documents.

John Campbell is thought to have sailed on the ship *Henry and Francis* to East Jersey from Leith, September 5th, 1685. He may have been banished to Jersey due to the Catholic/Protestant fighting going on in Scotland during this time. Banishment usually meant a person had to serve four years of bond service.

"In August 1683, David Barclay sent to East Jersey by the Ship Exchange, joint stock for his own and other proprietors advantage . . . servants were to remain four years . . . each servant to have 25 acres, the tradesmen among them 30 . . . other Scotsmen came at intervals, some of whom were Quakers and some Presbyterian . . . freedom of conscience being guaranteed by the proprietors".

Many of the early settlers were sent out, in the employ of the different proprietaries and land-holders, under such agreements as would afford them the benefits of the head-land grants for each individual brought into the province, fifty acres being allowed to each master of a family, and twenty-five acres for each person composing it, whether wife, child, or servant, each servant to be found three years, at the end of which time he or she was to be allowed to take up thirty acres on separate account.

Under this plan there was a shipment from Scotland in 1682, brought out by Rudyard and Groom,

and another the following year, on board the "Exchange," Capt. Peacock, which brought thirty-one men and women-servants under two overseers. This was but the beginning of an extensive traffic in servants, as the records of East Jersey show. Among the names mentioned as figuring in these importations we find Gawen Lawrie, William Haige, Thomas Pearson, William Dockwra, John Barclay, Robert Fullerton, John Campbell, Capt. Alexander Hamilton, David Mudie, Lord Neill Campbell, John Forbes, James Johnstone, George Keith, Charles Gordon, the Scotch proprietaries, etc.

Campbell's Brook (now Pleasant Run) was undoubtedly so named after John Campbell, the proprietor of the lands at its mouth, which he purchased in 1685. *("From Historical Notes of Judge Thompson.)*

By 1690, as says the Rev. H. G. Smith, the site of Matawan was occupied by a village of Scotsmen and known as New Aberdeen. Traditions, and the statement of Rev. Dr. John Woodhull in 1792 as to the date of the organization of the Scotch Presbyterian Church fixes it about 1692. If this be so, and it is thought it is, then the first organization of the old Scots meeting, in all probability was at New Aberdeen and not on the site of the meetinghouse of 1705.

". . . the return for the 100 acres on which the town of New Aberdeen stood, bears date some years after the actual settlement, in Secretary of State office in Trenton, Book 14, p. 438, "Surveyed and laid out for [a list which includes] . . John Campbell . . . granted to these persons by patent dated June 7, 1701."

In the **"The History of Somerset and Hunterdon Counties, 1881"** it was recorded that John Campbell had 1,874 acres of land on November 9, 1685. It would seem that if John came as a bond servant, he could not have accumulated this much land in so short a time period. Or, he was a very "crafty" Scotsman and never served as a bond servant but had personal funds to use.

By 1700 John along with other Scotsmen had settled in Matawan. In 1702-3 he was a witness for William Naughty's will using the (I.C.) marks. These marks help to identify this John Campbell from two other John Campbells in this general area of New Jersey.

John is named as a planter, in a deed for lands on Manalapan, conveyed by Campbell to another Scotsman named William Davidson (a carpenter) April 26th, 1695. This he also signed with his mark (I.C.). The witnesses to this deed were three Scotsmen, William Layn (Laing (?), John (I.H.) Oliphan, and Alan (A) Caldwell.

The boundary line between Monmouth and Middlesex was not perhaps, very well defined. At first account Perth Amboy had a number of Scotch among her citizens. One curious items is the will of Archibald Campbell, proved May 12th, 1702. After having given to Elizabeth Swan his goods and chattels, and having appointed John Campbell of Raritan River, his executor, he proceeded in his will to strike a balance sheet in the following account: "Rests due to me, Archibald Campbell:"

It is a fact not generally known at the present day that native Indians as well as negroes were at one time held in slavery in New Jersey. This is proved by occasional references to "Indian slaves" found in ancient records. Such an instance is found in the "Journal of the House of Representatives for the Province of Nova Cesarea, in the Second General Assembly and 1st Sessions, begun at Burlington this 13th day of Nov r, 1704," under date "Die Veneris, A.M. 24° g brl, 1704," as follows:

"*Ordered, that a Bill be Prepared & brought in for ye Speedy trying & Regulating of Negro & Indian Slaves; & y Mr. Hartshorn, Capt. Bown & do prepare and bring in ye same; And They Adjourned till 4 a Clock.*"

When John Campbell died, his wife Charity remarried George Davidson.

On 31 August 1731, the heirs of John Campbell completed a land sale begun before his death, whereby they sold land in Manatawny, Pennsylvania (land purchased from Samuel Bustil in 1716 and sold to Gershon Motto of Middletown, Monmouth County, New Jersey. This indenture (Phil Deeds, Liber F-1, 87) lists the following children together with the spouses of the married daughters. It also gives their residence in late April/early May of 1732. When they signed the release in their own right and did not have a guardian assigned it would indicates they were of age. Excerpts have been from this record as it is very lengthy: ***INDENTURE RELEASE OF PROPERTY OF JOHN CAMPBELL TO GERSHON MOTT BY***:

George Davidson and Charity, his wife, (widow of John Campbell) and his children: Walter Campbell, John Campbel, Margaret Campbell Parker, Joseph Longley and his wife Mary Campbell Longley, John Dimit and his wife Effie Campbell Dimit, Walker Wealson and his wife Jane Campbell Wealson , James Old and his wife Elizabeth Campbell Old, Priscilla Campbell, and Dorcas Campbell.

This Indenture made the second Day of October in the Year of our Lord One thousand seven hundred and thirty one Between George Davidson of the City of Philadelphia Cordwainer and Charity his wife, who was the wife of John Campbel late of Manhatawny in the County of Phildadelphia Yeoman deceas'd, Walter Campbel and Duncan Campbel, sons of the said John Campbel, Margaret Parker of Manhatawny, aforesaid Widow, one of the Daughters of the said John Campbel, Joseph Longley and Mary his Wife, another of the Daughters of the said John Campbel, John Dimit and Effa his wife, another of the Daughters of the said John Campbel, Walker Wealson and Jane his wife, another of the Daughters of the said John Campbel, James Old and Elizabeth his wife, another of the Daughters of said John Campbel, and Priscilla Campbel and Dorcas Campbel Spinsters, the other Daughters of the said John Campbel , of the one part and Gershon Mott of Middletown in the County of Monmouth in Eastern Division of the Province of the New Jersey Yeoman of the they hereby acknowledge themselves fully satisfied.

Other Part Witnesseth that they the said George Davidson and Charity his Wife, Walter Campbel, Duncan Campel, Margaret Parker, Joseph Longley and Mary his wife, John Dimit and Effa his Wife, Walker Wealson and Jane his wife, James Old and Elizabeth his wife, Priscill Campbel and Dorcas Campbel as well for in consideration of the sum of ten Pounds to them in Hand paid by the said Gershon Mott the Receipt whereof they do hereby acknowledge as of the sum of Twenty Pounds by him likewise paid unto the said John Campbel in his life Time wherewith

In Witness whereof the said Parties to these Presents have interchangeably set their Hands and Seals hereunto dated the Day and Year first above written.

> George Davidson (Seal)
> Charity Davidson her mark (Seal)
> Dorcus Campbell (Seal)
> Margaret W Parker her mark (Seal)
> Priscilla Campbell her mark (Seal)
> Walter Campbell (Seal)
> James Old his mark (Seal)
> Elizabeth E Old her mark (Seal)
> Duncan Campbel (Seal)
> Joseph Longley (Seal)
> Mary M Longley her mark (Seal)
> Walter Wilson (Seal)
> Jane Wilson (Seal)
> Epha Dimitt her mark (Seal)

Memorandum the first day of May, Anno Di 1732, before me Isaac Kerin, Esq one of his Majesties Justices of the Peace for the County of Hunterdon and Province of West New Jersey came the within named Joseph Longley and Mary his Wife and brought the within writing or conveyance which they acknowledged to be their deed and desired the same may be recorded as their deed according to law Witness my Hand and Seal the Day and Year aforesaid did Isaac Herin Seal___.

Listed were the children of John and Charity Campbell, their spouses and where they lived and the date they signed the document:

Heirs of JOHN CAMPBELL, yeoman, were listed:

George Davidson, cordwainer, and Charity his wife, who was the wife of John Campbell late of Manhatawny in the Co. of Philadelphia, deceas'd, signed 19 Apr 1732 Philadelphia.

Walter Campbell, signed 22 Apr 1732 Philadelphia
Duncan Campbell of Monmouth Co., NJ, signed and recorded 2 May 1732 Monmouth Co., NJ
Margaret Parker, widow, of Manhatawny, signed 22 Apr 1732 Philadelphia
Mary and husband Joseph Longley, signed 1 May 1732, Hunterdon Co., NJ and recorded as their deed
Effa and husband John Dimit, signed 24 May 1732, Province of New York
Jane and husband Walter Wealson/Wilson, signed 2 May, 1732 Monmouth Co., NJ and recorded as their deed
Elizabeth and husband James Old, signed 22 Apr 1732, Philadelphia
Priscilla Campbell, spinster, signed 22 Apr 1732, Philadelphia
Dorcas Campbell, spinster, was signed by her jurat: Penington Brockden, but no date found.

A record of Charity's death at this time not been located, but records indicate her second husband, George Davidson married again at a later date.

Speculation has been made that John Campbell's father was Walter Campbell. This is based on the naming pattern of that time in which the eldest son was named after the father's father.

Tartan of the Clan Campbell

The Ancient Campbell tartan is the same as Black Watch tartan, hardly surprising, since that illustrious regiment is a Campbell regiment, raised by the Duke of Argyll in 1739.

Francis Bodine and Winfried
Parents of Nancy Bodine Longley

FRANCIS BODINE was born 1768, probably in New Jersey. He came to Loudoun County, Virginia with his parents as a child in 1771 and remained there until 1796 when the part of the county in which he lived was added to Fairfax County. Having reached the age of 21 in 1789, he is first recorded separately on county tithe lists, but still in the household of his father. (In 1788, the Loudoun County tithe list places Francis Bodine in the age group 16-20 within the household of his father and in 1789, he is actually named, identified as aged 21 and over.)

On 22 December 1792, the Virginia General Assembly passed an act that required the formation of county militia companies and the enrollment of all able bodied male citizens over the age of eighteen. Incompliance, Francis Battalion, 57th Regiment Virginia Militia, Loudoun County. (Blincoe, Don. *Loudoun County, Virginia Militia Journals 1793-1829*, Iberian Pub. Co.: Athens, GA, 1993, p. 28.)

Francis was married first in Loudoun Co., Virginia about 1790, to Winifred, who with her husband, witnessed a deed in Loudoun County on 11 December 1795 (Loudoun County Deeds, W: 219-221). She died before the taking of the 1810 census in Fairfax County, and in 1830/1, in Sevier County, he married his second wife, Anna. Anna was born about 1794, survived her husband and was remarried on 6 January 1845 in Sevier County, to William Smith.

Sevier County, Tennessee

Francis Bodine purchased 50 acres of land in Sevier Co., Tennessee on 22 December 1821. The land document No. 258 surveyed on 22 February 1825 and recorded on 20 August 1825.

From 1796 to 1811, the Fairfax County personal property tax lists report Francis Bodine living in Truro Parish and from 1812 to 1816 in Fairfax Parish. In 1811, the county tax list reports Francis Burdine in possession of 186 acres of land. This is the only instance that land ownership on his part was reported. The General Index to Deeds for the period 1797-1841 records a sale from Francis Bodine to George Monroe (Deeds, CC-2- 250), but the actual deed book is lost. The Court Order Minute Books from 1798-1819 record only a Bill of Sale on 16 September 1800 from Francis Bodine to George Monroe and a suit filed by Israel Lacy, heard by the county court on 20 July 1803, directing Francis Bodine to pay.

In 1816 or 1817 he moved his large family to Sevier County, Tennessee, where his father had settled nearly two decades earlier. As a result of the loss of all county records for this time period, nothing is known of his activities in Sevier County. However, state records do show that on 22 December 1824 Francis Bodine was issued a 50 acre Tennessee Land Grant Entry on the waters of Flat Creek in Sevier County, adjoining the land of Joseph Manning, William Maples and Joseph Clark. The land was surveyed 22 Feb 1825 by Daniel Kerr, Surveyor for Sevier County. Wm. Maples and Nathaniel B. Barker were Chain Carriers.

A plat of these 50 acres was submitted to the General Assembly of Tennessee under file no. 32-3-1813-6. (Land Entry No. 258, Book 12: 395.) This land came into the possession of his widow upon his death.

Will of Francis Bodine

In the name of God, Amen.

I, Frances Bodine of the County of Sevier and State of Tennessee being weak in body, but of sound mind, blessed be God, knowing that it is appointed once for men to die, do this twelfth day of September in the year of our Lord one thousand Eight hundred and thirty-five, make this my last Will and testament, and for which I do

ordain and appoint my beloved wife Anna Bodine and Andrew Canatzer Executors. And first I recommend my soul to God that gave it and my body to be decently buried, and for my worldly goods which God has blessed me with: I do give and bequeath devise, as follows-

First I do give unto my beloved wife Anna Bodine all my original tract of land, house, goods & chattels to have and to hold during her widowhood or natural life, except one Bay mare, after another Season she is to be sold, and the money to go to the Estate. The said land after the decease of the said Anna Bodine is to fall to the two sons Frances & Wesly, and to be equally divided between the above named Boys Frances and Wesly Bodine.

I give and bequeath unto my beloved son James Bodine an Entry of fifty acres of land joining the old original tract. I do give and bequeath unto my beloved Daughter Lydia Maples one Dollar. I give to my beloved Daughter Nancy Langly one Dollar. I give to my beloved son Bowling Bodine two Dollars. I give to my beloved Daughter Charlotte Patterson one dollar. I give to my beloved Daughter Viney Maples one dollar. I give unto my beloved son John Bodine one dollar. I give unto my beloved Daughter Hannah Toby one dollar. I give and bequeath to my beloved Daughter Jane Bodine, one Bed and furniture and one heifer.

As witness hereunto I set my hand and seal date above written.

Frances (X) Bodine mark
In presence of Henry Houk, Daniel Layman

I certify the foregoing to be a true copy of the original Will of Frances Bodine Dec'd as Recorded in my Office this 8th June 1836.
I.A. Miller, Clerk of the County Court of S.C.

NOTE: The original will was lost in the destruction of the Sevier County courthouse in 1856, but a copy was re-filed in the 'Case of Calvin Clinton vs. Wm. Smith & others,' 25 October 1859 (Sevier Co Chancery Court).

James Bodine and Unknown Wife
Parents of Francis Bodine and Mary Ann Bodine Longley

JAMES BODINE was born about 1745 probably in Middlesex or Monmouth County, New Jersey. Although there is no direct record of his parentage, he is believed to have been a son of Francis and Abigail Bodine based upon a series of family naming patterns. These include naming children Francis (after his father) and Abigail (after his mother).

James Bodine married his first wife, whose name is unrecorded, about 1765 and came to Loudoun County, Virginia in late 1770 or 1771 in which year he is first identified on tax lists. County court records show his continuous residence in the county until 1791 in which year he is last named on a tax list. During his residency in Loudoun County, he appeared on many occasions before the county court involved in a variety of legal actions ranging from indebtedness to trespassing and the filing of petitions. In addition, the tax lists show James Bodine in possession of horses and cattle from 1782 on.

Land records make no reference to any land ownership on his part and it appears he probably leased whatever land was needed for the support of his family. He first is recorded in the Loudoun County Court Order Books on 11 April 1774 in a suit wherein Joseph Skelton Sr, for Joseph Skelton Jr, sued for a debt against James Bodine (Book F: 351). He is last mentioned on 10 September 1788 in the case of James Bodine assignee of Wm. Smith vs. Archibald Botts (Book L: 14).

In 1791 or 1792, he left Loudoun County and his whereabouts for the next twelve years are not known. James Bodine is recorded on the Loudoun County tax list of 1791, but not in 1792 or later. By 1803 he had settled near the French Broad River in Sevier County, Tennessee where he was later to be joined by his son Francis. (On 24 September 1803 Abigail Bodine was born 'on the French Broad River in East Tennessee' according

to the biography of her son, James B. Snow, published in Goodspeed's History of Tennessee, 1887. Francis Bodine arrived in 1816 or 1817 based upon tax lists for Fairfax County, Virginia from which location Francis had moved.)

Previous to that date he married his second wife, Sarah Russell, daughter of Daniel and Jemima Russell of Jefferson Co., Tennessee. James and Sarah Bodine lived on a plantation that her father subsequently devised upon her in his will of 14 September 1805 and which land came into her possession at his death the following month (Jefferson County Wills, 1: 261-63). This 29-acre tract was surveyed for James Bodine in 1807 and on 15 June 1810 he received title to it through an occupation land grant from the State of Tennessee, based upon an Act of the General Assembly of 23 November 1809 (East Tennessee Land Grant No. 1506).

On 24 April 1812, Sarah Burdine witnessed a bill of sale from Jemima Russell to Thomas Welch of a slave woman and her two children (Jefferson County Deeds, 1792-1814, p. 180).

There is no record of what became of James and Sarah Bodine as a result of a fire on 24 March 1856 that completely destroyed the Sevier County courthouse and its contents. Neither James nor Sarah Bodine appears in the 1830 Tennessee census; it is presumed that James Bodine had died long before that time as by this time he would have been in his 80.

Special Note: The information shown for the Bodine family was taken from Dave's Bodine Web site with his permission.

Francis Bodine and Wife Abigail
Parents of Francis Bodine

FRANCIS BODINE was born doubtless, on Staten Island, and crossed from there into New Jersey, settling at Cranbury, on the borders of Middlesex County, before 1745.

Cranbury, during the Revolution, frequently resounded with the tread of marching feet, and in 1778 the main body of the army spent the night of 26 June, the eve of the battle of Monmouth, at this place, which event was described by General Washington in his report to the Honorable Henry Laurens, President of Congress, under date of 1 July, 1778, in this manner:

"In the evening of the same day [26 June], the whole army marched from Kingston, where our baggage was left, with the intention to preserve a proper distance for supporting the advanced corps, and arrived at Cranbury early the next morning. The intense heat of the weather, and a heavy storm unluckily coming on, made it impossible to resume our march that day without great inconvenience and injury to the troops.
Our advanced corps, being differently circumstanced, moved from the position it had held the night before, and took post in the evening on the Monmouth Road, about five miles from the enemy's rear, in expectation of attacking them next morning on their march. The main body having remained at Cranbury, the advanced corps was found to be too remote, and too far upon the right, to be supported either in case of an attack upon or from the enemy, which induced me to send orders to the Marquis to file off by his left toward Englishtown, which he accordingly executed early in the morning of the 27th."

Information taken from Clute's History of Staten Island and New Jersey Archives, second series. Vol. ii. 286, 287.

In 1773, Francis acquired a tract of 20 acres from Amos Pharo at Tranquility Swamp and a part interest in another 22 acre piece. Also in that year, James Pharo made a quit claim to Francis Bodine, the III for five and a half acres on the Pappoose Branch.

On 1 November, 1775, Francis Bodine had some thirty acres of land surveyed in Tranquility Burlington County. Swamp, on Wading River, in Little Egg Harbor, Washington Township and moved to the vicinity with his three sons. The deed for this property is found in the Burlington County Deeds, Book M2, p. 335.

He died in Burlington County, probably at his home in Tranquility Swamp, Little Egg Harbor Township.

His first wife, Abigail, was the mother of all his children. She died between 1750 and 1754 probably in New Jersey. He later married Rachael Wilson in Middlesex County Jan 29, 1755. His four known children were baptized at Christ Church, Shrewsbury, Monmouth Co., New Jersey. In the *Annals of the Sinnott, Rogers, Coffin, Corlies, Reeves, Bodine and Allied Families*, by <u>Mary Elizabeth Sinnott, Josiah Granville Leach</u>" book, it also says he married Rachel Wilson, but she did not have the name of his first wife.

Sinnott says Francis was 'a farmer by occupation, an Episcopalian by religious conviction, and the founder of the Bodine families of Philadelphia and southern New Jersey' (p. 165).

Some of this information comes from an article on Judge Joseph Lamb Bodine in 'New Jersey. A History, Biographical & Genealogical Records,'1932.

His sons Joel, Francis and John appear to be the original Bodines of Burlington County, New Jersey.

Francis Bodine & Wife, Maria/Mary Dey
(Parents of James Bodine)

Our lineage continues through Francis, father of John Bodine.

Francis was probably born between 1690 and 1699. He was mentioned in his Brother John's will before he left for sea in 1707. Most likely he was named for his maternal grandfather Francis Bridon.

About 1717/1718, he married Maria Dey, daughter of James Hans Dey and wife Mary Molenaar.

He remained on Staten Island until at least 1736. In 1726, he was charged with an offence against the king. Rather than contend against the king, he confessed judgment and submitted to a fine' (Richmond County Court Records). On March 7, 1736, he witnessed to a deed at Charles Neck (Richmond County Deeds, Book D, p. 131). He then disappears from the records on Staten Island. He probably had moved to Cranbury, Middlesex County, New Jersey with his sons, Francis and Vincent, where he died. This information comes from the Mary Sinnott book, page 163.

He was born in Richmond County (Staten Island) around 1720 to 1725. Prior to 1745, he settled at Cranbury, on the border of Middlesex County, New Jersey. He had 30 acres of land surveyed in Tranquility Swamp on November 1, 1775, and on Wading River, Little Egg Harbor Township, and Burlington County. He died in Burlington County, probably at his home in Tranquility Swamp, Little Egg Harbor Township. His first wife, Abigail, was the mother of all his children. She died between 1750 and 1754 probably in New Jersey.

MARIA (MARY) DEY was one of two daughters of James and Mary Molenaar Dey. Her birth must be estimated based upon the birth of her son in 1719 and so may have occurred between 1695 and 1700, likely in Richmond County where her father was living at the time.

About 1717-1718, Mary married Francis Bodine as their first child, John, was baptized on 29 Nov. 1719 at the Port Richmond Dutch Reformed Church on Staten Island. Although they had other children, John was the only one baptized there. On 14 April 1723, Francois Bodin and Maria Dey were sponsors to the baptism of Johannes, son of Samuel Kierstede and Lydia Dey, and on 19 April 1724 Francois Bodin and Maria Dey were sponsors to the baptism of John, son of Thomas Greegs and Lena Dupuy.

In the will of her father, written 22 Oct. 1744, he makes the following bequest: "I give and bequeath to Mary, my Daughter [and] his heairs the forth pairt of what Estate I leave behind, after my lawful contracted debts is paid."

The fact that James Dey made a bequest to his daughter on 22 Oct. 1744 is the only indication that she was still living. There is otherwise no other known record of her. Her husband, Francis Bodine, was living 7 October 1758 when he was named in a State Island mortgage.

Middlesex Co. Will Book D, p. 348. The will proved 26 Nov. 1745. Therein, James Dey leave ¼ of his estate to his daughters Mary and Sarah and ½ to his (2nd) wife Margaret, the mother of 3 children, so noted in the will.

James Hans Dey was the son of Laurens Dyijs from Noorstrant. He was a laborer living in the Brouwersgracht, aged 26 years, and married Ytgie Jans from Amsterdam, age 18 years. This information was found in the Amsterdam Archives. Nordstrand is the island off shore from Husum in present day Schleswig-Holstein. Laurens' surname undoubtedly came from 'Deutsch', the German word for 'German'.

Laurens and his first wife had 3 children baptized in the New Amsterdam Dutch church: Margariet in 1639; Jan in 1642; and Hans in 1644.

Jean/John Bodine and Wife Esther Bridon

Parents of Francis Bodine

JEAN BODIN was born, it is said, in Medis, a village in the Canton of Saujon, District of Saintes, then located in the former French province of Saintonge, on 9 May 1645, based upon "a tradition universal in the family."

Esther was the daughter of Francois and Jeanne Susanne Bridon. Francois left France, leaving behind a fortune values at 800 pounds. Note: 800 pounds would be valued at around $2,064,450 now. Esther was the executrix of her father's will and made an inventory on his estate on May 22, 1704 (*NY Wills*, 5/6, p. 385).

Jean Bodin of Medis fled from Soubize, France in September of 1681 for England with his wife, Esther Bridon, and possibly two children (*Hands, A.P. and Irene Scouloudi, French Protestant Refugees Relieved through the Threadneedle Street Church, London, 1681-1687. Huguenot Society of London Quarto Series, v. 49, London, 1971).* They, including a son named Jean, and eventually settled on Staten Island.

"The Huguenots are in daily expectation of a very severe edict against them, by which any of their children shall be capable of choosing their religion at seven years old; how this will correct the chastisement of their parents, and how it will expose them to the temptations of the seducers is not apparent. In Poictou the quartering soldiers upon them has made so many proselytes that the same trick is to be tried in Languedoc, and five hundred dragoons are ordered to march thither for that purpose."

Again on July 2d, Henry Savile (1642-1687), the British Envoy in Paris from 1679-1682 writes, "The edict I mentioned in one of my last concerning the Huguenots and their children does so alarm them that they are making extraordinary deputations to the king to prevent it."

Indeed, the edict was enacted on 12 July 1681. It stated that all children aged seven or older could renounce the heretic religion of their parents and join the Established Church. Interference by their parents would be harshly dealt with. Children were enticed from their homes with cakes and candies and once in the clutches of the priests would be dragged away kicking and screaming. In this fashion thousands of Huguenot children were taken from their parents.

Dragoons, the King's troops, would enter Huguenot homes and force the occupants to kiss crucifixes tied to their musket barrels. The homes were then ransacked. All over, Protestant churches were torn down. King Louie XIV ordered his dragoons to put an end to the Huguenots once and for all throughout France.

In 1681 Jean Bodin was a newly married man. His wife, Esther, the daughter of François Bridon, belonged to a well-to-do family from Port des Barques, not too far distant, being situated opposite the island of Oléron. Thoughts surely turned to children and the likelihood of their living in an intolerant environment where they would be taken from them and raised as detested Papists. The future looked bleak and offered no hope to the young couple. The situation would only become worse. It was time to leave.

Jean Bodin, accompanied by his wife, Esther, fled his native country on Saturday, 13 September 1681, a date noted in the financial aid records of the Threadneedle Street Church in London.

Not being a seaman it would have been a very dangerous undertaking to escape under the watchful eyes of those guarding the ports and successfully navigate the Charente and make their way to England. To overcome this handicap, the couple joined a group of other refugees who did possess the know how to safely make this journey. Again, the records of the Threadneedle Street Church show the following refugees first receiving aid 14-16 September 1681 and all having arrived from Soubize the previous Saturday. Clearly, Jean and Esther Bodin had chosen their companions well.

Jean Bodin, farrier, with his wife; Etienne Bourru, seaman; Vincent Bourru, ship's carpenter, with his wife and 4 daughters; Antoine LeRoy, seaman, and his bethrothed Isabelle DuPas; Elie Du Pus, seaman and ship's carpenter, with his wife and 3 children; and Francois Gaultier, seaman, with his wife, 3 daughters, and a niece.

"Plymouth, 6th Sept., 1681. An open boat arrived here yesterday, in which were forty or fifty French Protestants who resided outside La Rochelle. Four others left with this boat, one of which is said to have put into Dartmouth, but it is not yet known what became of the other three." (Agnew, i, 29)

Within a very short time, days perhaps, the Bodins were safely joined by the Bridons, the family of his wife Esther. The financial aid records of the Threadneedle Street Church note the assistance first given to Francis Bridon, husbandman, with wife, 2 children and 2 servants, on 23 September 1681, and that 'He left £6,000 in France.' (Hands, 46) The escape of the Bridons, like that of the Bodins, did not go unnoticed by the French authorities, who duly noted 'Francois Bridon, sa femme, deux enfans, fugitif de Port des Barques', translated means: 'Bridon Francois, his wife, two children, a fugitive from Port des Barques'.

The Bodine and Bridon families spent several years in England where they received financial assistance due to leaving most of what they possessed in France.

The arrival in America of Jean Bodin can be ascertained only by 19 June 1701, when Jean Bodin, as a resident of Middlesex County, in the Province of East Jersey, purchased an 80 acre tract of land on Staten Island, New York from Johannes and Neeltje Messereau. Middlesex County was situated just across Hudson Bay from Staten Island.

On 1 December 1702, Jean Bodin, now 57 years old, if the date of his birth can be trusted, found reason to compose his last will and testament.

THE LAST WILL AND TESTAMENT OF JOHN BODINE, 1702

"In the name of god amen the first day of December in the year of our Lord god 1702, I John Bodine of Staten Island in the County of Richmond yeoman being very sick and weak of body but of perfect mind and memory thanks be to God hereof calling to mind the mortality of my body and knowing that it is appointed for all men to die do make and ordain this my Last will and testament that is to say prinsapally and first of all I give and Recommend my soul into the hand of God that gave it and for my body I Command it to the Earth to be buried in a Christianlike and desent manner at the discretion of my Executors nothing douting but at the generall resurrection I shall reseve the samee againe by the mighty power of god and as touching such worldly Estate as hath pleased god to bless me in this life I give devise and dispose of the same in the following manner and form.

Impris - I make my well beloved wife Ester mistress and dame of all my hole Effects moveable and unmoveable whatsoever freely to be possessed and enjoyed during her widowhood without any cost or bond whatsoever and if she shall come to marry againe the Estate to fall to my Children and then to be divided amongst all my Children Excepting seven pounds which I give to my son John Bodine and one mare with the proviso that my son John doe Live with his mother to help bring up the rest of the Children, Also not to have no more than his Equall share with the rest of his brothers and sisters.

Furthermore my will and desire is that if my wife shall marry again that I appoint Denis Rishe and Fransis Bridon my administrators of my Estate so long that my Children Come of age and then to be Equally divided amongst my Children Excepting the seven pounds and a mare which have giving unto my son John with the proviso herein, *spesefied restating and Confirming this and no other to be my Last will and Testament in witness whereof I have hereunto set my hand and seal this day and year above written*

Jean Bodin (SEAL)

Signed, Sealed, Published, Pronounced and Delivered by the said John Bodine as his Last will and testament in the presence of us the subscribers, viz: David Bourepos, Jacob Cariot, William Tillyer

New York March 24th 1707/8

Then appeared before me Edward Viscount Cornbury, Cap Gen & Gov in Chief & David Bourepos & made oath upon holy Evangelists of Almighty God & he did see the testator John Bodin sign seal publish & declare the within writing to be his Last will & Testament & at the time of his doing thereof he was of Sound & perfect mind & Memory to the Best of this Deposes & Knowledge and he that he did see Jacob Cariot & William Tillyer the other two witnesses to the said Will Sign as witnesses in the presence of the Testator.

(New York County Wills, File No. 234)

It would appear from the above probate that Jean Bodin, now better known as John Bodine, died shortly before 24 March 1708. His death likely occurred shortly before 3 January 1708 when his will was noted in New York Calendar of Land Papers, IV [1704-1709], p. 81.

A census taken of the inhabitants of Staten Island and usually assigned the date of 1706 seems, on the surface, to have overlooked Jean Bodine, yet recording his wife and three children:

WOMEN	BOYES	GIRLS
Hester Bodine (Esther)	Francis Bodine Jacob Bodine	Jane Bodine

THE CHEW FAMILY

Ancestors of May Chew, wife of Thomas Langley/Longley

Some of the information is from *"Genealogy of the Chew Family"*, by Richard Chew and from various Jamestown and Chew research sites.

The Chew surname is a very old English name. The Chewes mainly lived in Whalley Parish, Lancashire and Chewton, Somerset. The Chewes owned lands, estates, and married well for many centuries in England. Our immigrant ancestor begins with John Chew.

In Richard Chew's research, he found that John Chew of Long Island, was an adventurer. He was born in England, then moved to Virginia, from Virginia he moved to Maryland but later returned to Virginia.

John Chew (1587-1668), may have first come to the new world in 1607 with Captain John Smith when the first few hundred settlers landed in Virginia. If he did, he then returned to England, married and started his family. There is evidence to show that he was planning his permanent move for several years, as early as 1618.

Immigration records of Virginia show that in 1622 John Chew, "merchant from Somersetshire England," arrived at James Cittie (now Jamestown) with three servants aboard the barque 'Charitie,' which was owned by his wife Sara Gale's father. She followed in 1623 on the ship 'Seafloure' (Sea Flower) with several of her children and servants.

John Chew was a wealthy settler in the new world, with land granted to him in Jamestown, near the Governor's mansion, and a plantation on Hogg Island across the river from Jamestown. Some say he built the first brick house in Jamestown. There was some indication that he brought bricks from England to build his home in Virginia.

He also had a store and warehouse there and was later granted 1,200 acres in York County for helping develop that area. Governor Harvey in 1725 called John Chew "one of the ablest merchants in Virginia."

As a well-established businessman, John Chew became involved in politics shortly after arriving in Virginia. For a period of almost 20 years, starting in 1624, John Chew served Virginia in the House of Burgesses and also served as a Justice for York County.

Historical Marker in Jamestown
"John Chew, like several of his immediate neighbors, was a merchant, one of the oldest in the Colony. He acquired the small plot here "backstreet" in 1624, and put up a 'house by him now erected and builded in Newtowne within the precincts of James City'."

Another marker mentioning John Chew:

"This area, locally known as Dandy, was part of the land granted to John Chew July 6, 1636, and was sold by his heirs to James Goodwin, a member of the House of Burgesses from Jamestown, August 27, 1668. The area was strategically important both to British General Charles Cornwallis and to Confederate General John B. Magruder, who erected earth redoubts at the heads of several creeks on Goodwin Neck."

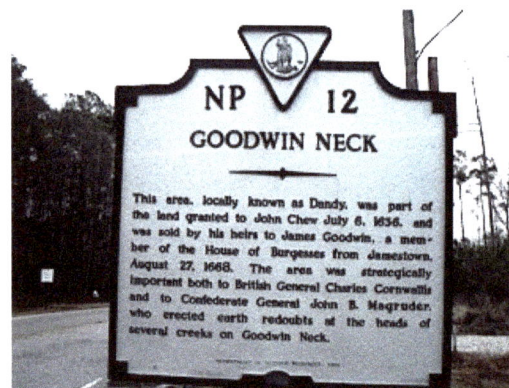

In 1649, however, after the Church of England began to persecute the Puritans and similar problems arose in the colonies, John Chew left Virginia with his family and moved to Maryland where Lord Baltimore granted them 500 acres in Ann Arundel/Calvert County (near today's Annapolis.

When John moved his family he had with him Sarah, and sons Samuel and Joseph. Sometime before 1651, Sarah died, probably in Maryland, and John decided to return to Virginia where he still held most of his original property. We know he returned to Virginia because in that year he executed a deed (recorded in York County) in view of his intended marriage with Mrs. Rachel Constable (Virginia Mag., I. 197).

A record was filed on August 24, 1668, under "York County", Virginia 16__ to 1668 Records". It names Samuel Chew, son of John Chew, deceased, as administrator his of estate.

So the life of this adventurer, original colonist and astute businessman came to an end.

John Chew and wife Ann Gates
Parents of Richard Chew

John Chew, II was a son of the immigrant John Chew. He would have been born about 1616 and would have been approximately seven years old when he accompanied his mother, Sarah, to Jamestown.

Life in Jamestown provided no comforts and was very primitive and hard so when some of his father John Chew's slaves ran away, John and his brother Nathaniel left in search of this runaway in 1643. Their search took them to New England and took over a year to before they landed in Massachusetts. The search took John and Nathaniel up the Atlantic seaboard into New England. The only way to get from Virginia north would have been by boat up the coast. It is very likely they made their stop in Boston as the area was centrally located between the Salem and Plymouth settlements.

It is not known if the slaves were found, but John apparently liked the English colonists religious belief and political way of life and remained there. He met and married Ann Gates, daughter of Stephen and Ann Hill Gates in Hingham, Massachusetts sometime between 1644 and 1650. The Gates family had come to that area from England in 1639 aboard the ship "Diligent".

Eventually some of the colonist began to migrate south into Connecticut and as Nathaniel was already established there, John apparently began moving south as well until he settled on Long Island in 1666. By 1644 the English had already begun moving into Long Island and settled in an area they called Hempstead.

The exact date of John's death is not known, but it is thought to be between May 1 and July 3, 1672. He left an estate large enough to pay off his debts.

Richard Chew and Frances Woodward
Parents of Mary Chew

Richard's childhood is unknown, but his birth date is estimated as 1655. The location of his birth is also unknown. We do know that his marriage to Frances Woodward was recorded in the *"New York Marriages Prior to 1784"* and was dated 1 March 1675, probably in Flushing, Long Island.

The settlement of Long Island was growing rapidly by 1675. Englishmen came from Connecticut, Massachusetts, and England daily. One family that came was the Nathaniel Woodward family, who settled in Newtown.

Nathaniel was the father of Frances, who became Richard's wife. Nathaniel emigrated from England with wife Margaret. He was a surveyor and mathematician and a freeholder of Newtown, Long Island.

Richard and Frances had their first child about a year after their marriage. By 1683, their family consisted of three sons and a daughter, named John, Nathaniel, Richard and Hannah. The family continued to grow and added Henry, Charity, Thomas, Mary and Elizabeth.

Political and religious persecution again took place in this area. When news of a place in West New Jersey where a good and peaceable life could be found, Richard investigated it. This area was under the guidance of William Penn and was found to be what Richard wanted for his family. Richard and Frances then moved their family to this new land and settled in Gloucester County in 1699.

Richard bought 300 acres of land for twenty-eight pounds and ten shillings—current silver money.

The family lived comfortably in that area, and as the children grew they began to marry.

Frances' date of death in not known but Richard died in 1726.

Our Dutch Heritage

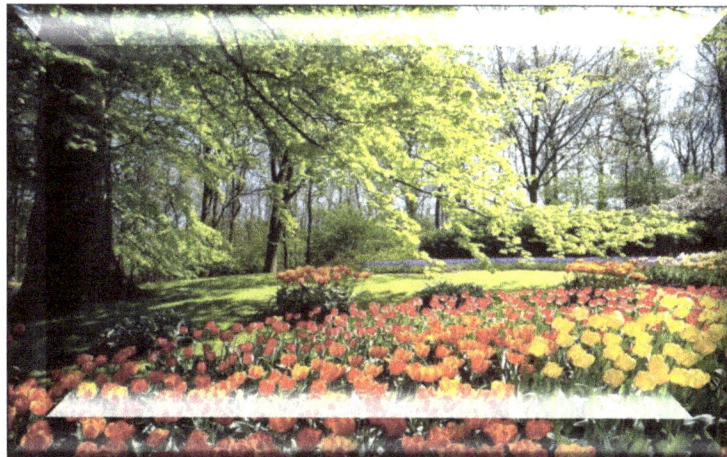

Those of us who are descendants of Dutch ancestors have a very rich heritage. We have been blessed to have inherited some of the characteristics of that group of people. They were religious, hardworking and industrious, to say nothing of being adventurous.

Just imagine getting on a ship, say in the year 1620, and travel from Holland to the new world. That world was unknown to them, with only a brief idea of the land, indigenous people, climate, and most of them had no idea of the living conditions and safety.

Conditions aboard the ships during this time period were harsh at best. Families with small children made this trip and many people died along the way, children as well as adults.   .

Some of our Dutch ancestors made the trip as early as 1629 and others traveled at different times until the 1650s.

We come from people of varying degrees of wealth, some with a substantial amount and others with little wealth, but most of them were people with skills that the new world needed.

They all left their mark on the settlement of the "New Netherlands" and their descendants are too many to try and numerate.

On March 31, 1624 a ship carrying settlers left Holland. It was the *Nieuw Nederland* and aboard were thirty families who were going to cultivate the land overseas. It was the first Dutch emigrant ship, and these were the first Dutch immigrants to North America.

Willem Verhulst was the name of the man who directed this venture. The *Nieuw Nederland* anchored near Fort Nassau in the Hudson, at a place called *Maeykans*, which means `Home of the Mohicans.' The same year, 1624, another fortress, Fort Orange, was built on the shore not far from there.

In 1625, eleven years after Fort Nassau was founded, a fort was put up on Manhattan Island and ships brought farmers from Holland who were to supply the food for its garrison. Five farms (*bouwerijen*) were established on the island to meet the needs of the colony. These farmers were in the service of the company. As soon as the moat surrounding the fort was completed, the fort-to-be was christened *Amsterdam* after the capital of The Netherlands, and the new town around it, *Nieuw Amsterdam*, which some time later would be renamed New York City.

There was an increase in population from an estimated 2,000 in 1648 to 10,000 in 1660. During its last twenty years under Dutch rule, New Netherland changed from a trading post to a real colony. Even so, because the traditional incentives for leaving the mother country were lacking, the trickle from Holland never swelled to a stream.

The British in New England and Virginia, on either side of New Netherland, continued to outnumber the Dutch at least four to one.

Clothing of the 17th Century

"On Long Island the oldest settlement was Nieuw Amersfoort, later Flatlands, which dates from 1636 and was named after the Dutch city of Amersfoort. Destined to become more famous was Breukelen, named by its settlers for their village of origin in The Netherlands. Breukelen became a town in 1646, and in 1661 it counted 130 inhabitants. It has been doing quite well for itself since then: in 1970 it had a population of 2,602,000. It is still carrying its original name, which -- slightly Anglicized -- is now spelled `Brooklyn.'

In 1664 fifteen hundred people lived in the capital. There were at least three hundred and fifty houses, and the town had received jurisdiction of its own, separate from the Governor's court. There were two windmills, a church, and many inns. The inhabitants were actually not one hundred per cent Dutch.

One writer reports, without doubt exaggerating slightly, that eighteen languages were spoken in Nieuw Amsterdam. The little capital was definitely more cosmopolitan than anything to be found in New England. Peter Stuyvesant himself, the son of a Frisian minister, was a severe Calvinist, but he had to obey his company. The Company, in the spirit of seventeenth-century Holland, did not allow discrimination and ordered the Governor to accept the settling of Lutherans, Quakers and Jews.

The cosmopolitan and tolerant atmosphere of New Amsterdam outlasted Dutch rule, and is perhaps the most important contribution that Dutch colonization made to the future United States. It was a Dutch minister, Balthazar Bekker, who later in that century wrote a book (*The World Turn'd Upside Down*), which became a classic denunciation of the belief in witchcraft. This same enlightened spirit could be found in New York in the very years when witch trials were being held in New England.

The relaxed social atmosphere of Nieuw Amsterdam also contrasted with the English colonies to the north, restricted by their rigid Blue Laws. This accounts for a Nieuw Amsterdam characteristic which was inherited by New York: the large number of places to eat, drink and dance. Sports were popular, too. The colonists loved boat and carriage races, and from Holland they imported the game of kolf, which later became golf." Note: The above information was taken from: *American History from Revolution to Reconstruction and beyond* website.

Map of The Netherlands

Territory call "New Netherlands in 1660"

Schenck Families

Our family connection to the Schenck ancestors goes back to both Roeloff Martense and his brother Jan Martense Schenck.

Alta Pearl Gage and Samuel Thomas Pointer were both 6th great grandchildren of Roeloff Martense and Neltje Van Couwenhoven Schenck and 7th great grandchildren to Jan Martense and wife Jannetje Stevens Van Voorhees Schenck.

Roelof's lineage goes from son Garret, son Roelof, son John, son Roelof, son Aaron and then daughter Kesiah, who married John Thomas Pointer.

Jan's lineage goes through his daughter, Jannetje, who married Gerret Dorland, their son, Gerret married Jannetje Probasco, then their daughter Anitje Dorland who married Rem Lupardus and Rem's daughter Jannetje/Jane Lupardus, who married Adrian Hageman. Hannah Hageman was their daughter who married Roelof Schenck and was the mother of Aaron Schenck.

It is through Jan's & Jannetje's line that we are related to the following Dutch families: Dorland, Probasco, Snedecker, Stryker, Vanderbeek and Rapalje.

Other connected Dutch families we descend from through Roeloff Martense Schenck and wife, Neltje Van Couwenhoven Schenck include Voorhees, Wyckoff, Van Dorn, Van der Vliet, Bloetgoet, Jans, Van Arsdale, Badie, Trico and other Dutch families less well known.

THE FAMILY OF SCHENCK.
Pronounced as Skenck

HISTORY OF MONMOUTH CO., NEW JERSEY by Franklin Ellis

The Schencks of Monmouth County are descended from Roelof Schenck Van Nydeck, who, with his brother Jan, immigrated to this country from Holland in 1650. The particular place from whence they came was probably Doesberg, in the province of Guelderland, where, it appears, their father was born. He was a son of Martin and a grandson of General Peter Schenck and his wife, Joanna Van Scharpenseel, and General Peter was a brother of the celebrated General and Sir Martin Schenck, with whom his brother fought and was one of the most successful, daring and enterprising commanders in Holland in the time of the war of the revolution there.

Tracing them back, they were descended from four Dericks in succession, and them from two Heinrichs, or Henrys, in succession, going back to 1346, and who were lords of the manorial estates of Afferden, Wachtendonk and Blyenbeck, Afferden and Blyenbeck lying on the Maas River, above the town of Gennep, and Wachtendonk on the Nioss River, above the town of Gelden. Passing back one or two unknown generations, they were descended from Ludolphus, Wilhelmus and Christianus, going back to 1225, and then through Christianus, a second son in the family of Schencks, the barons of Tautenberg, going back to 330 A.D. The descendants of Christianus were known as the Schencks Van Nydeck, so called from the town of Neideggen, lying on the river Roer, some eighteen miles east of Aix-la-Chapelle, where no doubt Christianus had an estate or residence.

Painting of General, Sir Martin Schenck, brother to General Peter Schenck.

Martin Schenck was apparently born at Goch, the exact date is not known. It is known that at the time of his death (1589) he was still "young in years".

He became a well-known soldier and fought many battles. In one such battle at Werl on 2 March 1586, he met with the English Earl of Leicester, Robert Dudley. Leicester informed Walsingham that on 8 May, he had knighted Schenck with great pomp and gave him a gold chain with a value of 2000 guilders, which was considered a great honor by the Englishmen at that time. After presenting the gold chain, Leicester writes from Utrecht to Walsingham on April 16th, "I assure you that he is a worthy nobleman and has performed exceptional services since my arrival here."

Martin, after many battles, began his last one at Nymwegen where in his rush to attack, dressed in a heavy, "shot-safe" suit of armor, he jumped into an overloaded ship. It sank and Schenck, whose heavy armor made it impossible for him to swim, drowned.

General Peter Schenck, Martin's sibling was the grandfather of Roelof Martense and Jan Martense Schenck. Peter was also very active in the wars of that time.

Bleijenbeek Castle (Dutch: Kasteel Bleijenbeek)

It is located in the small hamlet of Bleijenbeek in the Dutch province of Limburg.

Blyenbeck Castle

This is a sketch of the original castle when occupied by the Schenck family.

Photo taken from:
"*The History of the Family of Schenck Von Nydeggen 1225-1860*", written by Heinrich Ferber, January 1860.

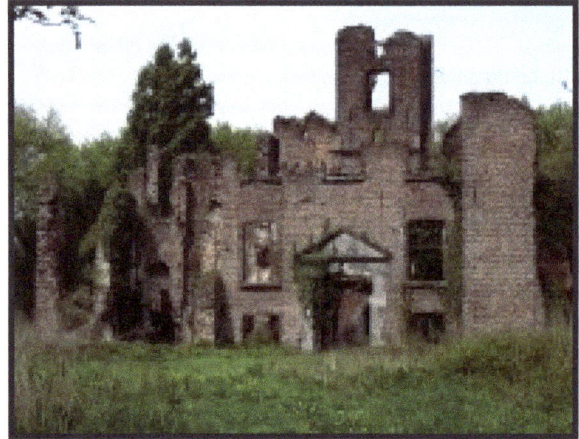

The photograph is what is left of the castle after the bombing of the Allies on 21 and 22 February 1945.

Bleijenbeek Castle
(Dutch: Kasteel Bleijenbeek)

The castle is situated in the small hamlet of Bleijenbeek in the Dutch province of Limburg.

According to the 19th century historian A.J. van der Aa, the castle is known for its numerous sieges by the armies of Guelders and Spain. In 1580, the castle was besieged by the forces of Guelders, but it was defended bravely by the lord of the castle, Marten Schenk. When the Duke of Parma sent cavalry, the besieging army had to retreat. In 1589, Schenk changed sides, and the castle was besieged by Marcus van Rije, the stadtholder (governor) of Guelders appointed by the Spanish king; this time, the castle was conquered.

In 2009, the property was purchased by the Bleijenbeek Foundation, which intends to restore the remaining structure, moat, and surrounding gardens and provide public access

After work is complete. Construction began in the summer of 2012.

Note: The duchy was named after the town of Geldern (Gelder) in present-day Germany. Though the present province of Gelderland (English also Guelders) in the Netherlands occupies most of the area, the former duchy also comprised parts of the present Dutch province of Limburg as well as those territories in the present day German state of North Rhine-Westphalia that were acquired by Prussia in 1713.

Jan Martense Schenck Home

Now Located in the Brooklyn Museum, New York City

Jan Martense Schenck House

The Jan Martense Schenck House represents the oldest architecture in the Museum's period room collection. It is also the most complex of the period rooms in terms of reconstruction and interpretation. The house originally stood in the town of Flatlands, one of six rural towns that were to become the borough of Brooklyn. Established under the Dutch colony of New Netherlands, which became the English colony of New York in 1664, Flatlands was first called New Amersfoort, after Amersfoort in the Netherlands. The area was originally inhabited by the Carnarsie Indians. The house is a simple two-room structure with a central chimney. Its framework is composed of a dozen heavy so-called H-bents, visible on the interior of the house, that resemble goal posts with diagonal braces. This is an ancient northern European method of construction that contrasts with the boxlike house frames that evolved in England. The house had a high-pitched roof that created a large loft for storage. The roof was covered with shingles, and the exterior walls were clad with horizontal wood clapboard siding. A section of the clapboard has been removed at one corner to expose a reconstruction of the brick nogging used as insulation. The interior walls were stuccoed between the upright supports of the H-bents. A kitchen was added at a right angle to the house probably in the late 1790s. In the early nineteenth century a porch with four columns was also added. Finally, sometime about 1900, dormer windows were installed above the porch. The interior of the house was also changed. The large central chimney was removed, probably about the same time as the kitchen wing was added, and new chimneys and fireplaces were built on the outer walls. Old photographs of the interior of the house on site in Flatlands show it with early twentieth century wallpapers and an assortment of nineteenth-century furniture, all of which was discarded when the house came to the Museum.

Note: 1664 The Dutch relinquish the colony of New Netherland to the English, and New Amsterdam becomes New York. **Early 1670s** Jan Martense Schenck marries Jannetje van Voorhees. **1675** Jan Martense Schenck purchases Mill Island (now known as Mill Basin) in the town of Flatlands, along with a half share in the island's tidal gristmill. He builds a house there by 1677. **1689** Jan Martense Schenck dies and leaves his house, mill, and farm to his son Martin.

The Schenck family owned the house for three generations, finally selling it in 1784. *The Jan Martense Schenck information was taken from the BrooklynMuseum.org website.*

The Jan Schenck House

Jan Schenck Home—1830

Jan Schenck Home—1830

Jan Schenck Home—1952

The Jan Schenck house was acquired by the Brooklyn Museum in 1952. The land the house sat on became the site of elementary school P.S. 236. The house was still extant after the school was built, it was located behind the school. In 1952 the house was dismantled and stored for ten years. The original portion of the house was rebuilt on the fourth floor of the Brooklyn Museum.

From the (1939) WPA Guide to New York City

Schenck-Crooke House, located on Avenue U between East Sixty-third and sixty-fourth Streets, is considered one of the oldest houses in New York City, the original section having been built in 1656. A white house with green shutters and red brick chimneys, it stands in a little hollow back of Public School 236, surrounded by old pine trees. Its Dutch origins are evident in the small twelve-paned windows and early round-end shingles. The slender-pillared front porch formed by an overhanging roof is an eighteenth-century addition.

166

Schenck and Hageman Homes in Early New Amsterdam

THE 'SCHENCK' LANDMARK AT CANARSIE. BUILT 1660

THE HAGEMAN HOUSE FLATBUSH AVE & KINGS HIGHWAY BUILT ABOUT 1780

COPYRIGHT 1901 BY E.A. BISHOP

The farm house is the Roeloff Martense Schenck home located in New Jersey.

I was told that the family who inherited this house went to remodel it and found the silver tea set. It was hidden in the back of the old fireplace.

This same man, who now lives in Nova Scotia, also inherited a trunk with Schenck records dating back to the 1600s.

Hageman Ancestry

ADRIAEN HEGEMAN (The Immigrant)

Adriaen emigrated from Holland and was the first of the American Hegeman/Hageman/Hagaman line.

Adriaen was born in Elburg, Gelderland in 1624, the son of Hendrick Hegeman, a minister of the Dutch Church at Vorchten. His two brothers were ministers of the Dutch church also. He moved to Amsterdam before 1649 to join the silk trade.

At the time Adriaen's bann's were proclaimed on 29 January 1649, his parents were deceased. Source: *'Ancestry of Adriaen Hageman of New Netherland'*.

On March 7, 1649 at the age of 25, he was married to Catarina Margits, the daughter of a London diamond cutter. What was Joseph Margits doing in Amsterdam? It was suspected that the English Civil War was a bit too hot for him. The 1640's were a tumultuous time in England. In fact, the King was executed on Jan. 30, 1649, two months before Adriaen and Catarina's wedding.

Adriaen arrived about 1652, with his wife and several children. He lived in New Amsterdam for a time then bought land on western Long Island, what is now Brooklyn and Flatbush, then called Midwout (middle of the woods).

Smit's *'Dutch in America'* says that Adriaen Hegeman purchased 59 morgens of land (a morgen is a Dutch unit of land equal to about 2 acres) in Midwout about 15 April 1661.

Midwout is one of the six early villages in Brooklyn and now is called Flatbush. It was the farm area of New Amsterdam and had lush forests with game, wetlands and good fishing. The swampy areas must have reminded the Hollanders of home. Trading was done with New Amsterdam by ferry (230 years before the Brooklyn Bridge) and settlers apparently went to church (Dutch Reform) in New Amsterdam as the Hegeman baptismal records are there.

Adriaen and his friend Jan Strijcker were involved in many political and legal affairs of Long Island. They functioned as the 2 schepens (judges) and Adriaen was the schout (sherrif) of the Long Island towns. The two men were close friends and were instrumental in building the first church on Long Island, the Dutch Reform Church at Midwout in 1654. The Church was rebuilt in 1698 and in 1776 its bell announced the advance of the British forces on New York. The present third church building, built in 1797, is still in the original location at the corner of Flatbush Avenue and Church Lane. The stones used in its construction were the main ones from the second church. Source: 'The *Stryker Family in America*' by William Norman Stryker, 1979.

There is a copy of Adriaen's signature from a legal document, taken from Stryker's Family History. The document from the Colonial Documents of New York deals with the shocking behavior of the English who were trying to take over the Long Island towns. Many of Adriaen's legal writings exist as abstracts or transcriptions in 'NY Colonial Documents'.

I have included six generations of Adrian Hageman's ancestors as the family has a rich history both in The Netherlands and in the settling of New Amsterdam and finally moving into New Jersey.

Adrian Hageman was born on 8 Aug 1745 in New Jersey. He married **Jannetje (Jane) Lupardus** and died on 22 Jun 1821 at the age of 75 in Hamilton County, Ohio. He was a Revolutionary War veteran and fought with the Somerset County, New Jersey Militia. He signed a will on 23 Sep 1818 in Sycamore Township, Hamilton.

Parents

Adrian Hegeman was born about 1720. He signed a will on 8 Aug 1754 in Somerset Co., New Jersey. **Sarah Wyckoff** and Adrian Hegeman were married on 14 May 1744 in Somerset County, New Jersey.

Grandparents

Adriaen Hegeman was born about 4 March 1685/6. He was baptized on 14 Mar 1685/6 in Reform Church, New Amsterdam. He died on 8 Aug 1754 at the age of 68 in Six-Mile Run, Somerset, New Jersey. Adriaen was a Farmer in New Jersey. **Maria Van der Vliet** and Adriaen Hegeman were married on 1 May 1713 in Flatbush, Long Island, New York. Maria was born before 1690 in probably Flushing, Long Island, New York. She died after 1740 at the age of 50.

Simon Wyckoff was born on 23 Nov 1683 in Amersfoort, Long Island. He was baptized on 23 Nov 1683, in Flatbush, now Brooklyn, Kings Co., Long Island, New York. He signed a will on 14 Jul 1759 in Somerset County, New Jersey. Simon died in 1765 at the age of 82. **Greetje Van der Vliet** and Simon Wyckoff were married in 1705.

Great Grandparents

Hendricus Hegeman was born in 1649 in Elburg, Amsterdam, Netherlands. He was baptized on 13 April 1649 in Amsterdam, Netherlands. He died about 1710 at the age of 61 in Flatbush, Kings Co., New York. **Ariaentje Bloetgoet** and Hendricus Hegeman were married on 26 April 1685 in Flatlands, Brooklyn, New York. Ariaentje was born on 14 Jan 1660 in probably Flushing, Long Island, New York. She was baptized on 14 Jan 1660 in New York Dutch Church.

Jan Dirkszen Van der Vliet died on 29 May 1689 in Flatbush, now, Brooklyn, Kings Co., Long Island, New York. He signed a will on 1 Dec 1722 in Six-Mile Run, Somerset County, New Jersey. In the record of their banns, they were: "Betrothed the 18th Nov. 1683, Jan Dirksz Van Vliet, young man from Well in Gelderland,

residing in Midwood; with Gerrtje Verkerkken, young lady from Buurmalsen in Gelderland, living at N. Utrecht. **Grietje Verkerk** was born in 1655 in Buurmalzen, Gelderland, Netherlands.

Cornelius Pieterse Wyckoff was born in 1656 in Flatlands, Brooklyn, New York. He signed a will on 4 Apr 1726 in New Jersey. He died on 4 Apr 1746 at the age of 90 in Middlebush, New Jersey. **Geertje Simonse Van Arsdalen** and Cornelius Pieterse Wyckoff were married on 13 Oct 1678 in New Utrecht, New York. Geertje was born in 1660 in Amersfoort, Netherlands.

Jan Dirkszen Van der Vliet are the same as shown previously.

2nd Great Grandparents

Adriaen Hegeman was born in 1625 in Elburg, Amsterdam, Netherlands. He died in Apr 1672 at the age of 47 in New Amsterdam, New York Co., New York. Katherine/Catherine Margits and Adriaen Hegeman were married on 7 Mar 1649 in Sloten, near Amsterdam. **Katherine/Catherine** was born in 1625 at Amsterdam, Holland in Noorderkerk (North Church). She was baptized on 4 Feb 1625 in New Church, Amsterdam. She died in 1690 at the age of 65 in Midwout (now Flatbush), Kings Co., Long Island, New York.

Frans Jan Bloetgoet was born about 1632 in Gouda, Ziud Holland, Netherland. He died on 29 Dec 1676 at the age of 44 in Flushing, Long Island, New York. **Lysbeth Jans** and Frans Jan Bloetgoet were married on 8 Feb 1654 in Reenwych, Gouda, Zuid Holland, Netherlands. Lysbeth was born in 1633 in Gouda, Ziud Holland, Netherland.

Dirk Janson Van der Vliet was born in 1612 in Rylevelt, Holland. He married **Geertgen Gerrits**. He died after January 1679/80

Jan Janse Verkerk was born in 1628 in probably in Bueer Maetsen, Gelderland Province, Netherlands. He died after 10 Nov 1688 at the age of 60 in Brooklyn, Kings Co., New York. **Mayke Gisberts** was born in 1640 in Holland, Netherlands. She died in 1688 at the age of 48 in New Utrecht, Long Island, New York.

Pieter Claasen Wyckoff Van Norden was born on 6 Jun 1625 in Nordingen, East Friesland, Holland. He died on 30 Jun 1694 at the age of 69 in Flatlands, Brooklyn, New York. **Grietje Van Ness** and Pieter Claasen Wyckoff Van Norden were married between 1645 and 1649 in Rensselaerwyck, Fort Orange, Albany, New York. Grietje was born in 1624 in North Overijssel, Emmeloord, Holland. She died in 1699 at the age of 75 in New Lotts, Flatbush, Brooklyn, Kings Co., Long Island, New York. She was also known as Grietje Wyckoff Van Norden.

Simon Jans Van Arsdalen was born in 27 February 1627/28 in Nukerke, Oost Vlanderen (East Flanders), Belgium. He died in 29 October 1710 at the age of 82. Abt. 1659 in New Amsterdam. He married **Pietertje Claes Van Schouw**, the daughter of Claes and Metje Harpentse. She was born October 28, 1640 in Amersfoort, Flatlands, New Amsterdam, and died in Flatlands, Long Island, New York.

Dirk Janson Van der Vliet was probably born in Nederhemert, just west of Well, a village on the south side of the Bommelerwaard in Gelderland, Netherlands in 1612/13; he died Flatbush (now Brooklyn, Kings County, Long Island), New York after January 1679/80. His third wife, **Geertgen Gerrits**, was the mother of his son Jan.

Jan Janse Verkerk was born in 1628 probably in Bueer Maetsen, Gelderland Province, Netherlands. Immigrated in 1663 to America from with his wife and five children. In about 1652 Jan Janse married **Mayke Gisberts**, probably in Bueer Maetsen, Netherlands. Jan Janse died after 10 Nov 1688 in Brooklyn, Long Island, New York.

3rd Great Grandparents

Hendrick Jacobse Hegeman was born in 1600 in Harderwijk, Gelderland, Netherlands, the child of Jacob Lambertse and Aertien Hendricksdr. He married **Marrieken Berendse** in 1637 in Vorchten, Gelderland, Netherlands. He died in 1637 in Vorchten, Gelderland, Netherlands, at the age of 37. Marrieken died in 1670 in Kings County, New York, at the age of 68.

Joseph Margits was born in 1597 in England. He died about 1660 at the age of 63. He was buried at Amsterdam, Holland in Noorderkerk (North Church). He married **Annetje Waerdenburgh**. She died between 1630—1635.

Jan Hendrickse Bloetgoet was born about 1590 in Gouda, Ziud Holland, Netherland. **Geertjen van der Gouda** and Jan Hendrickse Bloetgoet were married on 28 Oct 1612 in Gouda, Ziud Holland, Netherland. Geertjen was born before 1598 in Gouda, Ziud Holland, Netherland. She died in Holland.

Claes Cornelissen or Meutelaer Van Schouw Or Van Schouwen Or Van Wyckoff was born on 3 Apr 1597 in Boda-Oland Island, Kalmar, Holland. **Marritie\Margaret Van Der Goes** and Claes Cornelissen or Meutelaer Van Schouw Or Van Schouwen or Van Wyckoff were married between 9 Nov 1623 and 1639 in Holland. Marritie was born in 1601 in Boda-Oland Island, Kalmar, Holland. She died on 2 Aug 1631 at the age of 30 in Zierikzee, Zeeland, Walcheren Island, Holland.

Cornelis Hendrickszen Van Ness was born in 1604 in Holland. In 1641 he was a Farmer and was Councilor Cornelis Hendricksz van Nes in Rensselaerswyck. **Mayken Hendricks Van den Burchgraeff** and Cornelis Hendrickszen Van Ness were married on 31 Jul 1625 in Harvendijk, Zeeland, The Netherlands. Mayken was also known as Mayken Hendricks Van Ness.

Claes Cornelisen van Schouwen was baptized on 12 Feb 1606 in Brouwershaven, Schouwen, Zeeland Province, Netherlands. He married Metje Harpertsen.

The Van Dorn/Doorn Families

The Sam and Alta Pointer families are related to the Van Dorn/Doorn line with two ancestors. Our first Van Dorn connection is through Engeltje Van Dorn. She was the first daughter of Jacob Van Doorn and wife Marytje Andrianse Bennet, and was born on Long Island, 9 Oct 1696 and died 20 Sept 1747, when almost fifty-one years of age. In 1718 she married Roelof Schenck, brewer.

In Teunis G. Bergen's Book, he states that the baptismal records would give us proof of the parentage of the Roelof Scheck who married Engeltje Van Doorn. Baptisms for this couple are found in the Dutch Reformed Church of Freehold/Middletown, New Jersey. They confirm that the Roelof who married Engeltje Van Doorn was the son of Garret Roelofszen Schenck and his wife Neeltje Coert Van Voorhees. Roelof was the second child and oldest son of his parents, and he must have married Engeltje about 1718. Bergen said that Roeloff's and Engeltje's four oldest children were:

Gerret, baptized 3 May 1719 Wit: Nelke Voorhees (Paternal grandmother)
1. Marike, baptized 17 Jul 1720 Wit: Adriaan Van Doorn, Marike Bennet, widow of J. Van Doorn
2. William
3. Nelke, baptized 17 Jan 1724 Wit: none

Jacob Van Dorn was 'of Freehold, Monmouth County' when he wrote his will on 24 April 1719. The will was probated on 23 May 1720. In it he names his wife 'Marytye' and his children Aria [Adrian], **Angeletje [Engeltje], Christy**-Ian [Christian], William, **Jacob**, Angenyettie, Catherine, Abraham, Peter, and Isaac. The executors are (significantly) Gerret Schanck [sic] and Adrian Bennet.

Engeltje and her brother Jacob Van Dorn were both children of Jacob and Marytje Andrianse Bennet Van Doorn. Engeltje was the mother of Captain John Schenck who married Mariah/Mary Van Dorn, daughter of Engeltje's brother Jacob, who married Marytie Janse Schenck. Marytie was the daughter of Jan/John Roeloff Schenck and wife Saartje Van Cowenhoven.

Captain John Schenck's wife was the niece of his mother. To add confusion, Garret, (father of Captain John) and Jan/John were brothers and sons of Roeloff Martense Schenck and wife Neeltje Van Couwenhoven. This is presented in the ancestor chart on page 39.

Jacob Van Dorn and Wife Marytie Schenck
Father of Mariah/Mary Van Dorn

Jacob married first Marytie Schenck, and after her death married Rachel Schenck. Under Jacob's father's will, after his mother's death, which was about 1735, Jacob received half his father's farm comprising 317 acres.

On Oct. 23, 1756, Jacob, his brother Isaac, and his nephew Jacob (son of Aure), leased from Joseph Throckmorton, Jr., one half of the 1/16th part of all mines and minerals discoverable on the land of Nicholas Golder in Somerset County, but what minerals were found is not known. After having added more land to his original farm in 1743, Jacob bought still more land in Freehold Township at a sheriff's sale in 1772 but resold it May 3, 1774. In his youth Jacob had been a bit of a religious poet.

In his will Oct. 26, 1778, proved Apr. 19, 1779, Jacob left his wife Rachel 10£, 20 Lbs. of flax and 5 lbs. of wool yearly, the choice of one room in his dwelling, firewood and a negro boy to make her fires; to sons Isaac and Peter, who were also the executors, as tenants in common, his 'mills, lands and meadows, and all my real and personal estate;' to children of son John 250£ which was 'to come out of the money he owed me at the time of his decease;' to his other sons 250£ each and to his daughters each 200£. Jacob died Feb. 26, 1779.

Jan\\John Roelfse SCHENCK was born on 10 Feb 1670 in New Amersfoort, Flatlands, first Achtervelt, borough of Brooklyn, Long Island, Kings Co., New York. He was christened on 1 Mar 1670 in Flatlands, Long Island, Kings Co., New York.

Jan and Sara were cousins. Jan/John was a son of Roelof Schenck Van Nydeck, the emigrant to this country, and first wife, Neeltje. Sarah was the daughter of William Gerretsz Van Kouwenhoven and Jannettje Pieterse Montfoort. William and Neeltje were siblings and children of Garrett Van Kouwenhoven and Aeltje Cornelis Cool.

He emigrated in 1696 from New York to Pleasant Valley, New Jersey. He signed a will on 11 Sep 1746 in Flatlands, Long Island, New York. He died on 30 Jan 1753 in Pleasant Valley and was buried in 1753 in Holmdel Cemetery in Pleasant Valley, Monmouth Co., New Jersey. The cemetery is 1/2 mile from Holmdel village near the turnpike to Keyport.

Jacob Christianense Van Dorn and Wife Maria Adiaense Bennet
Parents of Engeltje Van Dorn

Jacob Christianense Van Dorn was born on 21 Oct 1668 in Gowanus, Long Island, New York. He died before 21 Mar 1718/9 at the age of 50 in Marlboro, Monmouth County, New Jersey.

(The following is from the book 'The *Van Doren Family'*, by Wilson V Ledley.) He was very detailed in his study of the Van Doren Family before 1800.

'Jacob was baptized Oct. 21, 1668, in the New York Dutch Church. Initially he went by the name Christiansen, his patronymic (ones father's ancestor), and it was as 'Jacob Christiaense, native of New Utrecht,' on Sept 26-30, 1687, that he took the oath of allegiance there to the English. Although then only about nineteen, as his father was then dead, Jacob was probably in possession of the family lands in Kings Co., and as a landholder was deemed of sufficient importance to demand his taking the oath.

It was about five years later that Jacob married Maria Adiaense Bennet, a neighbor first of New Utrecht and later Gowanus, Kings Co. That Jacob still adhered to the name 'Christiansen' is shown when stood as sponsor, on Dec. 10, 1694, in the Brooklyn Dutch Church, at the baptism of a child of Cornelis Van Brunt and his wife Tryntje Bennet, who was Jacob's eldest sister-in-law. It must have been in the following few months that he began to use the Van Doorn surname as it was under that designation that he was received into the membership of the Brooklyn Dutch Church on Oct, 19, 1695. Thereafter in Dutch records he was always referred to by the name without the patronymic, although it is to be noted that he used the English spelling 'Van Dorn' in signing his will in 1719.'

Jacob on Feb. 14, 1697, bought a tract of land near Middletown in Monmouth Co., New Jersey, bounded by 'Hop Brook, Penn's land and a deep gulley' from Richard Salter for £140, then on the following Apr. 2, Jacob and his brother-in-law Arie/Adriaen Bennet bought a much larger tract adjacent to the first, part of John Reid's estate 'Hortencie' near the present Hillsdale, described as 'on the east branch of Hop River' (between the present townships of Middletown & Holmdel; Monmouth.

Then on May 17, 1700, Jacob and Adriaen purchased another 200 acres from John Bowne, making in all about 675 acres in the Pleasant Valley, which in time Jacob alone owned it. On a stream encircling the valley he later built a grist mill which stood until 1829; his first residence was said to have been on a hill about a mile west of the present village of Holmdel, although it was generally referred to as of Hillsdale.

Jacob Van Dorn

In 1700 & 1701 the name of 'Jacob Vandorn' appeared on two remonstrances to the king against acts of the East Jersey proprietors who declined to recognize certain land titles in the count; in the ensuing dispute on Aug. 27, 1700, Jacob 'Vandorne',

Arian Bennet and fourteen others were indicted by the county grand jury for having assaulted Jacob Stewart, county High Sheriff, and one other, beating them and taking away their swords, but the indictment was never tried and nothing came of it

In 1702 Queen Anne took over the government from the proprietors and confirmed the county land titles.

'Jacob Vandorne' on Nov. 6, 1705, was appointed an ensign in 'that company of militia in the eastern part of Freehold wherein Captain Salter is Captain' in a commission signed by Lord Cornbury, Governor, but the extent of his service is not known.

Jacob was also instrumental in the establishment of the first Dutch church at Marlborough and he and his wife were charter members of the 'Reformed Congregation of Freehold and Middletown' at the installation of the first pastor, Oct. 19, 1709. Prior to that, the Dutch in Monmouth either had to bring in a pastor from Brooklyn or go there to church; it is worthy of note that although Jacob had been living in Monmouth since 1697, up till 1709 his children were either baptized in Brooklyn or recorded there. In his later years Jacob was referred to as 'the miller.'

In his will Apr. 24, 1719, proved Mar. 21, 1720, 'Jacob Van Dorn 'named his wife Marytie, who was to have use of all his estate during her widowhood; also he provided that the residue of his personal estate he divided among all his children and divided his mill and lands between sons 'Arria' & Jacob, on condition that they each pay the other heirs a sum of £357/10(shillings).

(in the case of Jacob after he became of age; friend Garret Schenck & Aria Bennet were named executors; witnesses were Jacob Sutphen, Jan Sutphen, & William Laurence, Jun'r (attorney who drew the will).

The estate was inventoried May 23, 1720, at £139/6 shillings, so although Jacob was a large landholder, he was not really wealthy.

Marytje Adrianse Bennet was born about 1672 in Gowanus, Brooklyn, New York. She died on 1 Nov 1756 at the age of 84.

Maria Bennet was half English. She was one of eleven children of Adriaen/Arie Willem Bennet, an Englishman, who was born in 1637, and of his wife, Engenietje Jans Van Dyck, a Hollander, who was the daughter of Jan Van Dyck of New Utrecht, Long Island. Her grandfather, **William Bennet**, who came to this country prior to 1636, at which time he purchased, with Jacque Bentyn, 930 acres of land at Gowanus of the Indians; subsequently buying in Bentyn's share.

Willem Bennet married Mary/Maria Badie in 1636.

Willem Adriaese (Bennet) was a cooper. In 1636, he was one of the first colonists to become land-owners at **Gowanus (Brooklyn)**. Ca. 1643, his home was destroyed by Indians. Willem and Maria were the parents of five children born between ca. 1637 and March 9, 1644. Soon thereafter Willem died.

Conclusion:

I have chosen to end the effort to present the history of our ancestors at this point. Many of our ancestors have roots going back into the early days of English, Dutch and French history that I have not included.

Some of the accounts researched by me are speculation, theories and/or "wishful thinking". Some accounts are accurate but at times it became impossible to differentiate between them.

I have attempted to show, as accurately as possible, the names, dates, places and living conditions of our ancestors and their families.

In compiling this work, I recognize that errors may have occurred. It is unintentional as I have attempted to show accuracy, not speculation, unless otherwise mentioned.

INDEX

177

www.ingramcontent.com/pod-product-compliance
Lightning Source LLC
Chambersburg PA
CBHW041612260326
41914CB00012B/1470